Rapid Prototyping
the management of software risk

Rapid Prototyping
the management of software risk

Tim Maude
Graham Willis

Pitman

PITMAN PUBLISHING
128 Long Acre, London WC2E 9AN

A Division of Longman Group UK Limited

First published in Great Britain 1991

British Library Cataloguing in Publication Data
Maude, Tim
Rapid prototyping: The management of software risk.
I. Title II. Willis, Graham
005.1

ISBN 0-273-03309-3

Reproduced and printed by photolithography
in Great Britain by Biddles Ltd, Guildford

ISBN 0 273 03309 3

Contents

Preface

The aim of this book is to explain the use of rapid prototyping within the software engineering discipline. It is intended for practising software engineers, both managers and developers. The knowledge gained from reading this book should enable them to use rapid prototyping in a variety of software development projects. They will find it a complementary approach, rather than an alternative one.

Although primarily written for software engineers, students will find this text a useful supplement to many software engineering courses, particularly those courses covering the software development lifecycle, project management, and software development methods. Students of business administration will also find much helpful material on the use of risk management within software development.

The approach taken by this book is to highlight the main purpose of rapid prototyping, that of controlling and reducing the enormous risks involved in embarking on large or difficult software projects. The proper management of risk is a crucial factor in the successful running of a project, and it is this that rapid prototyping addresses.

This book differs from other texts on the same subject in a number of ways. Firstly, it is comprehensive, covering all the major techniques of rapid prototyping. Secondly, it identifies risk management as the main task of rapid prototyping, and systematically follows this approach throughout the book. Thirdly, the authors, being full time software engineers themselves, have been involved in many rapid prototyping projects run on a commercial basis. This practical knowledge has been put to good use in the text, particularly in the final chapter, which contains four comprehensively documented case studies.

Chapters 1 and 2 introduce most of the major concepts in the book. Chapter 1 concentrates on the problems of software engineering and discipline of risk management. Chapter 2 continues this theme, and expands on the use of rapid prototyping as an approach to software development problems.

Although the subsequent chapters are ordered with the aim of taking the reader through the subject in a logical sequence, it is not strictly necessary to read them in order. After reading the first two chapters, the reader should have sufficient information to delve into those sections in the rest of the book that they find of most interest.

Chapter 3 explains a strategy for rapid prototyping, and discusses the relationship with risk management. It should be possible to incorporate this approach into current development practices after reading this chapter.

Chapter 4 is about the management of rapid prototyping projects. The management of projects is crucial factor in their success, and rapid prototyping has its own particular management problems.

Chapter 5 shows how rapid prototyping may be used in a wide variety of contexts, for example for prototyping user interfaces, database systems, or distributed systems.

Chapter 6 is an examination of the various tools and techniques that may be used in rapid prototyping. It is not intended to be fully comprehensive, but rather to cover the main categories which are currently available.

Chapter 7 gives four detailed case studies. Each case describes a commercially run project in which one or more of the authors was personally involved. They were chosen to show a range of different approaches to prototyping, and to illustrate how projects can succeed or fail as a direct result of the project managers' understanding of the risks involved.

We hope that you enjoy reading this book as much as we have enjoyed writing it, that is as an intellectual challenge in understanding rapid prototyping, a practical challenge in using prototyping, and with a few laughs on the way.

Acknowledgements

Thanks are due to the following people for their help:

Ciaran Byrne, Ron Clint, Tanya Heasman, Dave Linton, Kathryn Moore, and Martyn Reason, who read and commented on earlier drafts of this book.

Derwent Maude (T.M.'s father) and William Willis (G.W.'s father), who also read an early draft.

Ron Clint and Graham Turner, for their discerning management in giving us the opportunity to complete this book!

Ciaran Byrne, of Anvil Software Ltd, for many helpful discussions on the concepts of prototyping and problem solving.

Alicia Macleod, of Alicia Macleod Associates, for her comments on the layout.

Elizabeth Orna, of Orna/Stevens Consultancy, for much needed advice on presentation and design.

Nicky Tyler, for her help with the early versions of the diagrams.

Apple Computer, for the Apple Macintosh on which this book was produced.

Finally, many thanks are due to our publisher, John Cushion of Pitman Publishing, and our editor Roy Dowsing of the University of East Anglia, for their encouragement and helpful guidance.

Tim Maude
Level–7 Ltd
Centennial Court
Easthampstead Road
Bracknell
Berkshire RG12 1YQ

Graham Willis
British Telecom Research Labs
Martlesham Heath
Ipswich
Suffolk IP5 7RE

Trademarks

To my wife Becky, and my sons Jason, Daryl, and Alexander

T.M.

To my parents

G.W.

1 Problems and software development

Introduction

When software engineering graduates leave university and start their first job, they understand how compilers are designed; they can normalise a database schema; they have designed and built their own crossword compilation program, and any sorting algorithms that they don't know are not worth knowing. In short, they are convinced that they know everything there is about software engineering.

After working for a time on maintenance or testing, they wonder at the software that other people produce. They are amazed at the poor design, the messy formats, and the obscure constructions. They start to think that there might be one or two points of software engineering that cause difficulty.

They progress on to building new software, and are a little perturbed by the odd designs they are given to code. Coding to a design proves harder than they expected, and they are now prepared to admit that software engineering is not all that simple.

When they become designers themselves, they find it hard to believe that the specifications they are given are so ambiguous, and wonder why they can never get hold of the specifier to ask questions. They now know that software engineering has its hard parts, and that these are not exclusively confined to design.

Slowly, they slip into analysis and specification, and take on the task of specifying systems. They do not understand why the project managers take such ridiculous decisions. Software engineering, they now admit, is often a lot harder than it seems, quite tricky in fact.

As they become managers, they find that the projects they get are strange indeed, and do not seem to fit into the company strategy at all. Software engineering, they now know, is a very hard subject.

Eventually, they find themselves put in charge of two hundred people, running a project that will last at least three years, and possibly much longer. Faced with this problem, they sit back in the full knowledge that they haven't really got a clue as to how to do it, and wonder that any successful software systems are ever produced.

The purpose of this chapter

So what are the problems of software engineering, and how can they be solved? What solutions have been used in practice, and what are their successful points, and their failings? Some of these questions are examined in this chapter.

This chapter provides a general introduction to this book, and the rationale for looking at the new technique of prototyping. In order to do this, it examines the problems that software engineers face when developing software. The aim is to give the reader a feel for the size and scope of these problems, and an understanding of some of the techniques that may be used to solve them, of which prototyping is particularly important.

General organisation

Section 1.1 gives a short introduction to rapid prototyping, in order to gain a brief insight into the subject before it is defined more precisely later in this chapter. A simple example is given of prototyping.

Section 1.2 looks at the current situation of software development. It examines some of the problems that the industry faces with the growing demand for software, and the difficulties of a still young discipline. Although not wishing to overstate the situation, it can be said that a software crisis currently exists, where systems are almost expected to be delivered late, over budget, and with lots of bugs.

Having now seen the scope of the problem, section 1.3 examines the nature of software development, and in particular the characteristics that set the development of software aside from other production tasks, like engineering. Although software development is known to be problematic, little consideration is usually give to the risks, and in particular which parts are the most risky. This section introduces the concept of risk, and describes the top-ten software risk items.

The classic software development lifecycle model is described in section 1.4. This model was introduced to solve some of the problems of software development, but there are other problems which it does not solve.

Section 1.5 leaves the domain of software engineering, and takes a more abstract look at problem solving. The various ways of solving problems are examined, and related to prototyping.

1.1 Introduction to prototyping

The concept of a prototype will not be new to those involved in the manufacturing industries. Here, a prototype is often a full-scale model, which is built to test the feasibility and reliability of a particular design, and to discover the problems involved in manufacture. In software development the costs of manufacturing, ie replicating, software are not significant, and there is no concept of a full-scale model, since this would be the completed system. The software equivalent of the industrial prototype is a *partial* model of a system, which may also be used to test the feasibility and reliability of the design, but perhaps more importantly to investigate the system requirements and specification.

It is only really since the late 1970's and early 1980's that prototyping has emerged as a distinct software development technique. Although many software developers already use prototyping, there is not yet a general recognition of the important role that prototyping can play in systems development, and consequently it is often overlooked. However, prototyping should not be regarded as an instant solution to development problem. It is simply one of the many approaches available to developers.

1.1.1 Prototypes and prototyping

If a trial version of a system is regarded as a prototype, then prototypes have been constructed from the first time that man first constructed things, for example in building a dwelling of some kind. These prototypes were often trial versions simply because they were failures, and consequently had to be re-built. Eventually, with the experience gained from all the many problems, certain types of building became commonplace, and could be constructed reliably.

However, like most things, people sought to make improvements: a larger building, a higher building, one with a tall tower, etc. As these were new developments, and often required the use of new materials and techniques, many failures were experienced.

The flying buttresses which form such an attractive part of medieval churches are not decorative features, but were necessary to stop the walls being pushed outwards by the thrust of the roof – something which their builders had not anticipated. In many cases buttresses were added *during* the construction, in order to prevent an imminent collapse.

While some architects no doubt learnt such solutions the hard way, others were using scale models to investigate their designs. There are many examples of the use of scale models in architecture and engineering. For example, Robert Stephenson used wooden models during the construction of the Liverpool and Manchester railway in 1825, to calculate bridge angles.

In other areas, a prototype is still constructed as trial version of a complete system. In aircraft manufacture, a full-size aircraft is hand-assembled to test the design, which can't easily be tested in such a complicated product without a fully-working version being available.

Alternatively, a prototype is sometimes built as a full-size, but non-functioning mock-up, for example a model of a car. Although non-functioning, the model can still be used for measuring critical system parameters, such as the aerodynamic drag factor.

Even with prototyping, and many years of experience, engineering failures still can occur. A classic example is that of the Tacoma Narrows bridge in Washington State (Gordon, 1978, p350). At the time of construction in 1940, many hundreds of years of bridge building experience were available to the designers, yet it was built without adequate torsional stiffness. It swayed violently in moderate winds, and soon earned the nickname 'Galloping Gertie'. It collapsed in a wind of 42 mph only four months after completion.

The interesting point is not the mechanism of the failure, which was not unexpected because the designers at this time did not have the mathematical tools to perform the necessary modelling, but that some of the other bridges built around the same time did not subsequently fall down. This was not because their designers were more skilled, but because they recognised the limitations of their knowledge. Since they realised that there were important areas which they did not understand, they designed bridges that were massively over-engineered to compensate.

1.1.2 Software prototyping

The rapid growth of computing and the computer industry means that the commercial need to get error-free software systems to the marketplace on time – and within budget – gets ever more critical. Unfortunately, as the need for quality grows, software developers find that their progress is, if anything, getting far more difficult.

Computer hardware gets much faster and cheaper every year, but software systems get ever more complex, and their users much more sophisticated and demanding. Driven by worldwide market forces, the need for systems that can gain a competitive advantage by processing information faster or more accurately, or by being easier to use, shows no signs of decreasing. Future requirements are unlikely to be any easier to satisfy.

Although software development has some parts that are relatively straightforward and well-understood, where simple rules can be applied – for example in programming – a large part of the development process is difficult and complex. The hard parts of software development are unfortunately those where formal techniques are often of least use: in understanding the problem, in deciding what the goals are, and in choosing an appropriate solution. The easiest parts, those of implementation and testing, have the best techniques available.

Because of these difficulties there have been many attempts at finding a strategy which will allow average developers to solve a wide range of problems. However, the difficulty of these problems, and the skill of the developers, can vary quite widely. Where the environment and the system requirements are stable and well-understood, a specific strategy may be effective, but a better approach for the majority of projects is to have a range of techniques which can be tailored to the problems in hand.

This book concentrates on what many software developers believe is one of the most promising techniques for building software systems – that of software prototyping. The strategy proposed in this book, and discussed in detail, is that it is not possible to define the overall goals of a software project without seeing, at least in part, the operational aspects of a system designed to meet these goals – in other words a prototype system. A problem, like building a software system to meet specific requirements, can only be fully understood in terms of it's solution. The risks involved in attempting a project without a very clear idea of the project goals are very high – as evidenced by the large number of failed or unsuccessful software projects.

The problems faced by the early engineers, who did not have the understanding or mathematical skills needed to design reliably, could often be addressed by over-engineering their designs. An expensive solution – but one which prevented much more expensive failures. It is *known* that software development has problems which current techniques cannot solve, and so software developers should not neglect any techniques which may be helpful.

What actually is a software prototype?

A software prototype is similar to the idea of building a mock-up or model of something, for example a house or a car. It allows developers to understand complex problems by experiencing them first hand, and to use this experience to guide the development process. Prototyping recognises that all projects have some elements which are of higher risk than others, and the prototype can help developers to concentrate on them. The prototype must often be built rapidly, so that the major development problems can be understood before the development process is really started. The prototype can also be used as a means of eliciting and capturing the requirements, and communicating complex ideas to managers, customers, and developers.

Unfortunately, there is little real agreement on the definition of a software prototype. The definition given earlier – that of a partial model of a system – is open to interpretation, but will serve for now. According to Harel's article on folk theorems in computing (Harel, 1980), prototyping meets the criteria for being a 'folk theorem', being a concept which has anonymous authorship, is of uncertain age, and is currently popular. Many software developers will claim that they already use this technique, and have done so for years.

Already the signs of confusion about prototyping are showing. Some authors claim that prototyping is only an approach for requirements definition, and has no place during the rest of the development process. Others distinguish between modelling, scenarios, simulations, demonstrations, and prototypes. Tim Rentsch, in an article on similar confusion which exists in object-oriented programming, puts the point nicely:

> 'What is object-oriented programming? My guess is that object-oriented programming will be in the 1980's what structured programming was in the 1970's. Everyone will be in favor of it. Every manufacturer will promote his products as supporting it. Every manager will pay lip service to it. Every programmer will practice it (differently). And no one will know just what it is.' (Rentsch, 1982)

At the risk of blurring the definition, this book takes a broad view of prototyping. One of its mains aims is to get system developers to consider the use of prototyping during *all phases* of software development. For this reason it includes as many different aspects and applications of prototyping as possible.

1.1.3 An example of a software prototype

The following example is designed to illustrate the advantages – and pitfalls – of software prototyping.

The problem

A manufacturing company had a large team of field maintenance engineers. Each day the supervisors handwrote a timetable of jobs for each engineer, for the following day's calls. This job was time consuming and costly, as each supervisor had to perform a careful planning exercise, as well as writing out the results by hand. It was also error-prone, and engineers sometimes found that the scheduling of their jobs required so much travelling that they had to cancel appointments – much to the annoyance of the customers.

The solution

It was decided to implement a computer system to perform the above task. This would allow jobs to be scheduled according to their priority, and minimise the travelling time. It would also allow the company to expand their range of maintenance options. However, the manager in charge of the software development team was not entirely certain of the requirements for this system, and so decided to include a prototyping stage in the project plan to check that the requirements specification was correct.

Once the requirements had been gathered by interviewing managers and engineers, a user interface prototype was constructed. This was to have the 'look and feel' of the real system, although no system design had been done yet. In order to simulate the operation of the system, one of the software team typed the timetables into a disk file, which was picked up and displayed by the prototype.

As the initial reactions to the prototype were promising, the project manager decided to try the prototype out in a live experiment. The official list of jobs was supplied to the software team, who generated the timetables using the methods described in the requirements. The timetables were typed into the file, and the supervisors shown how to operate the prototype system, and how to print out the timetables. The timetables were then distributed to the field maintenance engineers.

Three days later there was near uproar among the field maintenance engineers, and some of them refused to go out on their calls. When it was all sorted out and the situation analysed, the problem was discovered to be due to the allocation of jobs. The supervisors usually allocated what were considered 'bad' jobs in rotation. The prototype system was not doing this – and some engineers were getting all the bad jobs. The requirements specification had to be rewritten, so that the supervisors could spread the jobs more fairly.

The prototype was updated to verify the new requirements, which were found to be acceptable. Several new ideas were suggested, tested with the prototype, and included in the requirements. When agreement was finally reached between all the interested parties, development of the actual system was started. Although it had been intended to throw the prototype out at this stage, the user interface was well liked, and so it was decided to keep it, rewriting some parts to include input error checking, which had been omitted.

Discussion

This rather simple example shows some of the key features of prototyping. The prototype allowed the requirements to be tested *before* a full-scale development was started, and prevented a costly mistake. This mistake in the requirements happened despite all the relevant parties being consulted during the analysis, and despite paper reviews of the documents. By allowing people to see and use the proposed system, new ideas were generated. In a conventional development the system would only be available for testing at the *end* of the development cycle, and so it might be too late to incorporate changes.

However, the use of prototyping in this project was not as effective as it might have been. By only building the prototype *after* the requirements specification had been written and reviewed, quite a lot of time was wasted. A better approach would have been to use prototyping *during* the requirements analysis, only completing the requirements specification after everyone was happy with the prototype system.

Furthermore, although this particular prototype was used in the final system, problems can occur if the developers are uncertain as to whether the prototype can be kept or not. The goals for the prototype should have been clearly defined.

1.2 Software development today

This section examines traditional approaches to software development. Many of these approaches have their origins in the early days of computing, when hardware was very expensive, and batch processing was normal. But in the software development environments of today, with powerful single-user workstations, and interactive programming, the traditional methods can lead to incorrect or inadequate systems being developed.

Before looking at the problems of software development in greater detail, some basic definitions are needed. These will be used in this chapter, and throughout the rest of this book.

Software development

Software development is the process of specifying, designing, building, and testing software systems that meet a set of needs, and that can be operated and maintained effectively. A software development project includes all stages of this process, from establishing what these needs are, funding and managing the project, through to handing over a completed system with operational instructions, and maintaining the delivered system.

Senior management

The senior managers are those people who are responsible for making strategic decisions, like defining the objectives of a company. Although they do not usually have a formal role in the development process, they have a responsibility for software development projects. Senior management must make realistic resources available to complete a project.

Customers

The customer is the person or group of people for whom the project is being developed. The customer may be a senior manager, or a representative of the management. The customer is usually the person who is paying for the project.

Developers

The developers are the people who actually build the system – the software and hardware engineers. They are normally organised into teams, controlled by team leaders. Overall control of the development project rests with a project manager. The project manager may just have a managerial role, in which case a technical leader will have the technical authority, or the project manager may combine both roles. Within the teams, individuals may have specific roles, including systems analyst, programmer, maintainer, system manager, and program librarian. Chapter 4 looks at the organisation of development teams in more detail.

Users

These are the end-users of the project, ie the people who will actually use the delivered system or product. It may be useful to distinguish between the users who are just operators, and those users who will actually benefit from the system.

Maintainers

These are the people who are responsible for implementing the bug fixes and upgrades necessary to keep the system running to the required operational quality levels. They may also provide user support. Small projects may not have a full-time maintenance team, any problems being fixed on demand by the original developers.

Project participants and their goals

All projects have goals and objectives, and for a project to be successful these must be met. However, in real life goals will conflict, and the participants in the project will have their own specific goals, some of which will be mutually incompatible. Typical goals are shown in Table 1.1.

Project role	Goals
Customer	Cheap to build Cheap to upgrade Cheap to maintain Product meets marketing requirements
Senior management	Meeting strategic goals of company within budget and timescales
Project manager	Product completed on time and within budget
Developers	Interesting systems to build Design and coding, not documentation and testing
User	Meeting user needs Good support Easy to use and bug free
Maintainers	Easy to maintain Good documentation Bug free

Table 1.1 The goals of the project participants

In an ideal world it would be possible for all participants to work together to achieve these goals, but as system complexity increases, and the more people that are involved in a project, the harder this becomes. Any approach to software development must not only take account of the technical problems, but also the goals of the project and the people involved.

1.2.1 Traditional approaches to software development

Many different software development models or techniques have been devised over the years. Most of these have been based on, or are variations of, the lifecycle model.

The lifecycle model encapsulates software development as a series of stages which are well-defined and closely planned:

- A detailed specification of what the system is to do.
- A design for a system to meet this specification.
- The implementation of this design in code.
- The verification of the code as being correct.
- The validation of the system as meeting the specification.

The lifecycle approach is heavily based on documentation, for example:

- The project is divided into well-defined stages.
- Each stage is closely planned and controlled.
- All stage products must be specified before they can be started.
- All stage products must be completed and reviewed before the next stage can start.

Starting with the specification, it is very easy to overspecify a system by proposing complex programming interfaces and elaborate standards. Design and implementation ideas often end up in the specification documents. The documents may achieve a validity simply because they exist, but in practice it is quite hard to write error-free, unambiguous specifications.

In many projects it is considered essential to make documents contractually binding, because the customer, concerned with ever increasing project costs, wants to get value for money. The developers, on the other hand, often promise what cannot be delivered, because they do not realise or understand the risk implications, and want to build interesting systems. This can lead to a lowering of overall quality levels, and because the development process cannot react quickly enough to changing situations, to the development of an inappropriate system.

The lifecycle model emphasises analysis and specification *before* implementation, and there is little interplay once the implementation has started. For example, in most lifecycle-based models the outputs of each stage must be carefully reviewed and checked before moving to the next stage. Any changes to the outputs of the early stages, like the specification or design, would be very expensive later, so a strict mechanism of change control is often used, and the specification must be fixed and frozen at an early stage.

Feedback between stages is not encouraged, and major changes are actively discouraged. The consequences of this are that a working system is not produced until near the end of the lifecycle. Since this is usually the first chance the customer has of using the system, errors in the early stages, like the specification, are not detected until the development is almost complete. These will be very expensive to correct.

Traditional results

While many complex and difficult software projects finish on time and within budget, an increasing number unfortunately do not. Some of the more common problems are:

- software projects finishing late
- high costs and budget overruns
- even higher maintenance costs
- low productivity and poor quality
- requirements not met

Not all projects suffer from these problems, but there are many examples of commercial software projects which have had quite catastrophic failures, despite being apparently well planned. The following article from Business Week illustrates this:

> 'A sampling of 'runaway' projects
>
> Allstate Insurance.
> In 1982, with software from Electronic Data Systems, the insurer began to build an $8 million computer system that would automate it from top to bottom. Completion date: 1987. An assortment of problems developed, delaying completion until 1993. The new estimated price: $100 million.
>
> City of Richmond.
> In 1984 it hired Arthur Young to develop a $1.2 million billing and information system for its water and gas utilities. Completion date: March, 1987. After paying out close to $1 million, Richmond recently canceled the contract, saying no system had been delivered. Arthur Young has filed a $2 million breach of contract suit against the city.
>
> Business Men's Assurance.
> In 1985 the reinsurer began a one-year project to build a $500,000 system to help minimise the risk of buying insurance policies held by major insurers. The company has spent nearly $2 million to date on the project, which is in disarray. The new completion date is early 1990.
>
> State of Oklahoma.
> In 1983 it hired a Big Eight accounting firm to design a $500,000 system to handle explosive growth in workers' compensation claims. Two years and more than $2 million later, the system still didn't exist. It finally was finished last year at a price of nearly $4 million.

> Blue Cross & Blue Shield of Wisconsin.
> In late 1983 it hired Electronic Data Systems to build a $200 million computer system. It was ready 18 months later – on time. But it didn't work. The system spewed out some $60 million in overpayments and duplicate checks before it was harnessed last year. By then, Blue Cross says, it has lost 35,000 policy holders.'
>
> (Business Week, November 7, 1988)

There is a belief that the lifecycle model is responsible for quite a few problems similar to those described above, and this has led some people to suggest an alternative strategy (Blum, 1982; McCracken and Jackson, 1982).

1.2.2 The software crisis

The problems of software development described in the previous section are, unfortunately, only the tip of an iceberg. Software development is fraught with many more serious problems:

- Demand for software outstripping the supply.
- Excessive time and effort spent on maintenance.
- Wasted effort spent on failed projects.

For some time now the world has demanded software at a faster rate than it can be produced. This is known as the *software crisis*. The world is in the midst of the information technology revolution, where computers are changing the way people live. This revolution has happened very quickly in comparison with the introduction of new technologies in the past. It has changed the world, but the world wants the changes to happen still faster. Thus the demand outstrips the supply, and the software crisis is the result.

Hardware costs are falling faster than software costs. In less than a dozen years, a personal computer, with the equivalent power of a minicomputer once costing many thousands of pounds, is now bought for a child's birthday present. The cost of software has also fallen, due to better development techniques, and combined with the low costs of hardware this has meant that there is a bigger market for software. Nevertheless, the fall in software cost has been nothing like the fall in hardware cost. Brooks summarises the situation thus:

> 'One must observe that the anomaly is not that software progress is slow, but that computer hardware progress is so fast. No other technology since civilisation began has seen six orders of magnitude in performance-price gain in 30 years. In no other technology can one choose to take the gain in *either* improved performance *or* reduced costs. These gains flow from transformation of computer manufacture from an assembly industry into a process industry.' (Brooks, 1987)

The software crisis that results from these events is that the demand for software outstrips the world's capacity to produce it. There is a constant search for a breakthrough in the software development process to solve this problem. Many tools and techniques have been developed, for instance fourth generation languages (4GLs) have speeded up the development of software, and object-oriented languages offer an easy way to reuse software.

Brooks (1987) in his excellent article 'No Silver Bullet' develops the analogy of the silver bullet that was used to kill the werewolf – and was thus an instant solution to a problem. He claims that there is no silver bullet to solve the software crisis, no instant solutions – only those that offer a general improvement of the situation. One of the solutions that he mentions is rapid prototyping.

The hidden costs of maintenance

Software maintenance is the modification of software after it has been delivered. The various studies that have been done on maintenance show that the cost of this stage is between 40 and 70 per cent of the total expenditure on software, and that a 'typical' company's expenditure on maintenance is around 2 per cent of its turnover. Such figures are frighteningly large. The interesting thing about these figures is that no matter how much effort goes into structured and formal techniques for design, coding, testing, and integration, in fact everything but the specification stages, the maximum decrease in the maintenance budget is about 20 per cent.

The cost of maintenance is sometimes mis-estimated. Pressman (1987) suggests that the budgeted cost is between 10 and 15 per cent, whereas the actual costs are between 55 to 70 per cent. Many developers will find that these sort of figures are familiar. One of the problems with managing a maintenance budget is that the cost is variable. Sometimes the maintenance team will be working nights for weeks on end, sometimes they have little to do except sift through the backlog of non-urgent changes (there is always a backlog). It is difficult to plan for maintenance.

Techniques for maintenance are not well-known. Many textbooks leave maintenance as an insignificant part at the end, dismissed in a few pages. One such book, whose name has been omitted to protect the guilty, creates a model of the software lifecycle which has twenty stages, the last of which is maintenance. It has 254 pages devoted to systems development, 12 of which are devoted to maintenance – less than 5 per cent. For detailed information on software maintenance see Lientz and Swanson (1980), or Martin and McClure (1983).

Thus the problem of maintenance exacerbates the software crisis. The continuing backlog of maintenance jobs, mostly due to user requests for different features, grows and the developers who work on these requests work with little or no methods to support them. Their work is a black art, which they cope with because they have to.

1.2.3 Why some projects fail

Software development projects can be said to fail if, for whatever reason, it would have been more economic not to have run the project at all. One way in which a project might fail is if the software it produces is not used. Some software will be used for purposes other than that for which it was intended. Some projects will deliver software that is subsequently modified, in order to fit the purpose for which it was intended.

Whichever way the software is used, a project cannot be considered to have failed unless the company makes a loss. Even though a project produces something which is not used exactly as delivered, it may still not be a failure. If the software is not used for the purpose for which it was intended, there is a high probability that not as much gain was obtained from the project as was possible.

A study done in the late 1970's for the U.S. government, on nine software projects totalling \$6.8 million in cost, examined what was done with the software at the end of the project. Table 1.2 shows the results, as reported by the US Government Accounting Office (1979). Although these figures are now a little out of date, they do give some indication of how many projects do fail in some way or another.

Result	Cost (\$M)
Used as delivered	0.1
Used after change	0.2
Abandoned or reworked	1.3
Delivered but not used	2.0
Paid for but not delivered	3.2

Table 1.2 Results of nine software projects for the US government

Projects can fail in a number of ways:

- They may run overbudget.
- They may run out of time.
- The product may not meet the requirements.

They run overbudget

Here the estimates made early on in the project were too small. The software actually costs a great deal more than was expected. This leads to a management decision – either to pour more resources into the project, or to cut the losses and cancel. The decision is best made as soon as an overrun on the budget is forecast. It involves re-calculating the cost-benefit analysis and making a decision.

If the project is cancelled, then it can be considered a failure. The only thing that is gained is some experience. If more money is put into the project, then the original expected profit from the project will be less than expected. This must be considered a partial failure. Other possible options exist, the most likely one being to reduce the size of the project. This is usually referred to as *descoping.*

Out of time

Every project has deadlines, sometimes based on the estimated time to build the software, and sometimes based on the estimated market window for the product. For example, a software package might be needed in 12 months time, as it is to be demonstrated at an exhibition. If the managers of a project realise that they are going to miss the deadline, they must make a decision – either to cancel, or to accept the late delivery.

At first sight it may seem a little drastic to cancel just because a project will finish a little late, but take for example an eighteen month project, where nine months into the project it becomes apparent that the deadline will be missed by six months. The marketing managers may decide that launching a product six months later will reduce the profits sufficiently to warrant cancelling the project there and then (perhaps due to rival products entering the market first).

Product does not match requirements

If the product does not match the requirements of its users at the time it is released to them, the project may be a failure. The system might have had its requirements poorly specified at the beginning of the project, or the requirements may have changed during the development stages. It may be that some requirements were not fully achieved, or it may be that the customers were not involved during the project, and so rejected the system when it was delivered. The result of any of these problems could be that the product as delivered does not meet the customers requirements.

Other reasons for failure

Other problems that give rise to project failure (or partial failure) are symptomatic of the above three. For example, a system may not be sufficiently robust because the requirements specification did not state the mean time between failures, so when the project team found they were running out of time and money, they cut a few corners and did not debug the system as thoroughly as they might.

1.3 The nature of software

Before a better solution can be proposed to the current problems of software development, it is necessary to understand why software development is difficult. This section looks at the nature of software to see what, if any, are the inherent difficulties. From this a classification of software projects can be made, according to their inherent risks of failure. Understanding the risks is the first step in proposing solutions to development problems.

1.3.1 Software characteristics

Software development is always likely to be difficult because of the nature of software. The most important factors to consider are:

- complexity
- accuracy
- visibility
- changeability

It is these factors that, to varying degrees, cause problems in understanding, specifying, designing, implementing, and managing software systems.

Complexity

Software can be quite complex. Even a small program of a hundred lines of code may be sufficiently complex that exhaustive testing of all the control flow paths is impossible. As system size increases, the complexity increases, and there are more interactions between the components of the system. This makes it difficult to test the components in isolation, because the interactions may be hard to reproduce, and testing the complete system more difficult because the way that the components interact is hard to predict. It is not uncommon to find software products which claim to have been rigorously tested, but when used are found to have major flaws.

Because of this complexity, it can be hard to understand a software system, and to communicate the 'essence' of such a system to others. Accurate documentation, even for quite a small software system, can fill several volumes, and programmers may take take several months before they are sufficiently familiar with a system to make any alterations to it.

Software engineers are always seeking to reduce the complexity by using diagrams or special notations, so that they can understand, design, and use these complex systems. However, in reducing complexity there is always a risk that the problem is over-simplified, and thus some key concepts are ignored or misinterpreted. Building a system model to aid understanding assumes that the system is sufficiently well-understood to know what to leave out.

Accuracy

Software is precise and logical. Unlike the traditional engineering concept of tolerance, where components within specified measurements are good enough to use, there is no equivalent concept of tolerance or closeness of fit in programming. A single logical error in a program can easily cause complete failure, rather than a gradual degradation of performance. A program must also conform to the standards of the programming language, and the implementation of that language must conform to the underlying hardware. When systems have to communicate with each other, they need to use an agreed standard to be able to exchange information.

Visibility

Software is invisible. The inner workings of a software system are hidden, and only manifest by virtue of their interfaces to the external world. This makes it hard to measure progress or quality in a software development project; one cannot state accurately that a system is, for example, 85 per cent complete. Because software is hard to visualise, written specifications can never capture the reality of the completed system. Software is not a physical entity, so it is difficult to model with anything else but software.

The difficulty of representing a system makes it hard to communicate key ideas to others. Yet without some means for visualising a system, there is a danger of the completed system not meeting the customers' needs.

Changeability

Software is easy to change, in the sense that the physical limitations on changing code do not vary with either code size or complexity. It is just as easy to change a line of code in a 100,000 line program as it is in a 10 line program. This does not mean that the programs will perform correctly after the changes, but that changes are often requested because of the perceived ease of change. These changes can be difficult to control, and because of this some kind of change control mechanism is essential.

But the driving forces for change are that the nature of the problem may alter during the development, and that once in use the system itself generates requests for changes. A development project is not a closed system, and external forces for change are always present. Not all changes may be desirable, and some should be resisted as they lead to poorer solutions, but others cannot be ignored without the risk of building a system that is out of date.

Software engineering and traditional engineering

One way of looking at what makes software difficult is by comparison with some traditional engineering problems, like the building of an office block, or the construction of a passenger aircraft.

The office building example is sometimes used to show how a software project is quite similar to other projects with which the reader may be more familiar. It has the same basic stages as a software project:

- project proposal (architects sketches)
- project costing and planning
- specification and design (the building plans)
- implementation (the building process)
- handover to customer (completion)

Both projects must conform to standards and regulations. In a software project this would be to the underlying hardware, and the chosen programming languages and interfaces. In the construction industry it is to the building and planning regulations. But there are some important differences between the building process and software development.

In terms of complexity, buildings are really quite simple in comparison to software. The building process is well understood, with a long history of past experiences. The modular nature of their design, construction, and use greatly reduces their complexity, as does the lack of interacting components. It is far easier to test a building component, for example a girder, since the loads and stresses on it can be reproduced in isolation. Many building components, like a window unit or heating boiler, can be purchased off the shelf, rather than being built from scratch.

Unlike errors in software, errors in constructing a building may have little or no effect. Individual components like a light or a window can fail, or even be omitted completely, but the building can still function reasonably normally.

Visualising an office is far easier. People are familiar with offices, since most people have worked in one at some time, and although the external and internal appearance varies according to the design, the major functional components remain unchanged. An office is a static, 3-dimensional entity, so scale models or perspective drawings will give a very good idea of the final product. Software is multi-dimensional and dynamic, so static modelling is not much use.

Because the various phases of construction of an office block literally build on top of each other, the requests for change are greatly reduced. Once the building process has started with the construction of the foundations, the major parameters are defined and fixed. The costs to re-design at this stage would be very high, and this fact is well understood by the customer. Changes to the external appearance would be quite easy to make, since the cladding of a building often just hangs off the framework. In software, top-level changes, eg to the user interface functions, may have considerable and hidden design consequences. But by virtue of being at the top-level, the user interface is seen by the customer as being very easy to change.

Apart from the differences in complexity, accuracy, visibility, and changeability, the cost components of testing and maintenance are also very different. Unlike software, there is no real concept of verification and validation stages in building, and the maintenance costs are very low in comparison to the total building cost.

A better example might be that of constructing a passenger aircraft. Building an aircraft is very complicated, and it is obviously critical that the aircraft functions safely. It shares several important features with software development:

- high complexity, comparable to the largest software projects
- many interacting components
- testing and reliability are very important
- maintenance costs are very significant

However, the research and development costs are so high in the aircraft industry that many aircraft must be sold to make any profit, so the product lifetime must be very long, with only minor changes being made. Because most aircraft are very similar in function, the impact of new models on the marketplace is restricted. In software, product lifetimes are quite short, and there is considerable scope for producing an innovative product that can change the marketplace overnight.

Summarising this, software is inherently difficult to develop because it is:

- complex and dynamic
- difficult to specify and model
- has a short lifetime before change

1.3.2 Software project characteristics

Software projects can fail for many reasons, some of which may be due to the nature of the software. However, a small project in a well-understood problem domain is far less likely to fail than a large project using unfamiliar technology.

The characteristics of software projects that largely determine how difficult they are, and thus how likely they are to fail, are:

- problem domain
- size of the project
- expertise of the developers
- project organisation and management
- project stability
- organisational stability

Problem domain

The problems that software systems must solve vary in many ways. Some problems have a high complexity, and will be difficult to understand and to solve, while others may be quite simple, or can be simplified because they are similar to those that have already been solved.

The degree of technical risk involved in a problem thus will vary from those that require state of the art computer science techniques, to those that can be solved with off-the-shelf application software.

Size of the project

The size of the project, to a large extent, determines the management and control problems in the running of the project, and hence the likelihood of a successful outcome. Projects with large budgets, large numbers of staff, long timescales, and many departments are much more difficult to run than those with small teams and a short timescale.

The greater the number of interacting departments involved, the greater the communications problems, and the increased chance of information being lost or misinterpreted. The longer the time to the first project delivery, the more the risk of the requirements changing, and the project delivering a system which no longer meets these requirements.

Expertise of developers

A project is limited by the experience of the developers, and it is difficult to compensate for inexperienced staff other than by increasing the timescales, or decreasing the functionality and quality requirements. Even then, this may not be effective. The developers must be sufficiently experienced in the problem domain, in systems development, and in the use of the hardware and software. The project managers must be familiar with the problems that can occur, and be able to monitor the project to make certain that the deadlines and requirements are met.

Project organisation and management

The organisational structure must be sufficiently flexible to cope with the changing needs of the project. Conflict can occur between the lines of technical authority, who are responsible for the major technical decisions in the project, and the managerial authorities who may have organisational responsibility, but not technical responsibility. The project management must be capable of resolving this, and of planning, controlling, and monitoring the project.

Project stability

It would be easier to run projects if their goals and requirements were fixed at the beginning, and didn't change throughout the lifetime of the project. However, the most successful projects are likely to be the ones that are the most responsive to these changes. For example the fundamental nature of the problem may change, or the requirements may vary. Unexpected changes in resources may mean that the project is suddenly short of funds or staff. Changing business needs may require the delivery date to be brought forward, perhaps making the original objectives impossible to achieve in the time.

Organisational stability

Unexpected changes can also occur within an organisation, where departments may be reorganised, or staff reassigned. This can threaten the success of any project. A particular risk occurs if the people that support the project, for example the senior managers, are reassigned.

1.3.3 Development project risks

It is useful to consider the essential characteristics of software projects, since this gives an insight into the types of problem that may occur. There is also a great amount of experience of failed projects to use in gathering statistics to identify the most likely risks to a project, and hence the most appropriate ways to avoid the risks.

The technical problems of writing correct software, or the complexities of managing a large software project might be expected to be primary reasons for the failure of a project. However, a large proportion of projects fail for far more mundane reasons; the delivered system does not meet the requirements of the customer, or the senior management reduce funding half way through the development. These are all part of the risk of software development. Boehm (1988) lists the top-ten software risk items as being:

1 Personnel shortfalls
2 Unrealistic schedules and budgets
3 Developing the wrong software functions
4 Developing the wrong user interface

5 Gold plating
6 Continuing stream of requirements changes
7 Shortfalls in externally furnished components
8 Shortfalls in externally performed tasks
9 Real-time performance shortfalls
10 Straining computer science capability

Personnel shortfalls

Personnel problems may be due to lack of manpower and skills, or to poor man-management. Some typical problems are:

- people promised are not made available
- a shortage of critical skills
- staff change during the project
- some people are in the wrong job
- personal goals conflict with project goals
- team members are not compatible
- project gets the most available people, not the ones with the appropriate skills

Unrealistic schedules and budgets

Budgetary and schedule constraints are common to almost all projects. They are usually imposed by the senior management, but if impossible targets are set, then it is up to the project manager to make this known. Some typical problems are:

- insufficient budget
- unrealistic schedules
- budgets likely to change
- schedules likely to change
- items to be delivered not prioritised

Developing the wrong software functions

If the requirements of the customer are not clearly defined and understood, then the wrong system functions may be implemented. If this is not discovered early in the project a large part or even all of the code may need to be thrown out. Some typical problems are:

- vague system requirements
- system requirements not fully understood
- system requirements expected to change
- system requirements confused with system design
- system functionality not demonstrated early enough

Developing the wrong user interface

It is just as easy to implement an unsatisfactory user interface as it is to build the wrong software functions, and potentially just as damaging to the project. Some typical problems are:

- unfriendly user interface
- user interface requirements not fully understood
- user interface requirements expected to change
- user interface not demonstrated early enough
- lack of involvement of user representatives
- the conceptual model presented is not the same as the user's model

Gold plating

There is a great tendency for systems to be over-specified in areas that are well-understood, and for developers to concentrate on interesting but irrelevant parts of a project. Some typical problems are:

- unnecessary features requested by customer
- unnecessary features implemented by developers
- key features omitted because of the above
- high performance systems with low performance requirements

Continuing stream of requirements changes

Requirements can rarely, if ever, be completely fixed. Projects that ignore changing requirements can end up with a system that is out of date. Conversely, if all the changes are attempted, then the project will become chaotic and late. Some typical problems are:

- no baseline for requirements changes to be related to
- requirements changes rapid or uncontrolled
- low threshold for requirements changes
- underestimate of effects of requirements changes
- no configuration management system

Shortfalls in externally furnished components

External components are those which are provided by a third-party external to the project development teams. This includes commercial software products. Since they are outside of the project, they may not have the same degree of management control as the project components, and thus not meet the requirements. Some typical problems are:

- components not suitable for required tasks
- expected availability not met, delivered late
- expected component quality not reached
- poor performance, reliability, functionality, etc.
- lack of support for commercial products

Shortfalls in externally performed tasks

External tasks such as project reviews, software which is contracted out, documentation, and audits can cause great problems if they are late or of poor quality. If an external task is on the critical project-planning path, then problems and delays can cause all subsequent tasks to slip, with a corresponding risk to the project delivery being on time. Some typical problems are:

- unpredictable costs
- expected timescales not met
- expected task quality not reached
- external tasks on the critical path
- reliance on non-existent products

Real-time performance shortfalls

Few projects have *critical* real-time performance requirements, but for those that do any problems here will be very hard to solve, unless almost all the other risks are avoided. Some problems are created by under-specifying the hardware requirements, or over-specifying the performance needs. Some examples are:

- performance impacts of design not determined
- performance requirements too high – no cost/benefit analysis
- critical performance areas uncertain

Straining computer science capability

Some areas of computer science are known to be difficult or even state-of-the-art. Projects should only be involved in a high-risk area when absolutely necessary. Areas of particular difficulty are:

- distributed systems
- real-time systems
- high-reliability/fault tolerant systems
- provably secure systems

Meeting these risks

Many of today's development strategies and techniques do not address the higher-level risks, eg the risk of having insufficient resources or uncertain requirements. For example, there are techniques which allow developers to write software which can be formally proved to be correct, and is thus error-free. These techniques are extremely useful, and of great significance in improving the quality of software, but such methods do not ensure that the *right* software is implemented.

Technical advances in computer science should not be expected to increase productivity by a significant margin without some of these higher-level risk items being solved, since the technical goals are in themselves not the major risk item. The major risks in managing a software development project are to do with people, and management; running a project given unrealistic resources, of coping with unexpected changes, and of not understanding the problem so that the right system is not built.

1.4 Systems development

The software development lifecycle has been modelled in order to control the development of software projects. More accurately, a set of similar models that are all variations on the same theme have been developed. This model shows the stages that software goes through from its original conception, through its specification and design, on to the creation of the software itself and its subsequent integration. It then goes through testing, installation, operation, and finally – in a position where some people hope it will quietly slip away unnoticed – maintenance. This section explains the classic lifecycle model, and some of the problems associated with it.

The original idea behind the lifecycle was that a carefully planned and systematic approach to software development would control the cost of using the expensive resource of a computer. By dividing the project into stages the complex problem of software development can be simplified, and each stage made a target that must be completed before moving on to the next stage. Detailed planning of each stage allows close control of project costs and resources, and progress can be measured easily by the stages completed so far. The linear approach means that different resources and tools can be applied to each stage as necessary.

1.4.1 The classic lifecycle model

The basic ideas for the lifecycle date back to the earliest days of computing, and the development of operations research and systems analysis. The lifecycle model is often called the *waterfall model*, and first appeared in an article by Royce (1970), although it was a later article by Boehm (1976) that really established the model.

The classic lifecycle model is shown in Figure 1.1. During each stage of the model it is possible to move on to the next stage, producing the waterfall effect on the diagram. It is also possible to return to the previous stage in order to correct any mistakes made there. Finally, after a period of maintenance, the software becomes obsolete. In order to start another development cycle going, it is necessary to return to the specification of requirements; thus a new system is built to replace the old one.

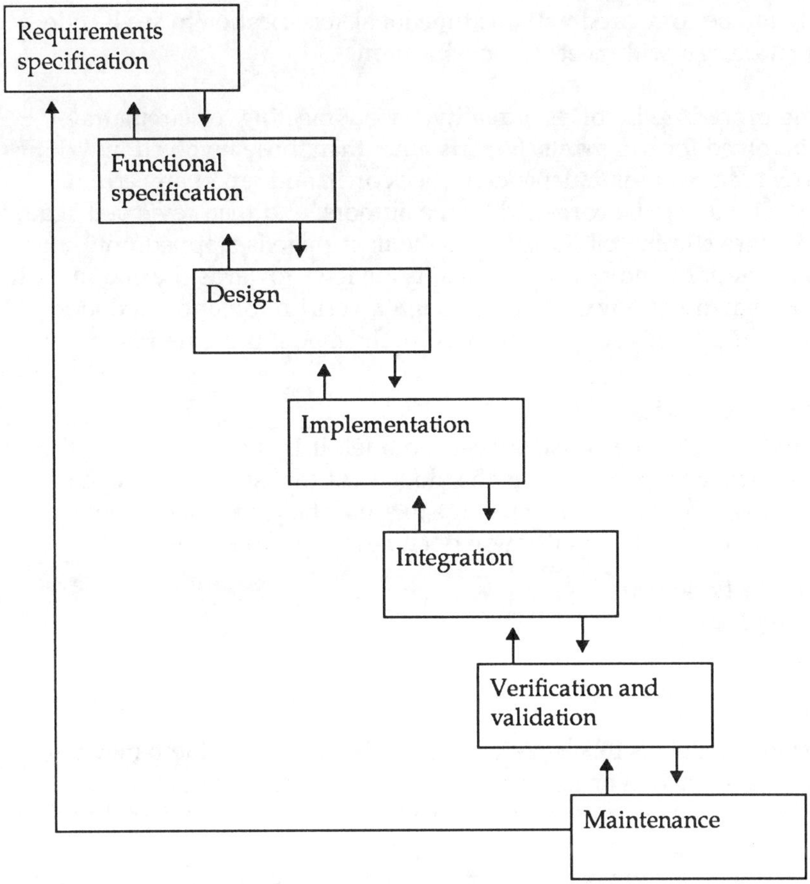

Figure 1.1 Classic lifecycle or waterfall model
Note: This is the conventional way of drawing this diagram

At the conclusion of each stage there is a specific end-of-stage product that is used by subsequent stages. This may be a document of some sort, such as a specification or a verification report, and sometimes modules of code. To be strictly accurate, there are often a number of end-of-stage products, but one of them is the main goal for the stage. For example, at the end of the coding stage the main product is the code; there are also documentation, installation notes, and other items, all of which are important, but are secondary to the code itself.

Before each stage is completed, the end products of that stage will be reviewed in order to verify that they are accurate, and fit for their intended purpose. This review procedure should check that the end product of a particular stage achieves what it was originally required to do. For example, the design document should be compared with the functional specification to see if code written to that design will meet the specification.

Typically, the procedure involves a quality review meeting, or circulating the documents involved for comments. Experts other than those involved in writing the end product can make an independent check on it, and report any errors. These errors will have to be corrected by the authors, and then reviewed again until the errors are eliminated. Progress to the next stage is stopped until this has been completed. In addition to the quality reviews towards the end of each stage, there is sometimes a need to go through a verification and validation stage in its own right. This stage is included in the model presented here.

Requirements specification

This is the first stage in the classic lifecycle model. It is the stage where the goals of the system are specified. It is this document that states the scope of the project; and will be used at a later stage to see if the project has been completed. A requirements specification document typically states:

- the problem to be solved
- goals of the project
- quality goals
- constraints

It does not state the details of system to be built; in fact the problem may not need a system to be built in order to satisfy the requirements, but that is a decision of the next stage – this stage only states the problem. The total project cost and timescales are usually set at this stage. The work that goes into producing this document can be done by the customer, or by the developers (for example by a systems analyst), but is likely to be done by a combination of both. The main end-of-stage product is a specification of requirements document.

Functional specification

This stage uses the requirements specification as a basis for producing the functional specification. This adds to the requirements specification any details that are necessary to build the product, but are not specific goals. The functional specification should give a complete picture of *what* the product is intended to do, but not *how* to do it.

Often the two specification stages are rolled into one, and no distinction is made between what is a requirement of the customer, and what is a function of the system. This is sometimes a matter of expediency; in a small project the addition of an extra stage can be an unnecessary administrative overhead. Sometimes they are rolled into one in the mistaken belief that they are the same. The wise will realise that the difference in the level of abstraction between these two stages is an important one. One stage specifies the goals, the other specifies what is needed to achieve the goals. The main end-of-stage product is a functional specification document.

Design

Whereas the functional specification states *what* is to be done, the design states *how* it is to be done. Design can be done to various degrees of detail. Sometimes this stage can be split up into high-level design and detailed design. The high-level design specifies the modules that are to exist, and the interfaces between them. This is analogous to a specification, in that it states what the module must do, but not how to do it. The detailed design is sometimes not documented, since the level of detail is so close to the code itself. The main end-of-stage product is a design document.

Coding

This, of course, is the stage that actually produces the code. The design should split the system up into 'chunks' that are then divided between teams. Each team develops code for a small sub-system which is specified in the design document, where all the interfaces to the other sub-systems are well defined.

If the detailed design has not been done during the design stage, then it is done here in the coding stage by the individual teams. Each team will test their sub-system to their own satisfaction. The main end-of-stage product is the code.

Integration

The separate sub-systems, which have been individually tested, are now brought together; this process is known as integration. The sub-systems are linked and tested, first in groups, two or three sub-systems at a time. When the small groups have been sufficiently tested, then they are linked together until, eventually, the system is tested as a whole.

It is at this stage that debugging becomes a lot harder, as the bugs that become manifest are the product of more than one team's work. Debugging requires close co-operation between the teams and the designers. The main end-of-stage product is a complete working system.

Verification and validation

Having got a complete working system, verification and validation can take place. Verification is the process of checking the working system to see if it matches the functional specification. Validation is the process of checking to see if the working system matches the requirements of the user, which can be done by checking the system against the requirements specification.

These stages are not always included as they are formal checking procedures that do not appear to add any value to the product, and can cost a lot. They are best done by a team which is independent of the development staff, in order to avoid the problems of assumptions made by the development team being carried on into the verification and validation stages. The inclusion of formal verification and validation increases the need to have a very precise requirements and functional specification.

Verification and validation occur at the end of all stages in some form, since the end product of each stage must go through a quality control procedure. It is sometimes sufficient to rely on this quality assurance procedure alone, in which case the verification and validation stage is omitted. The main end-of-stage product is a statement of the variance between the specification documents and the product.

Maintenance

The software is now complete and can be installed and run. This is sometimes included in the lifecycle model as installation and operation stages, although this is not appropriate if the software is sold externally, rather than used in-house. It is only now that some problems can be seen. These may be problems due to bugs in the software, that have escaped the notice of the testers. Some may be problems due to poor design. The worst kind of problems are those due to errors in defining the original requirements.

Maintenance[1] is the process of correcting these errors, and subsequently reinstalling or redistributing the software. At some point in time, it becomes necessary to rework the complete system, simply because the old one has become so patched and so far from the changing requirements that it is no longer feasible to modify it, or the need for it has changed.

A good overview of software maintenance can be found in Foster (1989). There are four major types of software maintenance, which are:

- Corrective maintenance
  This is the act of correcting bugs in software that were not found during the development stages. Bugs are defined as those parts where the software does not do what the specification states it should.
- Adaptive maintenance
  This is the act of altering the software to keep it in line with a changing environment, for example a new operating system or new hardware. Adaptation reflects changes in the constraints set out in the requirements specification, but not in the goals of the system.

---

[1] The modern term for maintenance is *software evolution*, which emphasises the fact that software evolves continuously, rather than being frozen when delivered.

- Perfective maintenance
  This is the addition of new features or improvements, like improving the performance, usually at the request of the customers. Perfective maintenance corresponds to the goals in the requirements specification, and the details in the functional specification, changing.

- Preventative maintenance
  This is done simply to avoid potential problems, and to make the whole process of maintenance easier. Preventative maintenance does not correspond to any changes in the specification. There is a body of opinion that is opposed to such work on the grounds that 'If it ain't broke, don't fix it'.

Table 1.3 shows the split between the different types of maintenance as estimated by Pressman (1987).

Type of maintenance	Percentage of maintenance cost
Corrective	21
Adaptive	25
Perfective	50
Preventative	4

Table 1.3 Cost of different types of maintenance

Summary
This, then, is the classic lifecycle of software, from the software's original conception, to its final demise. It has been well used in the past, in its many varieties. The fact that it has been used to great effect in the past demonstrates its validity. It is a useful basis from which to work, but one must remember that it is only a model and not an infallible law.

The model may be split into three distinct phases:

- analysis – the requirements specification stage
- implementation – the stages between functional specification, and verification and validation
- maintenance

The first phase deals with understanding the problem, the second with developing a solution, and the third with coping with the inadequacies of the solution.

Table 1.4 summarises the stages of the classical lifecycle model and shows the people that are required to do the actual work.

Stage	Description of output	Who does the work
Requirements specification	What the goals and constraints are	Analyst/Customer
Functional specification	What the system does	Analyst
Design	How the system works	Designer
Code	System components	Programmer
Integration	The system	Programmer
Verification	Is the system correct?	Designer/Programmer
Validation	Is it the right system?	Analyst/Customer
Maintenance	A modified system	Maintainers

Table 1.4 Stages of the classical lifecycle model

1.4.2 Problems with the classic lifecycle model

One of the features that should be noticed in the classic lifecycle model is how each stage, quite naturally, depends on the output of one or more previous stages. For instance, the design depends on the functional specification, and verification depends on the functional specification and the working system. Ultimately everything depends on the requirements specification, being the output of the very first stage.

Specification problems

The lifecycle model assumes that 'what' the system must do can be separated from 'how' the system is to be built to deliver the specified functionality. This separation is ideal, but very difficult to achieve, since it is hard to ignore implementation issues when writing a specification (Swartout and Balzer, 1982). Every specification is effectively an implementation of a higher level specification, a meta-specification. For example, a design is a specification for how a system is to be implemented.

During the implementation it may be realised that the original specification is in error, or could be extended to include new, useful features. A blurring of the boundaries between stages is inevitable in any stepwise model.

Changing requirements

One of the assumptions that the classic lifecycle model makes about system development is that it is possible to define precisely the requirements at this stage (Giddings, 1984). If it is possible to define the requirements of a system all in one short space of time, then the most that can be said about them are that they are the requirements at that particular time. The system is brought into operation after it has been developed, but depending on the size of the system, this could be a year or more later. The hidden assumption is that the requirements do not change over time. This is clearly not the case.

Conceptualisation

Another characteristic of the classic systems development approach is that it leads to a large amount of documentation. In particular the requirements and functional specification documents will be large. They may be several hundred pages long, each page containing many detailed items, each one of which may have a profound effect on the rest of the system. However, there is a problem with such large documents. It is assumed that if one reads the document one understands it.

This problem is really one of conceptualisation. It is almost impossible to read a specification document of several hundred pages and be able to conceptualise the system. Once a document gets to a certain size and complexity, it is impossible for one person to hold the complete picture in his/her head at one time. This inevitably leads to problems and errors that are not seen until after the system has been built.

Inaccuracy of model

The lifecycle model does not accurately reflect the true life situation. An interesting study by Zelkowitz (1988) on systems development work showed that it is not just specification that goes on in the specification stages, nor just design in the design stages, etc. In fact *all* activities go on during *all* the phases, it is just that they peak at their appropriate stage.

For example, some coding might be done during the specification stages, perhaps to explore an idea. More code will be written during the design stage, perhaps to try out design concepts, and also to work on parts of the design that are stable. The coding activity peaks during the coding stage, and continues, although at a reduced level, through the integration phase as there are often modules that are not quite finished. During validation it will still continue, perhaps for quick fixes on any bugs that are found, and of course there is always coding during maintenance.

Summary

Of course, ways are devised to get round these problems. Stage reviews are put into the lifecycle to check the continuing validity of the requirements specification. Documents go through a formal quality review process to ensure that as wide a view as possible is brought to bear on them. These techniques help the lifecycle model through its difficulties, but do not eliminate them altogether.

The linear approach of the lifecycle model may be restrictive, but it does not mean that structured design and development techniques cannot be used (Zahniser, 1983). Any technique that might be useful can be used at any stage of the lifecycle, for example the use of flow charts in the specification stage, or data flow diagrams and data structure charts in the design stage. Where the lifecycle has been questioned, however, is that some of the newer techniques of software development, like object-oriented design or evolutionary development, are sufficiently different that a new approach is needed.

1.5 Approaches to problem solving

Software development is, above all, about solving problems, yet many of the current strategies ignore some of the key concepts which have been in use for many years in other disciplines. This section looks in depth at various approaches to problem solving, and presents a simple model for how people solve problems. Although it might seem that this has little to do with prototyping, understanding how problems are solved is essential to understanding why prototyping is such a powerful systems development technique.

Types of problem

The problems which have to be solved may range from those that are either simple enough or sufficiently well-structured to be clearly defined and understood, to those which because of their complexity or uncertain nature are neither well-defined nor easily understood. In general terms, problems can be classified as:

- well-structured
- semi-structured
- unstructured

Well-structured problems have the following characteristics:

- A finite set of alternative courses of action.
- The solutions can be derived from an analytic model.
- The effectiveness and efficiency of the solutions can be measured.

In well-structured problems all the factors affecting the problem solving process can be identified and quantified. This often applies to problems similar to ones which have been solved before, since previous experience can be used. Unstructured problems do not meet any of the characteristics listed above. The significant factors affecting the problem cannot be identified precisely, and it is difficult to measure how effective a proposed solution may be. Many problems have both structured and unstructured aspects, and these are termed semi-structured.

The problems for which software systems are developed may be of any type. It is easy to write a program for a well-structured problem, since the problem structure can be reflected in the software itself. However, well-structured problems are quite rare, and the majority of software development deals with semi-structured or unstructured problems, which are far harder to solve. Furthermore, different parts of a problem may have different characteristics, eg the user interface is well-structured, but the algorithm only semi-structured.

1.5.1 How people solve problems

Techniques for solving problems are as diverse as the problems themselves, ranging from an informal heuristic approach, through to the more formal scientific method. The following descriptions of some of these problem solving methods have been simplified.

Heuristics

If the problem is unstructured, then the only approach may be to use heuristic methods. A heuristic method is a 'rule of thumb' which has worked well in the past, for example 'This technique worked well last time, so I'll try it again'. Not surprisingly, given the nature of unstructured problems, it is not a strict, analytic method, but is a plausible method to discover a solution to the current problem. However, there is no guarantee of finding the best solution. Heuristic solutions aren't usually particularly rigorous, and unexpected situations can cause problems when a heuristic approach is used.

The decision-centred approach

Most people, when faced with a variety of choices to a problem, try to collect all the available information, analyse the situation, and choose the solution that best balances all the various factors: the costs, the benefits, the risks, etc. However, important information affecting the decision may be lacking, and decisions may have to be made quickly, and under pressure. The decision-centred approach recognises that at some time it is too difficult, time-consuming, or expensive to perform a full analysis of the situation. In this case the goal of finding the 'best' solution is replaced by the goal of finding 'the best feasible alternative at this time'.

The scientific method

The scientific method of problem solving is an old and well-established technique which is widely used in the physical sciences. Figure 1.2 shows the steps involved.

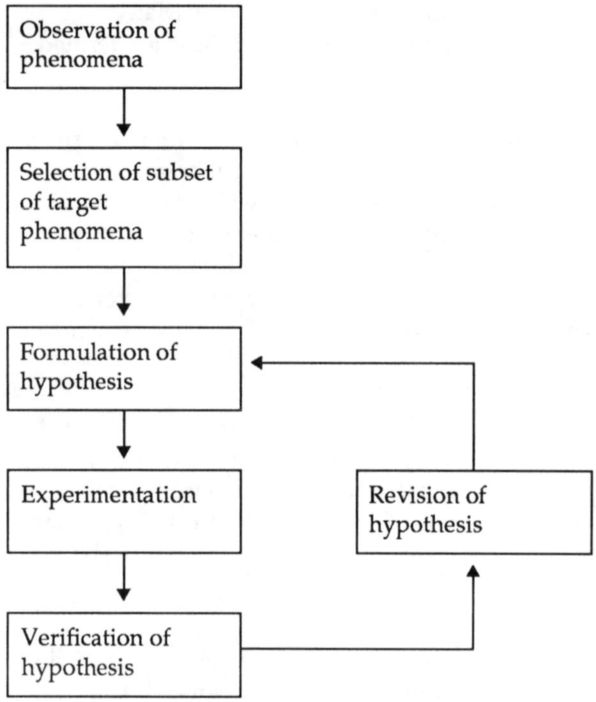

Figure 1.2 The scientific method

In this method the 'problem' is to formulate a hypothesis which gives an accurate and consistent description of the observed behaviour of the system being studied. The 'solution' is then the theoretical model used to capture and predict the behaviour of this system, eg an equation to fit measured data.

The cycle of hypothesis – experimentation – verification – revision is used to achieve a convergence between the predictions of the model, and the behaviour of the system being modelled. It is possible to check the degree of convergence between problem and solution by seeing how closely the hypothesis models the observed behaviour.

Comparison with software development

The problem that software development aims to solve is to build a system that meets the needs of the customer. In many cases there is no existing system to study the behaviour of, and so it is not easy to define the nature of the real problem, nor is it easy to formulate a precise specification of the required system.

In the lifecycle approach, the requirements specification is a *prediction* of the behaviour of a future system that *might* meet the customer's needs. It is not analogous to the formulation of a hypothesis in the scientific method, since it is a partial model of system behaviour. The only complete model of system behaviour is the implementation of the system itself. This is equivalent to the theoretical model used in the physical sciences.

However, the behaviour of this system can only be truly verified by reference to the customer's needs, ie the real problem. This is done in the lifecycle approach *after* the system has been implemented. Convergence between the problem, and the system intended to solve it, can only be achieved by starting again, or by trying to change the completed system, under the guise of system maintenance.

In contrast, the prototyping approach uses the cycle of prototype – verify – refine to allow a model of system behaviour to *evolve*, and as it is a working model, it can evolve into a complete system. Alternatively, the prototype might be used as a partial description of the system, and the system then built using a conventional lifecycle approach.

However, the prototyping method shares the same disadvantages as the scientific method, in that the evolution of hypotheses does not necessarily lead to an optimal solution. In the sciences, many hypotheses may be generated in an attempt to solve a particularly intractable problem. The 'best' hypothesis is the one that most accurately models the observed behaviour, and makes the fewest assumptions. The other hypotheses are discarded.

Similarly, in software development it may be necessary to throw systems away. This often happens because the wrong system has been built, but it should also happen as a necessary part of the problem solving process. The prototyping strategy recognises this, hence the evolutionary development cycle (see Chapter 2 for more information).

Finally, the scientific method emphasises the importance of better descriptive tools. The development of calculus and vectors led to profound improvements in science. Advances in software development, like new programming languages, new computational strategies, or new development methods like prototyping, can have an equally powerful effect.

A model of problem solving

Reasoning to solve a problem involves two basic types of information:

- The knowledge of the problem solver, based on personal experience (internal information).
- The knowledge of the problem domain, based on the type of problem (external information).

The reasoning process starts with the problem solver in a particular state of mind. This state of mind is represented in Figure 1.3(a) by the 'thinking' axis, which indicates everything involved in the thought process: perception, reasoning, knowledge, intuition, the problem, and many other factors. The state of mind shown in (a) does not change with time. However, a solution is rarely, if ever, reached without the problem solver progressing their state of mind, so this diagram is not realistic.

A better representation of the reasoning process is shown in Figure 1.3(b). Many factors influence the reasoning process, so the state of mind of the problem solver evolves with time. The thinking process, as people reason about a problem, changes; people revise their knowledge as they get new information about the problem, or make deductions.

However, Figures 1.3(a) and (b) assume that a problem has a single solution, although this is not very likely. Figure 1.3(c) shows a much more realistic scenario, where the problem has many plausible solutions, and the chosen one is not necessarily the optimum solution, if indeed an optimum solution exists.

The model so far shows the reasoning process evolving with time and reaching a solution to the problem, but it assumes that the problem is fixed, and cannot change. But external information can influence the problem domain, and cause change. The reasoning process itself may cause the problem solver to realise that a different problem should really be solved. Figure 1.3(d) shows the nature of the problem evolving with time. The problem space axis represents all the factors associated with the problem. A consequence of the changing nature of the problem is that the solution to the original problem will probably no longer be valid.

Problem solving and software development

The aim of the above discussion is to show that the task of problem solving, while it varies in difficulty according to the nature of the problem, also varies with time according to the state of mind of the participants, the knowledge available, and the influence of internal and external factors. This implies that, apart from very simple or well-defined problems, any problem solving mechanism needs to take account of these changes.

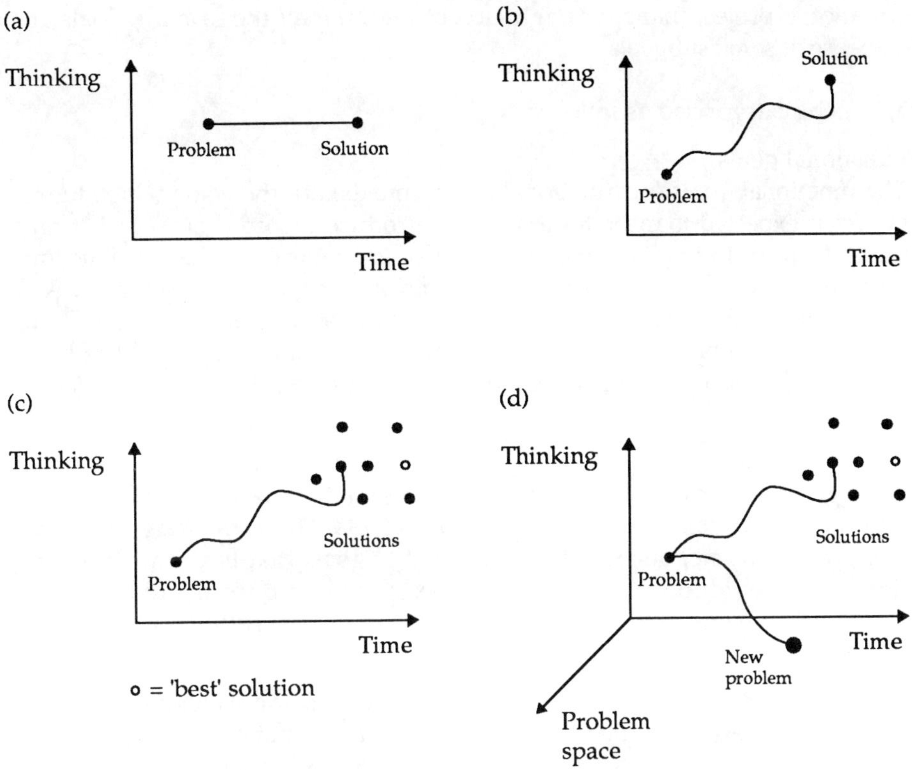

Figure 1.3 The thinking process:
(a) Unchanging thinking process
(b) Thinking process changes with time
(c) Multiple solutions
(d) Thinking process and problem change with time

1.5.2 Goals and solutions

The first step in the problem solving process is a statement of the problem to be solved. But in many instances either the problem cannot be stated accurately and unambiguously, or the real problem is not known. In order to understand better the problem solving process, some basic definitions are needed.

Goals

All projects have a set of goals which they must try to achieve. Although it is not always easy to state the goals of a project, failure to do so is a primary cause of unsuccessful projects, since it is impossible to know whether a project is off-target if the target is not defined. Goals can usually be ranked by degree of importance; a project manager might accept reaching all the primary goals at the expense of some subgoals.

Goals can be categorised as follows:

- Functional goals
  The functional goals (or functional requirements) are the goals which the system is expected to meet, for example to produce a word processor that runs under Unix, or to implement a menu-driven user interface. These are the top-level, primary goals of the project, and they are not usually negotiable. A system that does not meet a top-level goal is not acceptable. These goals can be prioritised, since some goals may conflict with others or be politically sensitive. Functional goals are either achieved or not; there is no partial achievement.
- Quality goals
  Some goals may express quality requirements, and can be quantified, for example performance or reliability requirements. They may vary with time, and are usually negotiable. It is these quality goals that have the most impact on the solutions, since they are measurable, and the degree to which these goals are met determines how 'good' a particular solution is.
- Constraints
  All systems must be implemented within a set of constraints on the resources available, for example the time, the people, or the money available to complete the project. Constraints can always be specified for a goal, since there is always an upper and lower limit for which it would be unacceptable to be outside.

All of these have an influence on the overall system goals, as shown in Figure 1.4.

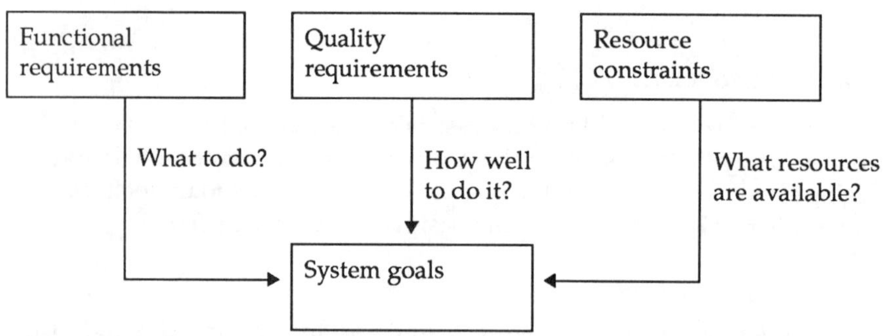

Figure 1.4 Factors influencing project goals

Specifying goals

Systems developers are very likely to have to sort out their goals from a document, usually a requirements specification, which is often written either by managers, or even worse by a committee. Such documents typically produce a long list of goals and objectives which are often no more than a wish list, and will need to be ranked in importance.

All projects must have their goals, requirements, and constraints clearly specified. The project documentation – the requirements specification and the functional specification – should answer, at the very least, the following questions:

- What is the project meant to *achieve*?
- What are the major project *goals*, in priority?
- What *functions* must the system actually perform?
- How *well* should the system do them?
- What are the *constraints* on doing them?

However, it is much easier to state these questions than to answer them. There are many problems in trying to specify goals, for example:

- goals may conflict with other goals
- goals change with time

Goals can conflict with each other. A goal of improving system response time may conflict with introducing comprehensive validation and error checking. Goals also evolve with time; this is why a business plan will specify long term strategic goals and short term tactical goals. The situation is no different in software development, as goals can always be expected to change throughout the lifetime of a project. Nevertheless, the project must start by specifying the goals.

Understanding the problem

The *problem* to be solved is how to achieve the project's goals, while being within the specified constraints. The statement of the problem must then describe these goals and constraints, using whatever language or notation is most appropriate.

Solutions

The *solution* is how to reach these goals within the required constraints. Since it is extremely likely that a project has several goals and subgoals, there will be several solutions which meet these goals, to a varying degree. This means that the solutions, as well as the goals, must be evaluated and ranked.

Solutions are specific to a particular problem, and the set of functional goals, constraints and requirements associated with the problem. Changing the constraints, for example, changes the nature of the problem, and hence the acceptable solutions. There are many techniques to help the process of choosing the most appropriate solution, for example critical success factors, impact analysis, and risk management (see Chapter 4 for more information).

It is very easy to make the mistake of treating solutions as goals. The real solutions are those which provide a positive contribution towards meeting the project goals. Solutions are accepted, or not, according to how they contribute. Some may have negative effects, and will not be acceptable. For example, a project might have the following goals:

- to build an efficient customer database system
- to use the B-tree file access method for data storage and retrieval

But the use of a B-tree is only one of the many possible ways of building an efficient system, and having it as a goal precludes other, perhaps more effective solutions. It is really a *solution* to the goal of building an efficient system, and is not a goal itself. Furthermore, the solution cannot be correctly determined unless far more information is available, for example:

- What are the access time requirements?
- How much data exists?
- What is the data volatility?
- Are search times more critical than insertion or deletion times?

Without knowing these basic parameters, the chosen solution may not meet the operational needs of its users. Figure 1.5 shows the steps from goal formulation through to solution formulation.

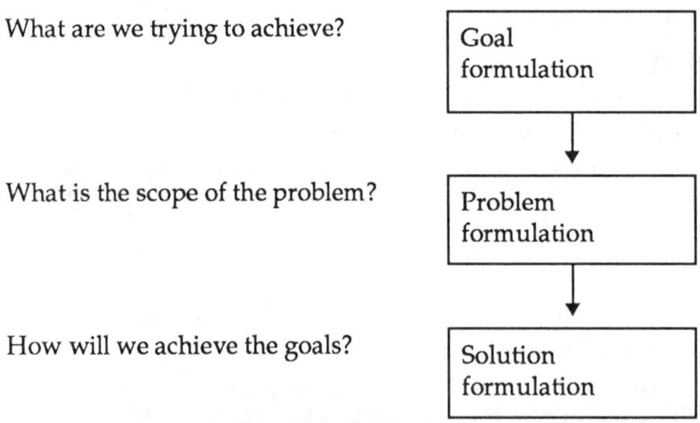

Figure 1.5 The process of moving from goals to solutions

Summary

Goals are important because only by knowing what the project is trying to achieve can the real problem be discovered. For example, a problem might be stated as: *build a system to save money on order processing,* whereas the unspecified goals for the system are to: *build an automated ordering, manufacturing, and stores processing system to be better able to react to a changing marketplace.*

If the project goals cannot be stated, it is very likely that the problem itself is of a vague and unsatisfactory nature. Any project that starts out with uncertainty is unlikely to have a worthwhile outcome.

1.5.3 Strategies for prototyping

Not all people are equal when it comes to making decisions. Some company managers make far better business decisions than other managers, and run successful companies, while others make bad mistakes, and their companies fail. But despite the thought that those successful people know something which the others don't, there is no unique decision-making strategy that is secret to those that are successful. Some people intuitively *know* what is right, some analyse the facts and figures in great detail before making a decision, and others rely on years of experience and lessons learned from their mistakes. Some just guess, and hope for the best.

It is the same with software development. Few software problems are well-structured and precise, and so most are not solvable by formal techniques. The less-formal techniques put the emphasis on finding feasible and plausible solutions, and on selecting the best solution from the available alternatives, but they cannot guarantee optimal solutions. However, the lifecycle model, with a strict sequence of specify – design – implement, places considerable emphasis on getting the correct solution first time. There is no explicit stage of gathering of information by looking at the nature of the problem, the goals, and the solutions, no chance to evaluate proposed solutions, and little recognition of the importance of interplay between the stages.

It is not entirely surprising that for some projects, the lifecycle and other methods don't work very well, but for others can be very successful. Projects don't fail because people don't know what the secret to success is. There isn't one. Projects do fail, however, if people think they have found it.

Is a strategy necessary for software development?

The real world, whatever it is, is non-deterministic. Unexpected problems occur every day, yet these can be solved because people are capable of reasoning about a problem, understanding their goals, and fixing up a solution on-the-fly.

Computer systems are deterministic, or at least people would like them to be. Since computers have no common sense, they cannot compensate for unexpected errors, and must assume that their programs are correct and complete. A strategy is an attempt to transform non-deterministic tasks into deterministic tasks for solution by computer, and so must attempt to prescribe all possible system problems.

Strategies do have some problems, though:

- They try to be all-embracing, and hence are very large.
- Development effort is expended in following the strategy, rather than in finding the best solution.
- There is a shift of blame onto the strategy if the project fails.
- Management can rely on the strategy without understanding the technology.
- The choice of a strategy is often subject to organisational politics.
- They prevent the best people from using the full range of their abilities.

However, there are very good reasons for having a strategy for software development. A single strategy cannot solve all development problems, yet some kind of strategy is needed to avoid the development process becoming degenerate. A strategy should provide a framework for software development, but it should be tailored to each individual project. The framework provides a common starting point for the development process, for example:

- setting goals, like software standards and managerial control
- specifying a range of tools, techniques, and strategies

Prototyping, and the goal-oriented approach to software development, put the emphasis on balancing the goals of the project with the available resources, and the expected risks. Prototyping is essentially a philosophy for software development.

1.5.4 Promising solutions

In Section 1.3.3 the risks to software development projects were examined. There are many potentially promising ways of attacking these risks; to discuss all of them would be beyond the scope of this book. However, all risks must be put into perspective, and the top risks attacked, rather than expensive resources being wasted on low risks with marginal benefits.

Boehm's ranking of the risks gives an interesting perspective on the problems:

- The technical risks are quite low in the ranking (items 9 and 10).
- The highest risks are due to insufficient resources (items 1 and 2).
- The requirements risks are very significant (items 3, 4, 5, and 6).

Technical risks due to attempting state-of-the-art computer science are not a major cause of project failure. The highest risks are of having insufficient resources for the agreed tasks: not enough people, not enough money, or not enough time. This is a serious problem for project managers to cope with.

The high risk of actually building the wrong system, and delivering something which does not meet the customers requirements means that the first step in any project should be a careful analysis of what the goals, problems, and solutions are. Even so, a project must deal with the risks of change during the project, for example requirements change, or resource reductions.

No easy solutions exist to these problems. Brooks, in his article 'No Silver Bullet', emphasises the key role of the system requirements:

> 'The single hardest part of building a software system is deciding precisely what to build. No other part of the conceptual work is as difficult as establishing the detailed technical requirements, including all the interfaces to people, to machines, and to other software systems. No other part of the work so cripples the resulting system if done wrong. No other part is more difficult to rectify later.' (Brooks, 1987)

As a possible solution, prototyping offers benefits in two main areas:

1 Understanding and defining the requirements (the problem-oriented phase).
2 Building the system (the implementation-oriented phase).

In the problem-oriented phase prototyping can be used for identifying the goals, understanding the problems, and evaluating the possible solutions. A clear statement of requirements should come out of this phase.

In the implementation-oriented phase, prototyping is used to help the technical development process, by prototyping critical or difficult problems.

Along with the use of prototyping, certain project management tools and techniques must be available, for example:

- risk management
- impact analysis
- critical success factors
- estimating techniques
- design to cost or design to time
- incremental or evolutionary development

Prototyping cannot be considered in isolation from project management, because the primary driving force is to build systems that meet the customer's requirements. Therefore developers must make certain the customer understands not only what is possible or impossible, but also how this can vary according to the resources available, and the constraints placed on these resources.

1.6 Conclusions

Software development is unlikely ever to be a simple process. The problems of taking a vague idea, and turning it into a precisely defined and carefully tested system are immense. The software crisis is the result of a demand for new systems that cannot be reliably met by current software tools and techniques.

The difficulties are not directly attributable to the software development strategies that are currently in use, like the lifecycle model, but are a consequence of the nature of the problem that is being addressed. Software systems can be complex and dynamic, and are often difficult to specify and model. There may be better development methods, but it is highly unlikely that they can ever resolve *all* development problems.

If the risks of software development are examined, then the highest risks, ignoring resource problems, are in building the *wrong* system. Even if unlimited resources are available, people will still build systems that do not meet their needs.

The trouble starts at the beginning of the project, with the analysis of the requirements, and their specification. The scientific method of problem-solving points the way here. The aim of the scientific method is to develop a hypothesis which accurately models the observed behaviour of a system. This is done by a cycle of experimentation, verification, and revision. It is not a static process. Hypotheses are revised or discarded if they do not fit.

In the lifecycle approach to software development, the requirements specification is an attempt to *predict* a system to meet a customer's future needs. What the lifecycle model does is to take a 'snapshot' of these requirements at the start, and keep it relatively fixed during the development of the system. The cycle here is specification, design, and implementation. But the revision of the system is only done *after* the system has been implemented, so the cycle is very long, perhaps months or even years. It is so long, in fact, that the requirements for the system are quite likely to have changed by the time the system is finished.

Prototyping takes a different approach, one which recognises that experimentation and change are an essential part of the development process. A prototype can be used in several ways to reduce the risks associated with software development – in understanding and defining the requirements, and in resolving implementation problems. It is not, however, a universal methodology that will solve all development problems, nor is it an excuse for abandoning current planning and development tools and techniques.

Selected reading

General overview of prototyping

Carey, T T and Mason, R E A
Information system prototyping: techniques, tools, and methodologies, *INFOR—The Canadian Journal of Operational Research and Information Processing*, Vol 21, No 3, August 1983, 177–191

Connell, J L and Brice, L
Rapid prototyping, *Datamation*, Vol 30, No 13, August 1984, 93–100

Software development

Berzins, V and Luqi
Software engineering with abstractions, Addison-Wesley, 1990

Page-Jones, M
The practical guide to structured systems design, Prentice-Hall International, 2nd edition, 1988

Pressman, R S
Software engineering: a practitioner's approach, McGraw-Hill, 2nd edition, 1987

Yourdon, E
Modern structured analysis, Prentice-Hall International, 1989

Software projects

Brooks, F P Jr
The mythical man-month, Addison-Wesley, 1982

Brooks, F P Jr
No silver bullet: essence and accidents of software engineering, *Computer*, Vol 20, No 4, April, 1987, 10-19

Problem solving and computing

Dromey, R G
How to solve it by computer, Prentice-Hall International, 1982

Harel, D
Algorithmics: the spirit of computing, Addison-Wesley, 1987

2 Prototyping software

Introduction

Before a company embarks on the manufacture of a new model of a car, it builds a prototype. The prototype is, in many respects, identical to the cars that will roll off the production line, so why bother to build it? Clearly, before starting the expensive process of setting up the production line, buying components and raw materials, and starting a marketing campaign, the company needs to make sure that the car will sell, will be easy to manufacture, and be mechanically reliable.

The risks of moving from a set of engineering drawings to full production, without any intervening stages, are high. If, for example, the new gearbox design is wrong, then the error will have to be corrected, and all the models sold recalled. Such problems are not unknown in the car industry. However, the risks of gearbox failure can be considerably reduced, at the cost of building a pre-production prototype which can be tested.

Likewise, the risk of the car not selling is also a problem. Maybe the body shape or the interior design are unattractive to potential car buyers. These factors, too, need to be tested before the expensive process of production can begin. The prototype can be used by the marketing teams to gauge customer reaction.

So, when developing a new model of car, the prototype is used to reduce the risk of failure. Why then is it unusual to produce a prototype when developing a software system?

The cost of producing a car is largely tied up with the manufacturing process. However, the cost of software manufacture is negligible in comparison with the cost of design and development. This is the key difference – to build a prototype car, almost identical with the planned model, is the cheap part of the whole process; to build a prototype software system, almost identical with the planned system, is seen as the expensive part of the whole process. The natural argument follows: why not simply reproduce the prototype, and sell it? Why is the prototype not just like the real thing?

The trap of equating the prototype to the real thing is one that must be avoided. Indeed, when introducing prototyping into a company, the arguments against this must be well-practised. There are many ways in which the prototype can be different from the planned system, and each can be used to reduce the risks involved with the production of a software system.

The purpose of this chapter
This chapter defines rapid prototyping in software. Its purpose is to make the reader aware of what prototyping is, why it works, what parts of software engineering it can help with, and its expected benefits and weaknesses.

General organisation
The first section of this chapter defines rapid prototyping as a model of the planned system. It explains how this model differs from the final product, where prototyping can fit into the traditional lifecycle model, and what some of the key aspects of prototyping are.

Section 2.2 examines the rationale of prototyping, ie why it works. In particular it relates prototyping to problem solving techniques.

In section 2.3 the problems of system requirements and specifications are discussed. This is seen as one of the hardest parts of the software lifecycle to get right, and the one in which prototyping can help the most.

The strengths and weaknesses of prototyping are discussed in section 2.4. These are particularly important when it comes to deciding whether to adopt a prototyping strategy.

2.1 What is rapid prototyping?

Software prototyping is, as already discussed, one of many promising ideas in software development. This section introduces a formal definition of prototyping, and looks at the various types of prototype, and how they can be used.

A definition of a prototype

A prototype is a software model of system behaviour which can be used to understand the proposed system, or certain aspects of it, and to clarify the requirements.

The use of the word 'model' needs explaining. A prototype is a representation of a system, something that is not the complete system, but has the important characteristics of the final system. The expectations of what these characteristics are, and how the prototype will be used, varies according to:

- the user of the prototype
- the information that is needed
- the application area

For example, in a well-defined application, the requirements may be known, but there is still a need to prototype the user interface, as the customer is not quite certain of the 'look and feel' of the proposed system. This type of prototype can have dummy functions, and may be thrown away once the user interface has been defined.

In a much more complex system, the prototype can be used to gain information on critical system components or aspects of the design. For example, the database could be prototyped to get a feel for the design, and an estimate of expected access times. Any serious problems can be identified before they can cause trouble.

Although the prototype may just be a model, and be thrown out later, a system prototype can be the first step in the implementation process. Successive iterations will add more detail and functionality, and because the early prototypes are available for evaluation, the refinements can be guided by the feedback from demonstrations to the customer. The customer may find that the early prototypes are useful in themselves, and the completed system will not give the customer any unpleasant surprises.

How rapid is rapid prototyping?

The commonplace use of the term 'rapid' in conjunction with prototyping implies that the prototype should be completed as quickly as possible. However, the value of a prototype is in the degree to which it helps meet the system goals, and not in the speed of development.

As a fundamental reason for prototyping is to understand the system goals, this must be done before the development can proceed. The need for this information determines how rapid the prototype should be. In some cases the speed of writing the prototype is traded for the quality of the prototype, and the prototype is ultimately thrown out. In other cases the prototype is used to investigate a particular problem, or to elicit information, and the prototyping continues as long as the problem remains unresolved.

2.1.1 The prototype as a model

A prototype can be regarded as a model of some system that one might hope to build in the future; it is a cut-down version of the real system. A scale model of a bridge has many of the characteristics of the actual bridge, with one notable exception – that of its physical size. In the same way, a software prototype may be regarded as a scale model of some other system, in that it has many of the same characteristics of that system – with some notable exceptions.

The model of the bridge may be used to determine some of the characteristics of the real bridge – the thickness of girders, or how the components fit together. Similarly, the software prototype may be used to determine some characteristics of the real system; the structure of the database, or the commands available through the user interface. The model of the bridge may be used to infer information about the real bridge, such as its strength or stability. The software prototype may also be used to infer information about the real system, such as the number of code modules, or the size of the data structures.

So in the same way that a physical model has some of the characteristics of the real thing and can be used to estimate some of the others, the software model, or prototype, also has some of the characteristics of the real system, and can be used to estimate others.

A scale model of a bridge is noticeably different from the real thing in its size. Clearly, there is no direct equivalent to a change in physical size in software, so there the analogy ends. There are many characteristics that can be chosen as the key differences between a prototype and the system it is attempting to model:

- user functionality
- underlying complexity
- user interface
- simpler data structures
- performance
- robustness
- hardware
- toolsets

User functionality

By reducing the functionality available to the user it is possible to include the essential functions of the system in the prototype. This allows the most important parts of the system to be tested without going to the expense of building a complete system. If a system that is used frequently is analysed, it will probably be found that about 20 per cent of the functions available are used about 80 per cent of the time. The other 20 per cent of the time is spent on the remaining 80 per cent of the functions. This '80-20' rule[1] is not always applicable, but it is surprising how often it turns out to be approximately true. If it is possible to predict the major 20 per cent of functions and build those into a prototype, then the goal of a rapid and cheap prototype is achieved.

Underlying complexity

The underlying functionality of the system can be reduced, as opposed to reducing the functionality available to the user. For example, a multi-user system can be built in single-user mode only – thus avoiding the need to worry about the problems of data locking and other cases of multiple access to the same resource. A second example is that of a system that is designed to be distributed. A prototype can be built which resides on a single computer system, thus avoiding the problems of the communications and their consequences.

User interface

A prototype that only has a user interface is important in showing potential users how the system might look. Screen layouts can be empirically tested, command names derived, usage of colour determined, etc.

These prototypes have little functionality under the façade of the user interface. The system commands can be entered, and example output can be displayed, but little or no processing goes on underneath. The simplest example of this type of prototype is a paper-based storyboard. Here the user interface is drawn onto sheets of paper and shown sheet by sheet.

Simpler data structures

Some applications rely on complex data structures to achieve their tasks. A lot of effort can be put into making these structures efficient. A common example of this is in a relational database. During the designing of a system, the data structures in a relational database have to be put through a series of transformations known as normalisation. This ensures the integrity of the database later on. If this stage is missed out during the building of a prototype, the database may work sufficiently well to demonstrate the principles of the proposed system, although the data cannot always be relied on.

---

[1] The 80-20 rule is an approximation of the law first observed by Zipf (1949), who noticed that in natural language text, the nth most frequently occurring word seems to occur with a frequency proportional to $1/n$. The 80-20 rule is also observed in file systems, where 80 percent of transactions deal with the most active 20 per cent of the records in the file.

Performance

A prototype can be a system with low performance. Whereas the final system reacts fast by using the most efficient data structures and algorithms, the prototype can be a slow system because one of the main aims is to build it quickly and cheaply. It is not necessary for a system to be fast to see if the user interface looks right, or to see if the database can hold all the relevant data. A prototype can also be used to explore performance aspects of designs, particularly in non-deterministic systems.

Robustness

Anyone who has written a significant piece of user interface code will know that a large amount of it is devoted to checking the validity of the user input. The 80-20 rule also applies here; 20 per cent of the code provides the functionality, the other 80 per cent provides the error checking (Mills, 1988). The same sort of checking goes on between any two items of software that are developed by different people. For example, a library module will generally perform a significant amount of checking on the parameters it is given. A prototype built without these checks can be built at far less cost than the real system.

Hardware

A prototype could be built on a different hardware base. The final product may be intended for a mainframe, but a prototype could be built on a personal computer (PC). This could be an advantage if, for instance, a good software tool was available on the PC with which the prototype might be built. The aim is to build rapidly and cheaply, and a special tool in a PC environment might be very useful. The PC system could then be demonstrated to the customer.

Toolsets

In order to build a prototype quickly, it is sometimes helpful to use a toolset that one might not intend to use in the final product. The tools for building the prototype may have some detrimental effect that would render the prototype useless for the real product. For example, some languages can be used to develop applications very quickly, but may produce inefficient code. The tools might be too expensive to sell with each copy of the product. This does not apply to compiled languages, but only to tools forming part of the runtime system.

Summary

A prototype may exhibit any or all of these characteristics. For example, a prototype might be built that had a complete user interface, together with a full implementation of the major system functions. The minor functions would not be implemented. Furthermore, the major functions could be built without proper error checking of the users' input. This prototype might be used to demonstrate to customers or users in order to obtain feedback.

The concept that people have of a prototype may not be correct. It is important that this is recognised and understood by those involved. It is no good creating a prototype on hardware X, and not explaining to a potential user that the system is actually being released on hardware Y. If one did, the knowledge gained from the exercise may be somewhat dubious, although this does depend on the use of the prototype.

2.1.2 Using the prototype

The prototype must serve a purpose. The important thing about using a prototype is that it serves to gain some knowledge. It is used for getting ideas, clarifying ideas, and confirming thoughts. Unless some knowledge can be gained from it, there would have been no purpose in building it in the first place; it would have been more valuable to develop the final system straightaway. In order to gain knowledge, some experiments must be performed and the results monitored. There are various ways in which the prototype can be experimented with:

- Showing it to potential users and recording their reactions and comments.
- Releasing it to potential users for a trial period, recording their comments, and recording the functions they use.
- Releasing it as a working system with reduced functionality, and similarly recording comments and functions used.
- Developers can run it and measure some characteristics, such as performance.

The knowledge gained from such experiments can be useful for developers in order to assess the specification or design, for managers in order to see if the work is progressing according to the plans, and for users and customers to see if this is what they really want.

2.1.3 Prototyping and the lifecycle model

In order to understand how prototyping can be applied to the problems of software development, it is necessary to return to the software lifecycle model. Figure 2.1 shows this in a slightly different perspective to that discussed earlier.

The lifecycle starts in step 1 with a definition of the problem to be solved. Once there is a sufficient understanding of the problem, a requirements specification can be written. This is shown in step 2 as an empty box, since none of the internal system details are known at this point. Step 3 specifies the functionality of the system, represented in the diagram by input and output arrows. Again, the internal system details are not defined. When the functional specification is complete, the design process can start. The design specifies how the system should work, down to the level of the internal system components. These are shown in step 4 by the internal boxes. Details of these components are resolved in step 5 during the implementation of the design. Finally, in step 6, the completed system is delivered to the customer.

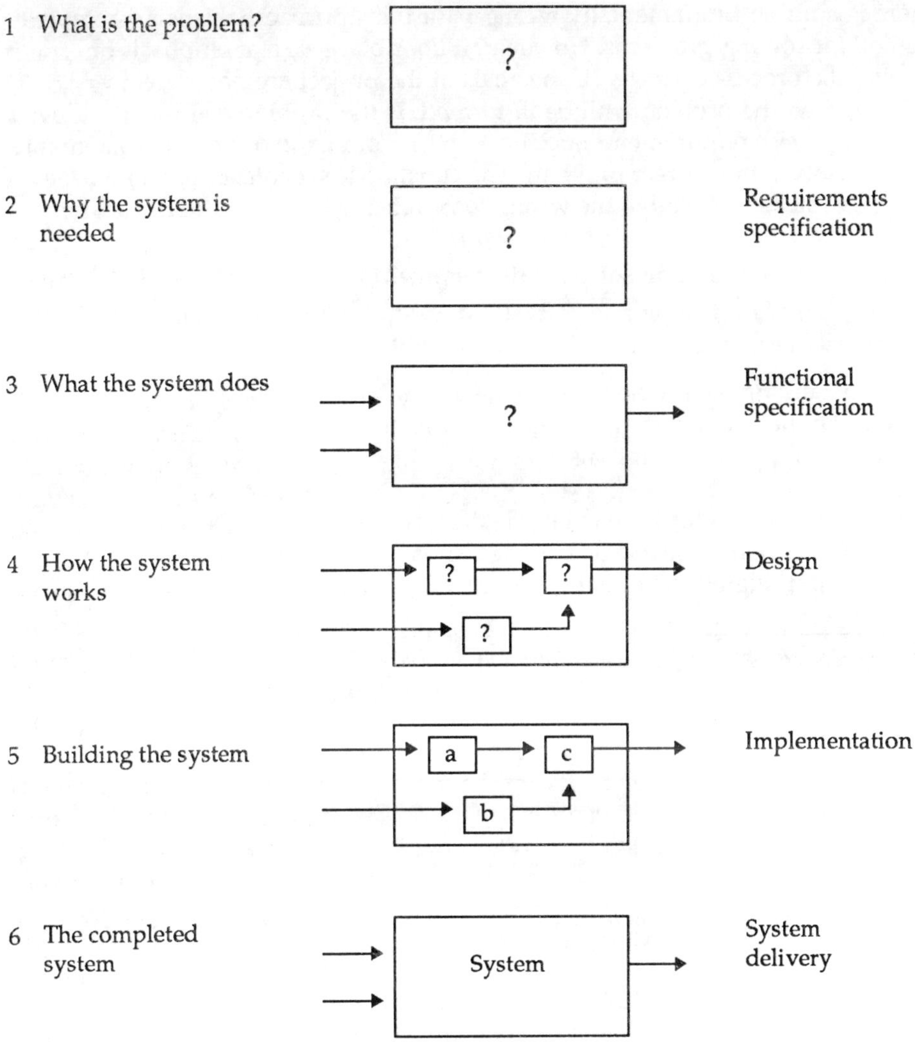

Figure 2.1 Conventional software lifecycle, illustrating the processes involved at each stage

The lifecycle is essentially a process of top-down decomposition, where each successive stage takes the 'black-box' of the previous stage, and refines the level of detail until finally the system is implemented. The difficulty is that if any stage is performed incorrectly, for example a specification is ambiguous or in error, the following stages build on this error, and the problems increase as the process continues.

There is nothing fundamentally wrong with this approach; this is an accepted method for solving problems. However, it does place a great emphasis on starting the process correctly. If the goals of the project are not correctly defined, then the problem will be ill-formed. If the problem is ill-formed, even the most precise requirements specification cannot turn the eventual system into one that solves the correct problem. The functional specification, and all the successive steps will lead to the wrong system being built.

The role of prototyping in software development

The key role of prototyping in software development is that it can help to get the critical start-up phases of the project right:

- understanding the problem
- defining the goals (requirements)
- evaluating possible solutions

This process covers steps 1 and 2 in the lifecycle model, and can be referred to as the problem-oriented phase, to distinguish it from the implementation phase of the project. Figure 2.2 illustrates this.

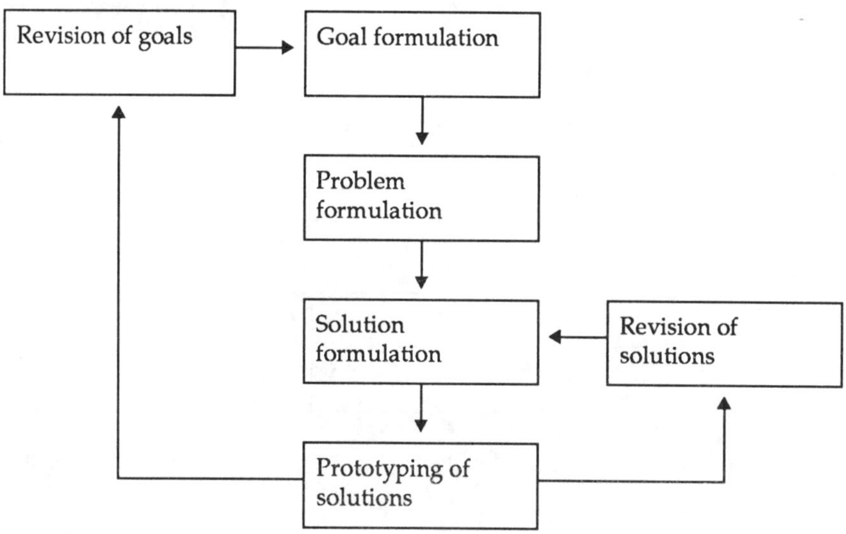

Figure 2.2 Use of prototyping for problem solving

Figure 2.2 does not show where the problem-oriented, prototyping phase fits into the implementation. This is because prototyping can be used at any point where there are implementation problems to be resolved, although it is much more likely to be used for the critical early stages of specification and design.

A project will normally start with a problem-oriented phase to understand the problem, and to define the requirements. The prototype may then be thrown away. But prototyping can also be used to find out information useful to the system design, for example the performance of a key component, or in any other phase of the implementation process.

The prototype does not have to be thrown out; a system may be built in increments, where each deliverable increment is essentially a prototype of the final system, or the system could evolve through a sequence of increasingly refined prototypes until a deliverable system is achieved.

The distinction between problem-oriented and implementation-oriented phases is a useful way of thinking about the role of prototyping. However, because an exact definition of prototyping is impossible, many authors have completely different views of what it means. The next section looks at the ways in which prototyping has been classified. But whichever classification is used, the basic role of prototyping is still in the problem-oriented process described in this section.

2.1.4 Key aspects of prototyping

The differing expectations that people have for a prototype, and the various ways in which prototypes can be used in systems development, have led to many attempts at classifying prototyping. The following list gives the most popular classifications:

- early/middle/late prototyping (Ratcliffe, 1988)
- data-driven prototyping (Appleton, 1983)
- exploratory/experimental/evolutionary prototyping (Floyd, 1984)
- horizontal/vertical prototyping (Floyd, 1984)
- throw-away/incremental/evolutionary prototyping (several authors)
- exploratory/experimental/organisational prototyping (Mayhew and Dearnley, 1986)

This section looks at the various classes of prototyping, although it should be regarded as more than just a theoretical classification, since it defines the key areas of prototyping which form the prototyping strategy defined in Chapter 3. From the viewpoint of software development the key areas are:

- how prototyping can be used in solving problems
- what to prototype
- when to prototype

Prototyping and problem solving

From the problem solving viewpoint prototyping can be classified as:

- explanatory prototyping
- exploratory prototyping
- experimental prototyping
- evolutionary prototyping

This classification is similar to that of Floyd (1984), but with the addition of explanatory prototyping. The role of prototyping in problem solving is not clear-cut, since there is no complete theory of how people solve problems. The categories indicate the general areas in which prototypes can provide assistance, rather than defining actual types of prototype.

Explanatory prototyping is the use of prototypes to explain, demonstrate, and inform. The prototypes tend to be horizontal in functionality (see later), and will usually be thrown away. Almost any type of prototype can be used in an explanatory role.

Exploratory prototyping is concerned with problem determination, clarifying the requirements and goals of the system, and in examining alternative solutions. Exploratory prototyping tends to be informal and unstructured, and the prototypes are usually thrown away once the necessary information is obtained from them.

Experimental prototyping evaluates the proposed solutions to find the optimum one. There is a wide variation in the literature about what experimental prototyping means, but in the view of the authors it is closest to the original definition of prototyping, as a means for modelling system behaviour. The prototype may be thrown away, enhanced, or even used in a product, depending on its quality.

Evolutionary prototyping is used to refine a solution. It assumes that the nature of the problem will evolve with time, that the system requirements evolve, and that when used the system will generate new requirements.

Evolutionary prototyping should not be confused with the use of prototyping for evolutionary systems development, which this book calls evolutionary development.

What to prototype

The functional aspects of a prototype allow two broad classes of prototyping to be identified (Floyd, 1984):

- vertical prototyping
- horizontal prototyping

Figure 2.3 shows an example of vertical and horizontal prototyping. A vertical prototype builds only selected functions, but these are implemented in their final form. Only the most useful functions are built, and this means that the overall system design is largely fixed. Even though only limited functions are available, the vertical prototype should still allow useful tasks to be performed.

Vertical prototyping can be used to provide an early version of a system, which is sufficient for the users to gain experience, and which can be enhanced by adding further functions. Used in this way, the vertical prototype becomes the system, and is not thrown away.

Horizontal prototyping provides a partial implementation of almost all of the system functions. It can be used to show how the target system will look or behave, but will not usually be of production quality. Horizontal prototyping is used to simulate system behaviour, and to help identify possible problems before they appear in the system. A horizontal prototype may evolve into the complete system, but is more usually thrown out because quality has been traded for speed of building.

In many prototyping situations the functionality is a mixture of both vertical and horizontal prototyping. This is sometimes called *diagonal* prototyping, although in reality it is not a particularly useful classification. The distinction between horizontal and vertical prototyping is useful in defining the scope of a prototype.

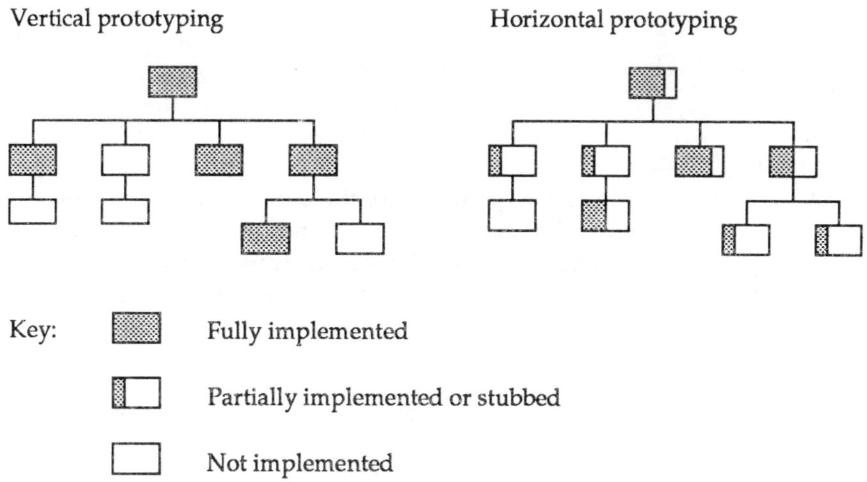

Figure 2.3 Vertical and horizontal prototyping
Note: In practice the distinction is rarely as clear as this

When to prototype

Prototyping is sometimes classified as early, middle, or late prototyping, depending on which position in the lifecycle it occurs. Table 2.1 shows the various possibilities. The choice of when to prototype depends on the purpose of the prototype.

Time	Stage	Purpose
Early	Feasibility study Requirements specifications	Elicit requirements Confirm requirements
Middle	Functional specification Design	Confirm behaviour Check design
Late	Implementation	Investigate operational parameters, eg performance

Table 2.1 Early, middle, and late prototyping in the software lifecycle.

Development strategies

There is no consensus of opinion on the strategies for running a prototyping project. Some authors propose that prototyping becomes an extra stage in the conventional lifecycle model. Others have suggested that a completely new strategy is necessary. This section uses one of the standard classifications of prototyping to describe the strategies:

- throw-away prototyping
- incremental development (or incremental delivery)
- evolutionary development

Throw-away prototyping

A throw-away prototype is an early, rapid prototype which is used, and then discarded. Although it is normally used for requirements analysis in the first stage of the lifecycle process, it can be used at any time during the development. The prototype can be a success even if it fails, since failure identifies problems. Because it is thrown out, this model is easy to incorporate into existing strategies.

Incremental development

Incremental development, or incremental delivery, is a prototyping strategy where the system is built and delivered in small units, each unit adding new functionality until the system is complete. Each incremental delivery moves closer to the final system, and so can be considered as a prototype.

The early increments are the high priority items. They may be simple, low risk items, or if they are sufficiently important, even high risk items. However, high risk items should only be attempted early in the project if their requirements are reasonably well-understood. If they are poorly defined or their requirements are unknown they should be deferred until later. The later increments are those of low priority.

Because the most important increments are built first, an incremental development project may still produce a useful system even if it is stopped before completion.

Incremental development assumes that the overall scope of the system is defined in advance, and is not expected to change much, if at all. Any changes are expected to affect primarily the implementation, and not the requirements.

Evolutionary development

Whereas incremental development is used for slowly growing systems, evolutionary development allows for rapidly growing systems with a high degree of change. The scope of the system is not rigidly defined in advance, and is allowed to evolve according to the changes brought about by demonstrations of the system, and early deliveries to the customer. In addition, changes in the organisation itself, and the environment in which the system is used, may cause the system to evolve. Although the process is open-ended, evolutionary development has a broad planning stage at the start of the development process.

Evolutionary development needs good communications between the customer, the developers, and the user, and places the responsibility on the customer and user to guide the development process. However, the customer and user must expect changes, and thus a new learning process, as the system evolves.

Since the programs are revised so frequently, and the specification, design, and implementation stages tend to overlap, good project management and a very disciplined work style are needed.

2.2 The rationale of prototyping

This section looks at the underlying reasons for prototyping. Whilst this might seem out of place in a book about software prototyping, it is the authors' contention that one of the reasons behind the success of prototyping is that it follows the way that people gain knowledge and understanding in everyday problem situations (Jörgensen, 1984).

2.2.1 Acquiring and using knowledge

The process of acquiring knowledge is known as *cognition*. This includes perception, learning, problem solving, intuition, reasoning, and many other factors. Cognitive skills are gained in many ways:

- by example
- by demonstration
- by solving problems

Often it is difficult to formalise this knowledge, for example, in the statement 'I know that this is the correct thing to do, but I can't explain why!'. Learning from a formal description, like a textbook or written document, is much harder than learning by watching a demonstration. For example, people learn a language by listening and speaking the language; it would be very hard to learn from a book by following the rules of the grammar. Interestingly, learning a language from a formal grammar assumes that the language used to present the grammar is known and understood.

It is also difficult to capture 'reality' with written specifications. A detailed description of a user interface, in terms of the screen displays, commands, and responses, does not capture what it is like to *use* the system, even if the specification can be formally verified as 100 per cent complete and correct.

In using knowledge, people usually prefer informal descriptions to the formal, for example, 'My house is the red brick one past the church', rather than 'Turn left 100 yards past the B209 junction with the A124'. Information that has been gained by experience, rather than a formal plan, is more easily recalled.

2.2.2 Problem solving

Solving problems is an important way of gaining knowledge. However, solving a problem may create new problems that also have to be solved. This is not intentional, but is an unavoidable consequence of seeking information. A solution to a problem will often affect the problem's environment in some way. It is not easy to predict exactly what these changes might be, since the environment is usually very complex, and is itself changing, often unpredictably.

The consequences of this are that when people build and use a new system, they may:

- Discover new useful ways of using the system which they had not previously thought of.
- Learn, by developing and using the system.
- Change their own perceptions, and hence their requirements for the system.

An important point to make here is that there is no way of predicting this in advance, even with training.

2.2.3 How this relates to software development

Systems development is a learning process for all project participants, but in different ways, and to different extents. By being involved in a project people learn new skills and concepts, gaining experience and intuition as a consequence of the development process. They also learn about the specific nature of the problem, how it can be solved, etc. This occurs irrespective of the nature of the experience. Even a failed project teaches something. For example, in the engineering industry, many significant advances have only been possible because failures have caused a fundamental reassessment of a particular technique. As Robert Stephenson said in 1856:

> '...for nothing was so instructive to the younger Members of the Profession, as records of accidents in large works, and of the means employed in repairing the damage. A faithful account of those accidents, and of the means by which the consequneces were met, was really more valuable than a description of the most successful works.' (Whyte, 1975)

The example of the Tacoma Narrows bridge discussed in Chapter 1 led to a fundamental reassessment of bridge design, and the replacement bridge was strengthened to avoid a similar failure.

Taking risks

Two types of error commonly occur in building any kind of system (Weinberg, 1982):

1 Attempting to build a system that *should not* be built.
2 Failing to attempt to build a system that *should* be attempted.

Type 1 errors are much more conspicuous than type 2 errors, for example cancelling a project is a type 1 error, and so are avoided if at all possible by managers. Type 2 errors, in contrast, are 'better' for a manager to make, being far less noticeable.

Managers need to balance these types of risk – building risky systems versus not attempting systems. The problems of balancing risks require difficult choices to be made, for example the trade-off between quality and cost. Most software projects which do not have explicitly-stated goals use delivery as soon as possible as their default goal – which leads to poor quality code being written.

Traditional development

Traditional systems development still has what may be termed 'batch processing' values:

- A low consideration of how the system will be used.
- A much greater concern about planning, specification, system architecture, and design.
- A dislike of change during the development.
- An assumption that written communications can capture the major requirements of the customer.

However, as discussed earlier, concern with the details of the system, and trying to keep the changes to a minimum, runs counter to the way that people learn and reason about a problem.

Prototyping has several advantages over the traditional methods of software development. It can be used as:

- a means of learning
- a means of communication
- a means of changing the development process

Learning

Learning is particularly important for the customer. Often, customers will not request changes, because of a lack of knowledge, or a fear of exposing their ignorance. Customers may have preconceptions based on established work practices, their position and status in their organisation, and do not want to change. Different customers will have different viewpoints, and hence differing requirements.

The rapid, iterative feedback of a prototype allows customers to learn by seeing immediately the consequences of their decisions. This solves the problem of understanding the system from written proposals and specifications.

Communication

Communication is essential in any process of problem solving, whether to communicate difficult ideas and concepts to others, or to elicit information to help solve the problem. Prototyping enhances the communication between all project participants, particularly between customers and developers.

Changing the development process

The traditional development process is an idealised process, which does not fit in well with the way that people think and reason about problems. Prototyping avoids these idealised development models, moving from a linear approach to an evolutionary, risk-driven approach.

Summary

The success of most development projects depends on a sensible approach to the decision making, for example balancing the choice of goals and solutions against the costs, the risks of failure, and the benefits of success. People are not generally very good at making balanced judgements, especially when dealing with risks.

For example, most projects that are stopped before completion are not stopped until the final stages – although if the factors that lead to the project being stopped were being evaluated rationally, the kill points would be spread evenly through the development cycle. But people's assessment of risk is not very good; most managers have a far greater aversion to losses than their desire for gains.

Prototyping cannot guarantee success, but since it allows people to learn and explore, without the costs of a full-scale development, they can have a far more balanced approach to software development.

2.3 System requirements and specification

This section looks at the critical early stages of requirements analysis and specification. These are the most important stages to get right, as mistakes made early in the development are often not detected until the software is operational. At this time any errors are most difficult and expensive to correct.

2.3.1 Why the real problem can't be defined

Many software development strategies have a deceptively simple first stage:

> 'Define the real problem to be solved'

The emphasis here is on the word 'real', the implication being that it should be possible to ignore all extraneous or ambiguous information, and understand the problem sufficiently well to define the *essence* of the development problem. Books on programming also use this approach as a first step in explaining how to write a program.

This is where the novice programmer immediately gets into trouble. A limited knowledge of what is possible in their chosen language, and an inability to state the problem, and to relate it to a programming solution, makes this apparently simple first step extremely difficult. It is not necessarily an incorrect approach, since it serves to focus the programmer's thoughts on stating what the program must achieve, but it does require a high degree of skill and experience.

In software development the difficulties are far greater. The problem is much more complex than that of writing a single program, and the nature of the problem may change with time. Many development strategies start with the customer's requirements, but without actually *seeing* a system in operation, it is very hard for a customer to know *exactly* if the system they have in mind is the most appropriate one. Even if a problem statement can be made at the start of the project, it is not realistic to expect it to be completely correct, and several iterations may be needed before it is satisfactory.

2.3.2 Requirements analysis

Requirements analysis can be divided into several phases, for example following Pressman (1987):

- problem recognition
- problem evaluation
- solution synthesis
- review of specifications

The analysis process is traditionally done by a series of meetings and interviews, particularly between the systems analyst and the customer, to establish the requirements. The analyst often builds a 'paper' model of the system, perhaps using data flow diagrams or other graphical means, to use as a basis for these discussions.

However, the requirements analysis stage has several major difficulties to resolve:

- What requirements are missing?
- Are the requirements acceptable?
- Are the requirements consistent and error-free?
- Can the requirements be achieved?

Good analysts are those who have the knowledge and intuition to separate out the answers to these questions, from all the mass of information that the analysis process generates. Not everyone can do this, and many systems fail because the analyst did not have a sufficient understanding of the steps needed to take the requirements, and turn them into a real system.

The problem of requirements analysis is that the only way to be certain that the system requirements are correct is to build a system to meet these requirements – an expensive exercise if the requirements are wrong. This turns out to be the case in rather too many projects, which perhaps explains the comment by Brooks:

> 'Plan to throw one away, you will anyway.' (Brooks, 1982)

A prototype can be considered as a partial implementation of a system, and hence it is far cheaper to build, and more practical to throw it away or change if the requirements are wrong.

2.3.3 What is specification?

The next stage after the requirements analysis is the specification stage. Specification is defined by the Collins English Dictionary as:

> 'A detailed description of the criteria for the constituents, construction, appearance, performance, etc., of a material, apparatus, etc., or of the standard of workmanship required in its manufacture.' (Collins, 1979)

In software engineering, 'the material, apparatus, etc.' is a software program; other than that, the definition is apposite. The main feature of a specification that distinguishes it from a design is that it states *what* is to be produced whereas a design states *how* it is to be produced.

In the software lifecycle there are a number of places where specification occurs. The first is the requirements specification stage, which specifies the goals of the system. Another stage, which is not always included, is the functional specification. This specifies the details that are not actual goals, but are needed to provide a complete picture, in other words the functionality of the completed system. It often fills in the details that the requirements specification left out.

An important feature of a specification is that it is used at the end of each stage, and especially towards the end of the development stages to verify that the system is correct. This involves checking each point in the specification for that stage to see if the system is correct.

The requirements specification should encapsulate the project goals and constraints. By doing this it should put a boundary around the problem being solved, in order to avoid the inadvertent expansion of the project into solving the problems of the whole world. The requirements specification should contain:

- A general description of the problem.
- A set of functional goals that the system must achieve.
- A set of quality goals.
- A set of constraints that the solution must exist under.

The general description of the problem should describe the current situation, and state what is wrong at present, giving no hint as to a way to solve it, for example:

> 'The telephone operators take too long to put a call through to the right person. This is particularly the case when the caller does not know the name of the person, only some other details, for example the Head of the stores department.'

The functional goals of the project should specify the metrics by which the final system can be measured, for example:

An electronic directory service will be developed which shall be capable of:

- being queried by surname, department, or job title
- holding 10,000 names
- allowing simultaneous use by up to 5 operators

The quality goals will state how well the system must behave, for example:

The electronic directory service shall:

- Answer each query within 5 seconds under any circumstances.
- Be 99 per cent available during normal office hours.
- Have less than 10 hours scheduled downtime per year.

The constraints limit the possible solutions. These are usually imposed for commercial reasons, for example:

- The system shall be developed on the Unix operating system.
- The user interface shall be developed in accordance with the company style guidelines.
- No changes to the existing accommodation shall be necessary in order to install the hardware.
- Operator training shall take no more than one working day.

The requirements specification therefore limits the problem, states the goals, and imposes constraints on the solution. The functional specification will expand on this to specify the precise details of the hardware, the user interface, and any interfaces to other systems.

2.3.4 Why specify?

There are a number of reasons behind the specification process. These reasons may seem obvious, but it was not that many years ago when the idea of fully specifying software before developing it was not common practice. Twenty years ago the term 'match-book specification' was used to refer to a specification that was so small that it could be written inside a book of matches. The term was used because such specifications actually existed.

There are various uses for a specification document:

- Communication tool
  A specification document is a communication tool that is used by managers, developers, customers, and users. It is usually written by the developers to state what they think the customer actually wants. The customer can then agree or disagree with it. When all parties agree that the specification adequately represents their point of view, the goal of communication is satisfied. Both requirements and functional specification achieve this purpose.

  A specification document is also useful for the developers. The specification is often done by an analyst, and the design by a designer, thus the specification document aids communication.

- A basis for planning work
  The specification will be used as a basis for planning the work. When the specification is complete, the rest of the project can be planned as it defines the scope of the work. The right resources can be allocated, the right personnel can be made available, timescales can be set, and the project can be put into action.

- Contractual agreement
  One of the most important uses of the specification document is that it forms the basis for a contractual agreement between the developers and the customer. The developers will be judged on whether they have completed their tasks on the basis of this document. If the work is done by a software house, the specification may be used as the basis for payment. If the work is done internally then the document forms a contract between departments, not legally binding, but nevertheless important.

- Protection from arbitrary changes
  Another important use of the specification is to protect the developers from apparently arbitrary change requests made by the customer. It is exceedingly difficult to manage a development project if the target keeps moving. It is also a severe morale crusher. A developer who has just completed a piece of code will not be pleased if it has to be thrown away because of a change of specification. Cost estimation is very difficult under these circumstances too. This reason, above all the others, caused the concept of a fixed specification to be introduced.

The importance of correct specification

It is extremely important to get the specification stages right. De Marco (1978) gives figures showing the distribution of the origin of errors, ie the percentage of bugs that could be traced back to errors made in the specification, design, or coding stages. He also gives figures estimating the relative cost of fixing a bug that originated in each of these stages. Both sets of figures are shown in Table 2.2. It is interesting to note that the stage where most errors originate is exactly the same as the stage where the cost to fix is greatest – the specification stage. The conclusion is obvious: it is vitally important to get the specification as accurate as possible.

Source of error	% distribution	% relative cost to fix
Specification	56	82
Design	27	13
Code	7	1
Other	10	4

Table 2.2 Distribution of errors by source, and relative cost to fix them

In all software development projects, the errors that are introduced in the early stages are not detected until the later stages. For example, specification errors are not detected until the end of the project, when it may be realised that the wrong system has been built, whereas design errors can be detected in the coding stage. This is shown in Figure 2.4.

Current approaches to specification

The common approach to specification, particularly when working under the classic systems development lifecycle model, is to start a complete and thorough analysis of the situation. Every person involved is interviewed, every last detail is sought, no stone is left unturned. This is the most crucial part of the lifecycle. Should a mistake be made here it will be very expensive to correct later on. It will be difficult to notice a mistake made here until the code has been written, installed, and is being used.

Having performed the detailed analysis, a specification document is written. For a large system, this document will not be written by just one person, but a whole team of analysts will work on it. For large systems the specification may be hundreds of pages long. It should be written in a precise, formal and detailed language. If it is not written in a formal specification language such as Z, then it is only as precise as one can get in natural language!

The specification is necessary because it is to be used as the basis for the contract. When the software is delivered, the customer has to be able to pick up the specification, choose any paragraph and check to see if the wording is true of the delivered system. The language it is written in must, therefore, be precise enough to be verifiable.

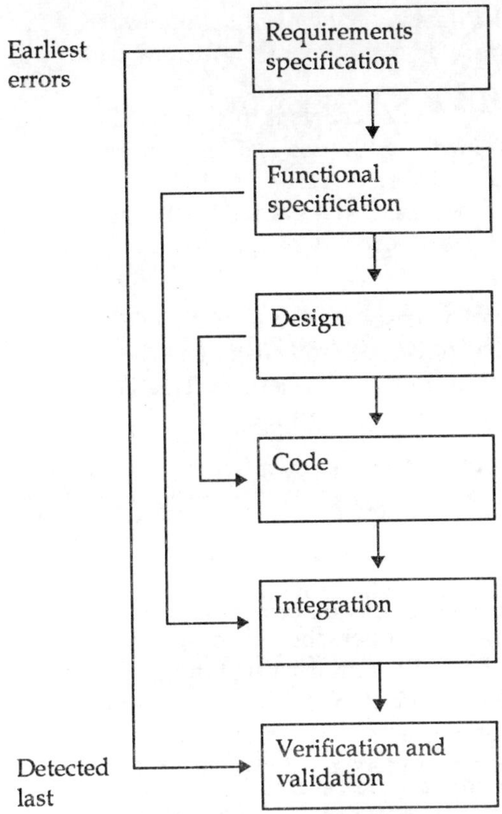

Figure 2.4 Software development errors, and when they are detected

Having developed the document itself, it must be formally reviewed by the customer. This process may be through formal review meetings, where the document is examined page by page and problems found and noted; the reviews being held until the number of errors is very small. The process may be more informal. The finale of the review process is when the customers sign (in blood if necessary) to say that they agree with the document as it stands.

Should the customers find, at a later stage, that they were wrong, and there is something else that is required, then the developers will wave the signed specification in front of them and say that negotiations will have to start again.

2.3.5 Difficulties in specification

The following problems, some already mentioned, occur with the traditional approach to specification:

- poor communication tool
- conceptualisation
- hidden details
- ambiguity and inconsistency
- missing functionality
- frozen specifications

Poor communication tool

The first problem that arises in specification arises from one of the main purposes – that of communication between developer and customer. The developer will often write the specification in technical jargon. This is necessary for the sake of precision. It is no good stating that:

> 'A local area network will be provided'

as there are many different types of local area network. The specification may state instead:

> 'A network conforming to IEEE 802.3 will be provided'

This statement is all well and good for the developers, but the customers may not understand it. The customers must then take it on trust that the developers know what they are talking about (even though they will have to sign the agreement). Even if the customers are happy with taking individual statements on trust, they are in no position to understand the document as a whole.

This problem is alleviated by using a prototype. If the system is prototyped during the specification stages, then the prototype itself can be used as part of the specification. The customers can then see what is going on. They still have to take it on trust that the wire at the back of the computer is an IEEE 802.3 local area network, but at least they have an understanding of the whole.

This is all part of a larger problem of clarifying the users' requirements. Once the developer has performed the analysis and 'knows' what the customer wants, it is important to clarify this idea. This is particularly difficult when it comes to clarifying the information requirements. Information is a large part of a system. For many systems, the information that is held outlasts the system, and must be passed on to the next one. It is therefore vital to clarify that this is correct. It is much more difficult to change the information in a system than it is to change the functionality, as changing the information will almost always imply a change of functionality, but not necessarily the other way around.

Conceptualisation

A second and related problem is that of the large specification. When a specification is several hundred pages long, even the developer must have a problem conceptualising the system, let alone the customer. The problem of conceptualisation arises when a system becomes large and complex, and it is therefore very difficult to analyse.

Hidden details

When the specification is written in a precise manner, details that take up only one line in the document may have major implications. A sentence such as

'The user interface will be written using the X Window System'

will have a major impact on the product[2]. It is easy to miss major items in a detailed specification and thus to focus on the less important problems. People tend to concentrate on what they understand. Building a prototype helps the developers to focus on the problems.

Ambiguity and inconsistency

In a large document ambiguity and inconsistency are difficult to discover. If the document is split up between a set of people and each reviews his or her portion, then such problems can slip through the net.

Table 2.3 shows the relationship between the number of people in the reviewing process (each reviewing one part), and the number of interperson checks that need to be carried out to check for ambiguities and inconsistencies. The figure grows with the square of the number of people.

Number of people	Number of interrelationships
2	1
5	10
10	45
20	190

Table 2.3 The number of people versus the number of interrelationships

[2] The X Window System is a network transparent window system developed at MIT, which runs on a wide range of computers.

The review process itself often just corrects the details, but misses the major problems – like is this the answer to the customer's needs?

Missing functionality

Another problem with a large specification is that the probability of missing vital functions, or including useless ones, increases with its size. The larger it gets, and the more authors it takes on, the greater the problem of communication between them, and the greater the likelihood of there being a problem. By prototyping the system, vital functions that are missing become obvious, and useless functions are more likely to be noticed.

Frozen specification

The signing of a specification marks a major turning point in the lifecycle. At this point everything is frozen. If a feasibility study or experimentation preceded the specification, it must be brought to a stop at the point of signing. Once the specification is frozen, the system is fixed – even if the requirements subsequently change. Figure 2.5 illustrates this problem, where the delivered system does not match the changed requirements.

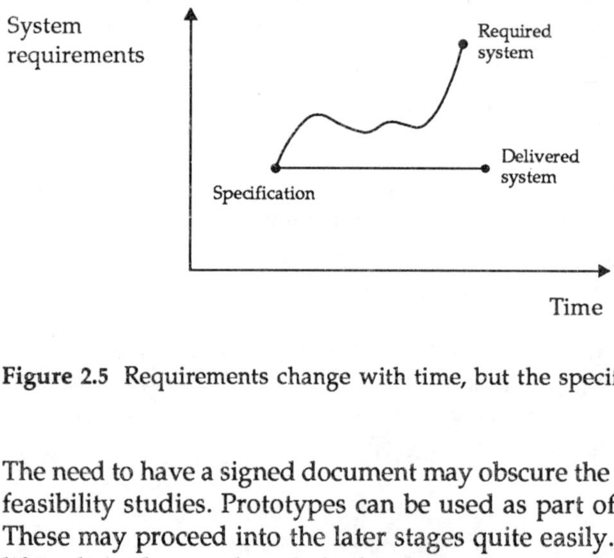

Figure 2.5 Requirements change with time, but the specification is frozen

The need to have a signed document may obscure the need to carry on with feasibility studies. Prototypes can be used as part of the feasibility study. These may proceed into the later stages quite easily. If an evolutionary lifecycle is chosen, the whole development may be considered a feasibility study. If it fails, then only a small project will have been wasted.

The product affects the requirements

One of the interesting aspects of the computer marketplace is that in its current, highly volatile state, selling a new product can change the state of the market. For example, when the first pointing device was launched, a market for new and better pointing devices was created in a very short space of time. This not only reflects on other companies building similar products, but also on the original company, as it will now have competitors. It will have to react to the market trends and perhaps produce a second version of its product in order to keep up with the market.

This process also happens, to a lesser extent, to an internal product. An in-house system will generate comments back from the users requesting changes and additions to the software. These changes would never have been requested if the software had not been produced in the first place. Thus the introduction of a system can change the requirements. This is a problem if one has adopted the traditional approach – the requirements are set in stone at the beginning of a project, but the act of using the system changes the requirements. Prototyping can help the users gain experience of the system early on in the life of the software, and so account can be taken of their changing requirements.

2.3.6 Can specifications be frozen?

As was stated earlier, specifications are frozen early in the traditional lifecycle because it is difficult to cope with a moving target. It is difficult to allocate resources, difficult to manage, and causes severe morale problems. It is extremely difficult for the developers to work in a situation where the specification changes. On the other hand the customers live in an ever-changing world, where constant change is a permanent feature. In the time it takes to create a new system the whole world can have changed.

The more effort that is put into getting the requirements specification right, the longer the time between starting the project and delivering a product. This means that the actual requirements of the customers have had more time to change, and are therefore further from the specification. On the other hand, if only a short time is spent investigating the requirements, they are less likely to be right and so they are still further from the actual requirements – even if the development is faster. This leads to:

> The software requirements uncertainty principle:
>
> 'At any given time, it is not possible to determine exactly the requirements of a user population and, at the same time, have a system that meets these requirements.' (Maude and Willis, 1991)

When the new system arrives it changes the work itself. So what is the solution to this dichotomy?

Unfortunately, there is no simple solution. Prototyping can help by focussing attention on the major risks, and thus avoid people concentrating on the parts of the system that they understand. If the requirements really do change very quickly, then the only way to cope is to build systems quickly. This prevents the specification getting too far out of date before the system is delivered. It is well known that one cannot simply halve the production timescale by doubling the personnel, and hope to get the same results, so pouring more resources into a product is not the answer. By developing software in an evolutionary fashion, building small parts quickly and releasing them to the users, the software can react to the changes in requirements.

2.4 Strengths and weaknesses of prototyping

In any software development project there many unknown areas. There is always some part of the system that the developers have little experience of. This leads to a statement that is often heard at the end of the development:

> 'I wish I could do it all over again, as I know how to do it now.'

Of course, one never can do it again as there is hopefully another project to move on to. Some problems occur regularly, and the developers get to understand them. It is at this point that they realise that as they are a frequent problem, a software tool would be helpful in solving them. Thus report writers became common in business oriented languages, fourth generation languages have arisen, compiler compilers are now used.

New unknowns now occur – how to build the tool, or how to use the tool? When a software tool is available, the developers make full use of it and use it to its limits, often in ways unexpected by the tool builder. Thus when a problem is common enough to be understood, a generic tool or technique is created which in turn creates new unknowns. So it is impossible to get away from the fact that when software is developed, there are always new problems.

When there are unknowns in a problem, the developers will quite naturally try things out first – to see if they work. This is prototyping in another form. It happens in a small and uncontrolled way, but needs to be recognised and its use brought out into the open. Prototyping is a natural way of working during the software development process.

The effectiveness of prototyping can vary according to the type of project, the experience of the developers in prototyping, and how the project is managed. This section examines strengths and weaknesses of prototyping in the software development process. The factors that are examined are generic, and should apply to most projects, but specific projects may be influenced in different ways.

2.4.1 Strengths of prototyping

Why is a systems development lifecycle model needed? Apart from giving us an interesting insight into the development process itself, there are two main reasons for having the model:

1 Management and control
2 Levels of abstraction

Management and control

The managers of a development project need to have some sort of perspective of the work that tells them what is happening. This is achieved by the lifecycle model. It gives the managers specific points in time at which they can expect specific end-of-stage products, so they can monitor the progress of the work.

Levels of abstraction

The developers working on the project need to develop a set of levels of abstraction to the solution of their problem. The solution they aim to achieve at the end of the project is a working system. This is the most concrete level of the system. Working back through the lifecycle, the process of abstraction continues until the requirements specification is reached, which is the most abstract solution.

The systems development lifecycle model helps to control the levels of abstraction that the developers need to go through.

Specific strengths of prototyping

The concept of varying levels of abstraction is the most general statement about the advantages of prototyping. The following is a more specific list:

- understanding the problem, goals, and solutions
- common system model
- improving communication
- early view of the impact on requirements
- risk management
- evolving development

Understanding the problem, goals, and solutions

When something is going wrong, it is often not possible to see the source of the problem. In many cases no-one may be aware that a problem exists. When the problem is understood, it may be very difficult to state a set of goals to aim for, and when a solution is presented to achieve these goals, it is often hard to understand how it can help achieve them.

A good example of this is the problem of running the country's economy. Politicians cannot even agree on the problem – is it high inflation, high interest rates, or high unemployment? – never mind agree on any goals or solutions.

In business the same difficulties exist, to a lesser extent. Some problems, when recognised, will require a software solution. If a prototype is built early in the lifecycle, then it is easier to understand the situation. If the problem is not clearly defined, then the prototype will help to clarify it. If the prototype is demonstrated, someone will say:

> 'That won't help'
> or 'That's just what we need'
> or 'Why don't you do it this way'

and it will act as a focus to identify the problem, the goals, and the solution. The concrete form of the prototype will help people to understand the abstract problem.

Common system model

When discussing a system that does not yet exist, the customers, users, and developers will all try to imagine what it will look like when complete. This mental image of the system is a conceptual model, and each person involved will develop their own. As natural language is so imprecise, and everyone will interpret it in a slightly different way, the conceptual models that are built will all be different. If they are slightly different, there is no major problem; if they are very different, then there is.

A prototype provides a basis for a common conceptual model for each person involved. It provides a reassurance that everyone is talking about the same thing, and there are no misunderstandings.

Improving communication

System developers are well-used to computer jargon, and tend to use it as everyday language, just as any other profession will use its own jargon. The developers have to explain things to the users and customers, and it is often difficult without using this jargon. For example, the word 'toggle' is used to mean a switch to change between two different modes, whereas the everyday use of the word is a button or peg on the end of a string, which is not very relevant to software.

A prototype can act as a communication tool between users, customers, and developers. The developer can show the users what they are getting, the users can point to the screen and say:

> 'But couldn't you do this instead?'

Early view of the impact on requirements

It is sometimes difficult to see what the effect of a software program will be before it is developed. The use of a prototype in a live or simulated situation can test the effect of the program. This leads to a better requirements specification.

Risk management

One of the duties of the project manager is to manage the risks, for example to reduce or transfer the risks. Building a prototype can reduce the risks involved with producing the wrong product. Incremental or evolutionary development may also reduce the effects of budget cuts, as some worthwhile code may already have been developed by the time the budget is cut.

Evolving development

The problem of freezing specifications has already been discussed. Prototyping by evolutionary development avoids this problem.

2.4.2 Weaknesses of prototyping

When considering the use of prototyping, the various weaknesses of the technique must also be examined:

- poorly defined strategy
- retraining of staff necessary
- confusion with the real system
- fewer tools and techniques
- not a universal strategy

Poorly defined strategy

If the strategy of prototyping is not accepted or understood by the customers, the approach could fail. The customers have to accept that software may be thrown away, they must realise that they will be shown incomplete software. If they do not understand this strategy, or if it is poorly defined, then the project could fail.

Retraining of staff necessary

The staff involved in the development of the prototype will need retraining and re-educating. In order to build a prototype rapidly, it may be necessary to use specialised tools. This will require retraining. All staff involved will require re-education in the strategy used. They must understand what they are building the prototype for, and what different philosophies are required.

For example, the programmers on a throw-away prototyping project will have to realise that it is less important to document the code, and that they may not need the degree of rigorous testing that they are used to.

Confusion with the real system

It is often difficult to explain to customers, or even one's own marketing organisation, that what they see is a prototype and not the real thing. If it looks like what they expect, and behaves like it too, then they may ask the question:

> 'Why can't I use this, it looks and behaves exactly as I want it to?'

Even if it is explained that there are some functions that it does not do, it is often expected that the missing functions are only a minor part of the system. The fact that is often missed is that the whole system may need redesigning and rebuilding from scratch, in order to get a worthwhile product.

Fewer tools and techniques

There are few strategies that have been tried and tested which involve rapid prototyping. Most of the well documented strategies are variants of the classic lifecycle, because it has been around for longer. This also means that what prototyping strategies do exist tend to be less formal, and this in turn means that prototyping projects are more difficult to control.

Not a universal strategy

The classic lifecycle and its associated strategy is designed to be universally applied to any software project. This is not the case with rapid prototyping. Only some projects would benefit, and each project would benefit in a different way.

The project manager has to understand the project sufficiently to be able to choose when to prototype and how much to prototype. This is not an easy decision, as it requires a careful play-off between using the prototype to develop a better understanding, and paying out more money to develop the prototype.

2.5 Conclusions

A prototype is a model of system behaviour. The aspects of the system that are being modelled can be chosen according to the problem under consideration, eg the user interface, performance-critical modules, or the requirements. As the prototype is only a partial model of the system, it can be implemented much faster than a full implementation – hence the term *rapid prototyping*. The actual speed of developing the prototype depends primarily on the need for the prototype. The development can be as fast or as slow as is necessary.

The ways in which a prototype can be used are also varied. Prototyping has an important role in software development, particularly in the critical start-up stages. It might be used for promoting ideas and understanding the problem, in clarifying and checking the system goals, or for comparing and evaluating potential solutions.

In order to apply prototyping to real software development problems, rather than keep it as an abstract, theoretical idea, more precision is needed in the terminology. The key aspects that should be of concern are the ways in which prototyping can be used in a particular problem, the functionality of the prototype, the time at which the prototyping is done, and the development strategy.

However, these are not precise categories, but rather points on a continuum. For example, the distinction between horizontal and vertical prototyping, while useful to a developer in order to consider the implications of what is or isn't being prototyped, is far less clear in practice. These categories should not be thought of as rigid, but serve to illustrate the potential scope and applications of prototyping.

The prototyping approach may not only be justified by considering it as the 'scientific method' for software development, but is also supported by the psychology of problem solving. From the psychological viewpoint of acquiring knowledge, the process of development itself causes people to re-assess their ideas and to learn new things, and consequently their own expectations for the system change – irrespective of any external influences which might affect the requirements.

In comparison, the lifecycle model is on rather shaky foundations. The notion that a 'real' problem can be defined clearly at the start of the development is not at all certain. Furthermore, the task of requirements analysis is difficult enough without being unable to see and test ideas on an operational system, and the idea that the specifications can be frozen is unrealistic.

If the software requirements uncertainty principle is believed, then traditional development methods are creationist – the origin of the system is the fixed requirements specification – rather than evolutionary.

Prototyping should not be regarded as a magic solution to all these problems. The notion that building a prototype will make everything all right is no more acceptable than the idea of finding a development strategy that guarantees success if followed. If anything, it represents a change in philosophy, from idealised development methods, to an evolutionary risk-driven approach. However, like any philosophical doctrine, attempts to define the creed often lead to disputes amongst the practitioners as to the real meaning.

Selected reading

Lifecycle problems and prototyping

Agresti, W W (ed)
New paradigms for software development, IEEE Computer Society Press, Washington, DC, 1986

Software specification

Gehani, N and McGettrick, A D (eds)
Software specification techniques, Addison-Wesley, 1986

Software prototyping overview

Computer
Special issue on rapid prototyping, Vol 22, No 5, 1989

Connell, J L and Shafer, L
Structured rapid prototyping: an evolutionary approach to software development, Prentice-Hall, 1989

Ince, D C and Hekmatpour, S
Software prototyping, formal methods, and VDM, Addison-Wesley, 1988

Ince, D C and Hekmatpour, S
Software prototyping – progress and prospects, *Information and software technology (GB),* Vol 29, No 1, 1987, 8–14

Lipp, M E
Prototyping: state of the art report 14:4, Pergamon Infotech, 1986

3 Developing a prototype

Introduction

A prototype has been defined as a model of a system that is yet to be built. However, defining a prototype does not explain how to go about building one, just as explaining the syntax and semantics of a programming language does not reveal the secrets of being a good programmer. Neither programming nor prototyping is a skill that can be acquired by reading a textbook. Nevertheless, a book may suggest some good ideas, and the correct approach to start. After that, the skills must be learnt by experience.

The reasons for prototyping are based around the need to reduce or off-load the risks of embarking on an expensive project. Risk management is the science of analysing and controlling the risks of failure. It is impossible to eliminate completely the risks of failure, but it is possible to reduce them to an acceptable level, usually at a small cost. Risk management is used in our everyday lives. Before crossing a road, it is advisable to look and see if any cars are coming. This costs a small amount of effort, but it dramatically reduces the risk of being hit by a car.

Prototyping is used for risk management in engineering projects, by building a model that can be tested. Any strategy using software prototyping should also involve some kind of risk analysis. It is important to understand the risks that are being reduced, in order to know that they have actually been reduced!

It is for these reasons that this chapter concentrates on risk management as being the key strategy in the production of a prototype.

The purpose of this chapter

This chapter provides an outline strategy for prototyping. It can only provide an outline because any strategy must be tailored to the specific task in hand. Software projects vary far too widely for any generic technique to be useful. The reader is urged to understand the reasons behind this strategy, and to apply them to according to the needs and merits of each project.

General organisation

Section 3.1 outlines the strategy. The aim of this section is to show how the various parts fit together to form an overall strategy. The subsequent sections examine the individual parts in more detail. The basis of the strategy is, as discussed earlier, risk management. Prototypes are built to assess and reduce project risks, the process being repeated until the risks are acceptable. If the risks are acceptable from the outset, then prototyping may not be necessary.

Section 3.2 looks at the crucial subject of risk management. The main risks to do with software projects were outlined in Chapter 1, and this section explains the background theory.

After performing the risk analysis, it is important to decide upon the reasons for building the prototype. This subject is covered in section 3.3, which looks at prototyping as an aid to problem solving, the problems being defined by the risk analysis.

The choice of the exact strategy is discussed in section 3.4. The decisions to be made are the development strategy (throw-away, incremental, or evolutionary), what exactly to prototype (the functionality), and when to build the prototype (early, middle, or late in the development).

Section 3.5 looks at the building of the prototype, starting with the vital area of designing a scenario with which to demonstrate the prototype. Few specific guidelines are available in the building of the prototype itself, as this is closely related to the specific type of program being written.

The use of the prototype in some kind of experimentation process is the last step of the method, and this is examined in section 3.6. A prototype is built to gain further knowledge, and this can only be obtained by experimenting with and using the prototype.

3.1 A strategy for prototyping

The aim of this chapter is to explain a strategy for prototyping, ie a technique for applying prototyping in software development projects. Of course, there is no guaranteed way to do this; what may be correct for one project will not necessarily work in another.

Books on programming may *attempt* to explain how to write programs, but they never really succeed in doing this. They might explain the steps that can be taken, eg the use of top-down programming as a strategy for writing programs, but this can only ever be an approximation. The only way to learn programming is by practical experience, and trial and error. Books may point the way to strategies for reaching the goals, but in the end they do not state exactly how to achieve them.

It is the same with prototyping. All that can be realistically done is to explain a strategy that points the way. This will provide some guidelines as to where to start, and where to go onto next, but it comes with a warning – the method must be applied to a project with some thought. It cannot be blindly followed, but must be used with careful consideration of the details of the particular project.

When applying the strategy prescribed here, each of the stages *must* be performed at some time, but the overall strategy can be combined with a full lifecycle development if necessary. The way that this is done will depend on the circumstances of the project.

For example, if the goal of the prototyping is to clarify the requirements, then the method described here might fit completely within the requirements specification stage. Alternatively, if there are some critical unresolved performance issues, then the method might be applied late in the systems development lifecycle, during the implementation stage. The basic issues are the same – there are specific projects risks which need to be resolved, irrespective of which stage in the development they occur.

Alternatively, if an evolutionary development is being performed, then this strategy becomes the whole of the development lifecycle, and any requirements analysis fits into the loop before implementation takes place. The use of the method needs to be tailored to the project.

The prototyping strategy described is outlined briefly in this section, and the individual parts of it are covered in much greater detail in the rest of this chapter.

The overall strategy is summarised in Figure 3.1. The prototyping loop is repeated until the risks are reduced to an acceptable level, ie the risks can be accepted. It is at this point that a classic software development cycle may start. It should be realised that the prototyping cycle may never finish, eg during evolutionary development. It may also be necessary to return to the prototyping cycle, eg if it is subsequently found that the risks involved in the project have changed.

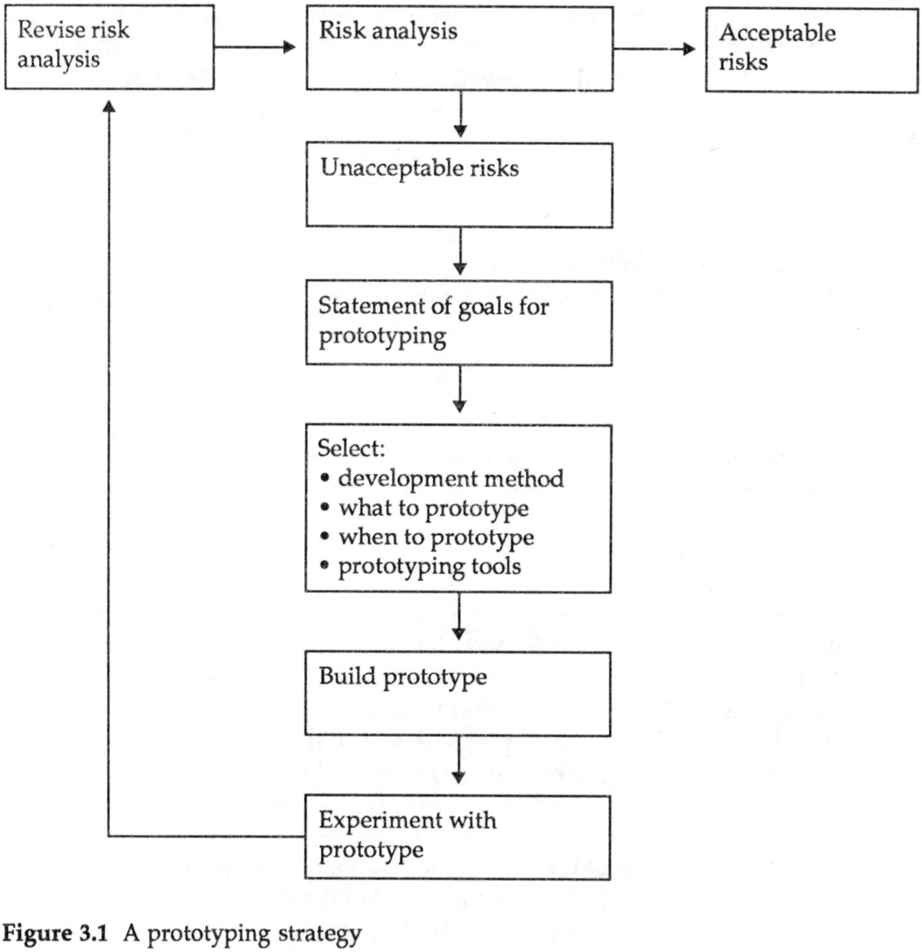

Figure 3.1 A prototyping strategy

Risk analysis

The first stage of the prototyping technique is risk analysis. The aim of this stage is to discover the main risks of failure in the project, and attempt to assess the chances of failure. Each risk item, if it happens, might mean that one or more of the goals of the project would not be met.

The result of this exercise is an ordered list of risk items, ranked by their relative likelihood – the highest risk item at the top, down to the lowest risk item at the bottom. If it is possible, an estimate of the percentage chance of the risk occurring can also be included, although this is often a guess at this stage. Along with the risk items there should also be an estimate of their effect on the project, ie the cost of a particular risk occurring.

Analysis of unacceptable risks

The top risk items should then be assessed to see if they are acceptable or not. This should take into account both the cost, and the expected chance of the risk happening. If a risk is unacceptably high, then some way of off-loading or reducing the risk must be found.

Statement of goals for prototype

Once the risk items have been examined, and it has been decided which ones are worth reducing, and how they can be reduced, a problem statement must be written. This should state what the goals of the prototype are. Of course, they should differ from the statement of goals for the whole project.

Prototyping may be used to help achieve some of the goals of the project, eg to produce a module, or it may be used to help achieve one of the subgoals of the project, eg in producing a requirements specification. Stating the goals will focus the cycle of prototyping.

The development method

The development method can now be selected. The choice will depend on the goals for the prototype, eg:

- If the requirements are unstable, evolutionary development is a good idea.
- If the funding is unstable, incremental development is useful.
- If the customer is uncertain of the requirements, then a throw-away prototype can help.

What to prototype

A prototype never builds the complete system, so a decision has to be made as to what to prototype. This is a choice of vertical or horizontal prototyping, as well as a choice of exactly which functions to include, eg:

- If evolutionary development is being used, then a vertical prototype is needed, developing the complete functionality of only one part.
- If the nature of the user interface is uncertain, then only the user interface should be prototyped.

When to prototype

This decision needs to be taken if a throw-away prototype is being created. It will depend on the goals, eg:

- If the requirements are uncertain, then prototype early.
- If the design needs to be checked, then prototype later on.

What tools to use

The choice of tools will depend on what is available, and on the functionality required. Often a special tool can be purchased for the project, although this might require extra training. Sometimes specialists in a particular tool will need to be called in to do the programming.

Building the prototype

This stage may involve a development lifecycle; design and specification may be required before the coding can start, or this may have been done during the earlier stages. For example, the specification may have already been provided by the customer.

It is at this stage that the experiments should be planned. This is particularly true if the system is to be demonstrated to an audience, as a scenario will need to be written. A scenario gives the demonstration a theme that makes it easier for the audience to follow.

Experimentation

This is not necessarily an experiment in the classic sense of the word, although it might be. In order to reduce the risks, it is necessary to gain some information, and to do this it is necessary to experiment, or to use the system in some way. The nature of the experiments will depend entirely on the goals of the project. They may involve real users, demonstrations to customers, comparative experiments by the implementors, or something else that exercises the prototype.

Repeat the risk analysis

At this point in the cycle, the procedure repeats itself. After the experiments, some knowledge must have been gained, and it is this knowledge that should have reduced the risks in some way. The cycle must be repeated indefinitely until the risks are acceptable.

Before examining the details of this strategy, it should be repeated that it needs to be put into the context of a real problem before it is useful. A real project will need to modify the strategy, and fit it in with its own needs. All that can be done here is to point the way.

3.2 Software risk management

Almost everything people do has a risk of failure. In most cases the risks are so low that people do not even think of them. Walking down a street to buy a newspaper is not regarded as particularly risky. Where the risks are higher, for example in choosing to travel in an aircraft, the benefits (fast journey, relative comfort) are weighed against the risks (delayed flights, aircraft failure), and a decision is made. Even then, most people think that flying is risky, whereas statistically it is probably much safer than driving a car. Risks are not very well understood, but although it is *known* that software development is very risky, few books on software project management mention this subject.

Risks exist in software development for many reasons:

- It is difficult to determine the requirements.
- The requirements may change during the development.
- It is difficult to estimate costs and resources.
- There is insufficient information at the start of development.
- The development itself may have technical risks.

Knowing that risks actually exist and must be carefully considered is a discipline called *risk management*, which is widely used in business. Economists have long recognised the importance of risk:

> 'One of the most rigorous theorems of economics (Boehm-Bawerks Law) proves that the existing means of production will yield greater economic performance only through greater uncertainty, that is, through greater risk. While it is futile to try to eliminate risk, and questionable to try to minimise it, it is essential that the risks taken be the right risks...
>
> We must be able to choose rationally among risk-taking courses of action, rather than plunge into uncertainty on the basis of hunch, hearsay, or incomplete experience, no matter how meticulously quantified.' (Drucker, 1975)

Risks cannot be completely eliminated, and even if this were possible there would be no progress if people only did things that were 100 per cent safe. Minimising the risks is not always productive either, since in some cases it might be better to take a risk which promises a high payoff, rather than try to avoid it. However, it must be known what the consequences of accepting a risk are, in terms of losses and gains. The problems when several risks are taken at the same time are even greater. Good managers take educated risks, learning as they progress, but also knowing when to play safe, or if things go wrong, when to stop.

3.2.1 Software and risks

What is a risk? Obviously the nature of what constitutes a risk varies from person to person, and from project to project. The following list gives some examples of situations which most managers would consider unacceptable, and therefore a risk:

- The system may not meet the requirements.
- The system may not provide the expected benefits.
- The project may finish late or over budget.
- The system performance may be below expectation.
- The system may contain undetected errors.

There are situations where a parameter that is acceptable in one system would be a critical risk item in another. For example, a response time of 0.5 second may be acceptable for an interactive user interface, but would not be sufficiently fast for a real-time flight guidance system. Risk management must not only identify the risks, but also assess the impacts of the risks on the particular type of system.

There are three parts to software risk management:

1 Risk identification
2 Risk analysis
3 Risk control

These are related as shown in Figure 3.2.

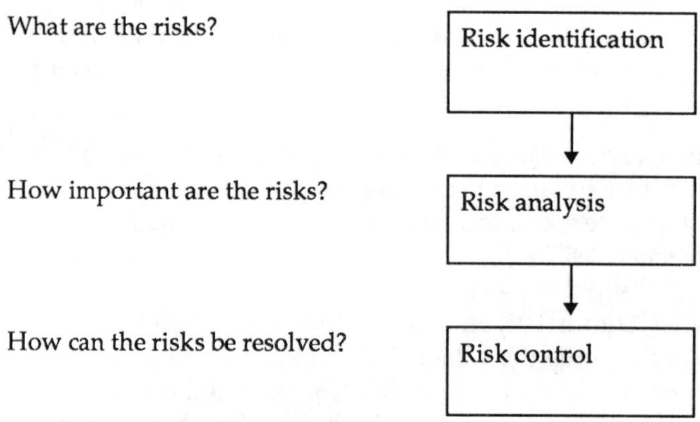

Figure 3.2 The stages of software risk management

Risk identification finds the risks that are specific to the project under investigation. Risk analysis assesses how the risks will compromise the project, and puts them in order of importance. Risk control provides the plans to control the risk, and the techniques to resolve the risks.

3.2.2 Risk identification

The first part of the risk management process is to know what the risks are. This is necessary to bring people's attention to the possible risks, so that the risks can be analysed and controlled. People normally do the things that they *can* understand first. Risk identification forces them to think about the things that they *can't* understand – even if they don't know how to solve them.

The top-ten risks described in Chapter 1 may be used to generate a check list for managers to start this process. For example, a risk item check list for schedules and budgets might contain questions like:

- Will the project really get all of the allocated budget?
- Is the project politically sensitive?
- Will the promised hardware and software support facilities be made available?
- Have hardware and software maintenance budgets been allocated?
- Is the required-by date stable, or fluctuating?

Other good methods for risk identification include:

- studying the driving factors behind the project decisions
- analysing the project assumptions (if stated)
- analysing the existing plans and specifications

Risks in project decisions

Quite often important decisions in a project are made for politically-motivated reasons, rather than for sound business or technical reasons. The marketing department may want features that will look good in the sales brochures, but are not of much practical use. Some decisions may be the result of confusing problems with solutions, ie the requirements specification states the expected solution, ruling out better alternatives. Decisions may ignore long-term factors, such as maintenance, and concentrate on short-term objectives.

Risks in project assumptions

Many projects are founded on optimistic assumptions, for example that all third-party software will arrive on time, and will be bug-free. There may be a temptation to agree to delivery deadlines on the assumption that the project will get all the best people, or simply in order to continue the funding and avoid cancellation. Obviously, the more assumptions that are made, the more likely it is that one or more of them will not be met. Most projects tend to be optimised around a standard set of assumptions, like the ones described above. Analysing these assumptions may identify some which could be potential risks.

Risks in plans and specifications

Plans and specifications should also be examined. Plans which are very detailed, with many tasks and sub-tasks, and precise dates and costs, should be carefully checked. Quite often some of the details will have no firm foundation; the first technical problem then throws the whole plan out of step. It is also easy for major items to get ignored in a large plan; the writers concentrate on the parts they understand or find interesting. Major parts of the system, like data acquisition, data conversion, or tasks performed by subcontractors, do not get the detailed attention they deserve.

Project planning charts, like PERT or GANTT charts, enable critical path analysis to be performed. The tasks which make up the critical path can then be studied further. Charts allow tasks which have a high fan-in or fan-out to be identified. A high fan-in means that if any of the input tasks are late, the task cannot be started. A high fan-out means that any delay in the task will delay all the dependent tasks.

Output of risk identification

The output of the risk identification process is a list of potential risks. No attempt should be made to put the risks in order, since this is the job of risk analysis. If needed the risks can be grouped into common categories, or divided into risks and sub-risks.

3.2.3 Risk analysis

Risk analysis takes the list of potential risk items, considers the probability of risks occurring, the expected losses if a risk does occur, and assesses the importance of each risk to the project.

The risk analysis phase utilises two fundamental risk management concepts:

- Risk exposure (RE)
- Risk reduction leverage (RRL)

Risk exposure

Risk exposure (sometimes called risk impact) is a measure of how risky an activity is, and is defined by the relationship:

$$RE = P * L$$

where P is the probability of an unsatisfactory outcome, and L is the loss to the project if the outcome is unsatisfactory. Risk exposure increases as both P and L increase, so there are two ways of reducing the exposure for a particular risk:

- Reduce the probability of the risk occurring.
- Reduce the loss if the risk does occur.

Risk is high when there is uncertainty about the outcome of a particular situation, in other words when the knowledge is incomplete. In contrast, complete knowledge of a situation means no uncertainty – and no risk. A *certain* outcome, even if it means a loss, cannot be considered as a risk because it must happen. Figure 3.3 illustrates the relationship between knowledge and risk. The more knowledge that is available, the less the risk, and vice versa. The shape of this graph may vary according to the nature of the situation, although the trend is always as shown.

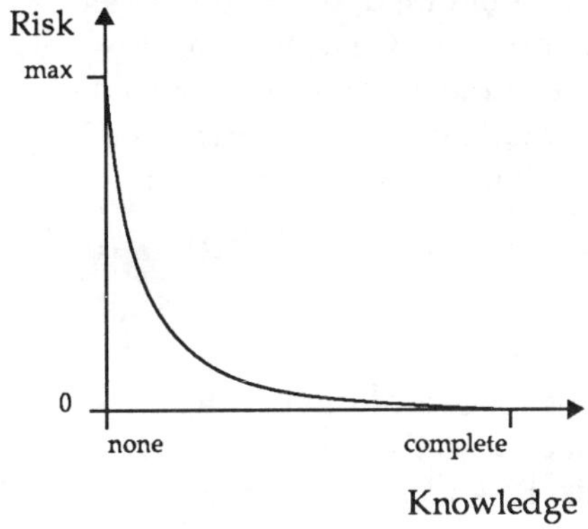

Figure 3.3 Knowledge and risk

Risk reduction leverage

The other measure, risk reduction leverage, shows the relative cost-benefit of a particular risk reduction strategy, and is defined by:

$$RRL = (RE_{before} - RE_{after}) / C$$

where RE_{before} is the risk exposure *before* the risk reduction, RE_{after} is the risk exposure *after* the risk reduction, and C is the cost of the risk reduction. The greater the value of RRL, the better the reduction strategy.

RE and RRL can be used in conjunction with a variety of techniques to assess risk, and order risk items. Possible techniques include:

- decision analysis
- cost and schedule modelling
- project planning charts

In decision analysis, a tree is drawn of the possible decisions to be made in the project, and the risk exposure calculated for each option. This will identify the 'best' solution, in terms of the one with minimum risk exposure, or show those decisions which are particularly sensitive to the estimates of probability or loss.

Cost and schedule modelling can be used to estimate the project's cost and development time, which can then be compared against the planned figures. Project planning charts, like the PERT charts mentioned under risk identification, can also be used to estimate the degree of risk.

Output of risk analysis

The output of the risk analysis phase is an ordered list of the risk items. The list must be updated regularly, as new risks are identified, or existing risks resolved. Whichever techniques are used, the process of risk analysis is essentially a matter of human judgement. None of the techniques discussed in the previous sections can produce accurate estimates of risk, since risks are by their very nature future events which may not happen. All estimates are subjective, and will require interpretation.

3.2.4 Risk control

Risk control takes the ordered risks, coordinates the resolution of these risks with the overall project plans, and monitors the project's progress towards resolving the risk items and meeting the goals. Risk control is the most important phase of software risk management.

There are three main aspects to risk control:

1 Risk management planning.
2 Risk resolution.
3 Risk monitoring.

Risk management planning

Risk management planning is not a separate project planning activity. It must be part of the normal planning of the project, and must not be overly complex or tedious to perform. The plans for resolving the risks must be coordinated with the plans for the project, ie meeting the goals, delivering products on time and within budget.

A simple technique for risk management planning is to have a plan for each risk item, together with a list of the top-ten project risks.

For each risk item, the plan should detail:

- What is the risk, and the priority?
- Who is responsible for resolving the risk, and by when?
- How will the risk be resolved, and what resources are needed?

The risk management plans are coordinated with each other so that the most effective risk reduction strategies can be identified. The top-ten risks give a good feel for whether the risk reduction strategies are effective, or if the results are not following the plan. Corrective action can then be taken. Risks that cannot be resolved, for one reason or another, may be sufficiently serious that the overall project plan needs to be changed.

Risk resolution

The measures of RE and RRL will be useful to determine the best risk resolution technique. Risk resolution may be done in several ways:

- avoiding a risk by changing the system
- reducing a risk to an acceptable level
- transferring a risk, eg to someone else
- accepting a risk, and taking the chance that it won't happen

Risks can be avoided by choosing a lower-risk solution. It may be possible to relax the requirements sufficiently for other alternatives to become viable, for example the memory space requirements could be relaxed to allow a simpler algorithm to be used.

Risk reduction can only be done if sufficient information is available to understand both the risk, and the ways in which it might be reduced. System modelling or prototyping can be used to 'buy' this information. The prototype may, for example, show that a preferred option has a higher than expected difficulty, and should be changed. Alternatively, the system may be built using an evolutionary development strategy, where the goals, solutions, and the risks are constantly evaluated.

An interesting application of prototyping in risk reduction is to build prototypes of key items on the project's critical path, for example external deliverables, or critical software modules. If an item is late, or otherwise unsatisfactory, then a prototype is immediately available to allow the project to continue. This buys time so that the critical item can be finished.

Risks may be transferred to a third party, perhaps by contracting out part of the development work. The contractor then takes on the risks. The contractor chosen must be sufficiently experienced to perform the expected tasks; the contract may contain a penalty clause in case of failure, or a bonus for early delivery.

Finally, it may be necessary to just accept some risks, and prepare alternative or fall-back options in case the risk should occur. In some situations, like a speculative research project, there may be no fall-back option.

The major risk resolution technique covered in this book is, of course, prototyping.

Risk monitoring

A table of the top-ten risks provides a good means of monitoring progress, since it can highlight new risks, risks that are increasing in importance, or risks that have been unsolved for a long time. This is illustrated by the example shown in Table 3.1, which describes a hypothetical project. The table shows that risk item 2 has increased rapidly in importance, and has been unresolved for quite a long time. This means that it needs careful consideration. Item 1 is unchanged, so this risk has not yet been resolved. Items number 5 and 6 are falling, as risk resolution takes effect. The items 7, 8 and 9 at the bottom of the table are static. Items 3 and 10 are new risks – item 3 being particularly important. RE and RRL may be used to help prioritise the risks, although the ordering may still be subjective.

This week	Last week	Weeks on list	Risk item
1	1	3	Functional specification must be changed to meet new project goals
2	4	7	Senior systems analyst leaving
3	–	1	Bug in sort module for large data sets
4	5	2	User interface software is late
5	2	2	Performance problems with communications software
6	3	4	Intermittent hardware fault on workstations
7	7	3	Delays in scheduling QA reviews
8	8	3	Porting of database not finished
9	9	3	Configuration management system is still losing files
10	–	1	Finance department has lost order for disk drives

Table 3.1 Top-ten risk items

3.2.5 Risk resolution by prototyping

Business risk management techniques are often mostly concerned with actively trying to *avoid* risks. In software, the marketplace is such that in many cases risks must be actively *taken* to gain an advantage over competitors, as well as trying not to take unnecessary risks.

A prototype, or a series of prototypes, allows managers to:

- identify the risks at the earliest stage (risk identification)
- quantify the risks by experiencing them, on a small scale (risk analysis)
- gather the knowledge necessary to reduce the risks (risk reduction)

Prototyping for risk identification

The prototype gives much needed information on the risks at the best possible time – as early in the development as possible. In the classic lifecycle model, the errors introduced in the early stages are detected last, with the completion of the final product. Prototyping identifies the risks right at the beginning. Even the most sophisticated method for finding coding errors is wasted if the wrong software is coded.

Prototyping for risk analysis

The prototype not only identifies possible risks, but because the prototype can be a scaled-down model of the real system, the risks are experienced in the development. The degree of difficulty in building the prototype, and the time and cost, may be used to help assess risks to the project.

Prototyping for risk resolution

Prototyping can assist risk resolution in several ways. Early identification of problems allows the appropriate risk resolution strategy to be chosen. The prototype may show that certain parts of the development are too difficult, and that the specification or design should be changed. This is risk avoidance. The information gained in the prototyping process also helps to reduce risks, for example in ensuring that the system meets the customer's requirements. It may suggest that some risks are best resolved by transferring them elsewhere, or should just be accepted.

3.3 Defining the reasons for prototyping

It is necessary for the developers to understand the reasons for prototyping in their project:

- What is the role of prototyping in the problem solving process?
- What are the goals for the prototype?
- What are the expected benefits?

Developers need to answer these questions in order to plan the prototyping, to divide the tasks between the development teams, and to choose an appropriate strategy.

3.3.1 Prototyping and problem solving

A prototype can be used to provide information on several aspects of problem solving. To recap on the discussion in Chapter 1, the following kinds of prototyping can be used:

- explanatory prototyping – to explain, demonstrate, and inform
- exploratory prototyping – to determine the real problem, clarify requirements, and investigate solutions
- experimental prototyping – to evaluate the proposed solutions
- evolutionary prototyping – to choose and refine a solution

Remember that the prototype is not always built during the early stages of the project. For example, an explanatory prototype could be built late in the project to explain an important new concept, or an experimental prototype built late to help solve an unexpected implementation problem. From the pragmatic viewpoint of the developer, it is highly likely that several aspects of a problem must be considered at the same time.

3.3.2 Goals

If the prototyping goals are not clearly stated, it is impossible to plan the prototype, or to know if it has met its goals. For example, if one of the goals is to elicit the requirements specification from the user, then the developer must plan for demonstrations. Failure to state the goals might mean that a lot of effort is wasted, perhaps in building a high quality prototype that is thrown out, or in delivering a 'quick and dirty' prototype, with many inherent problems, to the customer. It may also mean that the expected benefits are not achieved.

3.3.3 Benefits

The benefits of prototyping should outweigh the extra costs of building the prototype. Listing the expected benefits may be useful in providing justification for the prototype, or conversely if the benefits are not high, in choosing not to build the prototype.

Prototyping should be a learning process. If the expected benefits are noted at the start of a project, then an analysis of the results of the prototyping can be done at the end of the project. It will be useful for the next project to know how successful the prototype was. The importance of gathering measurements in estimating is discussed further in Chapter 4.

3.4 Choosing the strategy

This section examines the selection of the prototyping strategy. This is the key part of the overall strategy, and should be given very careful consideration by developers, as it is the major factor in determining the success or failure.

3.4.1 Choosing the development strategy

The choice of strategy determines the ultimate fate of the prototype:

- thrown-out, not delivered to customer – throw-away prototyping
- early delivery to the customer – incremental development
- early delivery, continually enhanced – evolutionary development

In a large project some prototypes might eventually become part of the product, and some may be thrown away, but it is still important to know what the underlying strategy is. It is possible that the choice may have already been made, perhaps by the requirements of the customer for early deliveries, or by the project management deciding that a specific strategy should be used.

Importance to developers

The strategy determines several factors:

- How the prototype is to be developed.
- The tools and techniques that can be used.
- How the prototype should be demonstrated.

Incremental or evolutionary development may need a team effort, the software being built to production coding standards, with full documentation, quality assurance (QA) reviews, and code walk-throughs. In contrast, a throw-away prototype can often be developed by a single person, and may use 'quick and dirty' coding techniques.

The strategy determines whether production or non-production languages and software tools can be used, and if the prototype can use the target environment, or, if it would be easier or faster, different hardware. For example, a user interface prototype could be developed with a 4GL and forms package on a PC, and the actual system built using the X Window System on a Sun workstation, assuming that the performance of the prototype is not a primary concern.

All prototypes must be demonstrated at some stage; this may be anything from a formal presentation to the customer, to an informal demonstration for a few fellow developers.

3.4.2 Choosing what to prototype

All prototypes should have the primary aim of meeting the goals of the project, and this includes prototypes to solve specific problems highlighted by the development. The functionality expressed in a prototype will obviously vary widely according to these goals, but as discussed in Chapter 1, a distinction can be drawn between horizontal and vertical prototyping.

Horizontal prototyping is similar to the concept of top-down design. It can be used to find major system flaws early, and makes a partial, early system demonstration possible. Vertical prototyping is similar to the bottom-up idea, and can provide early working sub-system prototypes.

In practical terms, however, the distinctions between horizontal and vertical prototyping are not particularly important, and most prototypes cannot be neatly classified. The choice of functionality depends on the functional and non-functional goals, and on the problem solving requirements. It depends to a lesser extent on the choice of strategy.

Functional goals

The functional goals are the top-level goals for the project, and are the essential things which the project should achieve, and which must usually be delivered at specified times. Functional goals are not prototyped directly, since they are absolute statements which are either achieved or not achieved, eg:

> 'The system shall use the X Windows System for the user interface'

is a statement which cannot be partially achieved. If the system does not use X, then this functional goal has not been met.

However, the aim of prototyping in any project must be guided towards achieving these goals. In the above example, prototyping cannot have a direct impact on whether X Windows is used, but it might help in resolving specific user interface design difficulties.

Quality goals

The quality goals, in contrast, specify *measurable* system requirements, like performance or reliability. Prototyping can be used to assist developers in achieving the required quality goals. This may be done in two ways:

1 Estimating the parameters of proposed systems.
2 Determining the feasibility of meeting the quality requirements.

Table 3.2 gives a range of quality goals, as defined by Gilb (1988), although the list is by no means complete.

Goals	Parameters
Performance	process capacity responsiveness storage capacity
Availability	reliability maintainability integrity
Adaptability	improvability extendability portability
Usability	starting requirements learning requirements handling ability likability

Table 3.2 Quality goals, and their major parameters

Of the goals listed in Table 3.2, prototyping can only really be used to assess the performance and usability. The goals of availability and adaptability are difficult to measure until the system is complete, so prototyping may be of little benefit.

System performance

If the system, when complete, does not perform as required, the costs to re-build the system may be prohibitive. So it is important for the developer to know, as early as possible in the project, what the *likely* performance will be, and which areas may have *poor* performance.

There is obviously a great deal of interest in system performance, and many statistical and modelling techniques have been developed to assist in estimating performance. However, these techniques can be very difficult to apply to complex systems, and are often too expensive or time-consuming. Many estimating techniques require information collected from the operation of similar systems, which is difficult if the proposed system is novel, since there is little historical data to use in predicting behaviour. Furthermore, unless the application area is well understood, it may just be the validity of the model that is actually being tested, rather than the performance of the system.

An alternative is to use prototyping techniques, either to build prototypes that can be run in the target environment, or from which the performance can be extrapolated. This is much harder.

The basic measures of performance can be defined as follows:

- Throughput – the ability to process units of work per unit of time, eg 100 data records processed per minute.
- Responsiveness – the time taken to respond to a single event, eg the disk access time.
- Storage capacity – the capacity of the system to store items, eg Mbytes of data records.

System usability

Determining the usability of a system is one of the key applications for prototyping. This is normally done by prototyping the user interface. Usability is a measure of the ease of use of a system, the user friendliness, and the productivity gained by using the system. Usability relates to the intended *users* of the system, so it cannot be measured by the developers using the system, since they have expert knowledge which is not normally available to a user.

The basic measures of usability can be defined as:

- Starting requirements – the basic training and knowledge needed to start learning to use the system, eg an introductory computing course.
- Learning requirements – the time needed to learn the system, and to perform a useful task, eg 30 minutes training is needed to perform 20 tasks with 99 per cent accuracy.
- Handling ability – the productivity expected after training is completed, eg 100 forms processed by the user per hour.
- Likability – the attitude of the users towards the system, eg 90 per cent of users prefer the new system to the old one.

Usability is important to the developers, since they need to know if the users like the system, even if it does not yet meet all of the functional requirements. Unlike the developers, the users may have to use the system on a regular basis. Measures of usability can be helpful in maximising the benefits of the system. There may be greater potential gain in building a usable system which meets 90 per cent of the functional goals, than in building a system which meets *all* of the functional goals, but is unusable. If usability is a key requirement, then it should be made one of the top-level functional goals.

Resource constraints

Resource constraints include both the constraints imposed on the development process, and also the operational constraints. Some typical resource constraints are listed in Table 3.3.

Constraints	Parameters
Development constraints	people time costs
Operational constraints	hardware performance storage capacity memory size

Table 3.3 Resource constraints, and their major parameters

In all software projects it is important to know if the allocated resources are sufficient for the tasks in hand, and to estimate the resources needed for a specific task. Prototyping may be useful in helping the estimating process:

- by prototyping part of the system, to get an approximate measure of the degree of difficulty
- by using incremental or evolutionary development, since each successive version allows a better estimate of the overall costs

Estimating is not easy, and it is hard to scale-up an estimate based on a prototype to an estimate for the complete system, especially if the prototyping is not done in the target environment.

Resource constraints are important to developers, since if there are insufficient resources, the team leaders and project manager must be informed, and they then have to make a decision either to increase the resources, re-allocate tasks, or reduce the functionality.

3.4.3 Choosing when to prototype

The choice of when a prototype should be built in a project will normally be decided by the project goals, and the choice of prototyping strategy. But it is worth considering that there may still be a degree of flexibility. For example, there may be some requirements that are difficult to establish, even with prototyping, until key system components are available quite late in the development. A typical example of this is in measuring the system performance.

Early prototyping

Early prototyping covers prototypes built during the pre-requirements and the requirements specification stages. Early prototyping is important to developers to avoid problems in the project goals and requirements, and a consequential detrimental effect on the project. The major risks during the early part of a development are:

- not discovering or understanding the customer's real needs
- incorrect goals – missing, ambiguous, or inconsistent
- dependencies between goals
- conflicting or impossible goals

The main goals of early prototyping are:

- to help understand the real problem
- to help define the project's overall goals
- to reveal goal conflicts and dependencies
- to elicit and understand the customer's requirements
- to refine the requirement specification

Applications of prototyping during the early stages concentrate on demonstrating what the system will eventually look like, and what it will do, so they include user interface prototyping and demonstration scenarios.

Middle prototyping

Prototyping during the middle stages of the project, the functional specification and the design, has a shift in emphasis from the goals and requirements of the early stages, to the investigation of the functional behaviour and the verification and validation of the design. The major risks during the middle part of a development are:

- the functional specification is inconsistent with the requirements
- the functional specification incorrectly defines the required behaviour
- the system design is incorrect, or is inconsistent
- the system design does not meet the quality goals or the resource constraints
- the system will be excessively complex
- the requirements have changed since the beginning of the project

Consequently, the main goals for middle prototyping are:

- to define the system's behaviour and structure
- to help refine and verify the functional specification
- to help verify and validate the system design

There are many different applications for prototyping during the middle development stages, for example:

- prototyping to complement the specification, or as a working specification
- prototyping to assess the performance and cost of a particular design
- prototyping to investigate the feasibility of the high-level design
- prototyping detailed design algorithms
- prototyping the database design

Late prototyping

Prototyping during the implementation stage is particularly concerned with quality goals such as performance. The major risks during the implementation are:

- the requirements have changed
- the system design proves to be unimplementable
- the implementation does not meet the system design

The major goals for the implementation stages in a project are:

- to implement the system specified by the design
- to implement the system to the required goals, within the constraints
- to ensure that the completed system is correct

Prototypes built during the course of the implementation may be used to test or measure the system as it is being developed, and to help solve unexpected implementation problems. Unlike early and middle prototyping, late prototyping tends to be more concerned with practical problems, and so demonstration of prototypes to the customer and user are of less importance.

System evolution

All systems evolve with time, and the cost of system maintenance is very high. The major risks during the system evolution are:

- project's overall goals have changed
- requirement specification changes are not tracked
- system evolution introduces new errors

Prototyping has a role in evolving the system after the system is delivered (Luqi, 1989), and the main goals for prototyping in this phase are:

- to discover changing goals and requirements
- to prototype system evolutions to meet the changed goals
- to help verify the proposed system

Quite often, as a system evolves, changes to solve one particular problem introduce new problems, or suggest interesting topics for future development. By prototyping proposals which look at systems for several years ahead, the customers and users have time to change their concepts and ideas, and hopefully will be able to define their goals better when the new developments are actually started.

3.5 Building the prototype

There are some simple guidelines for the process of implementing a prototype, but as is the case in a conventional software project, the actual coding phase is not the most difficult. More important is considering how the prototype should be demonstrated to gain the maximum benefits.

3.5.1 Designing scenarios

The preceding sections have discussed prototypes and prototyping from the viewpoint of a prototype as a single entity, eg an individual model of a system, or a prototype of a particular aspect of a system. This simplification has been necessary in order to describe the fundamental aspects of prototyping, but in looking at the different kinds of system that really need prototyping, for example distributed systems or large-scale systems, it is clear that the prototype itself may be quite complex.

The prototypes might have several interacting users, rather than a single user, or be implemented on a small computer network rather than a single machine. In these cases it becomes important to consider not only the basic concepts of prototyping, but the wider aspects of how to present the prototype system to the best advantage.

Demonstrating a prototype

Demonstrations are very effective ways of presenting the prototype. The presenter is the only person who operates the system; the customers and users watch, listen, and ask questions. This is often best done with a well-rehearsed script. Experience has shown that demonstrations are better if a clearly thought-out scenario is presented. The scenario should demonstrate all the major features of the system, and a typical sequence of actions can be chosen with a short story to explain the various activities.

If the scenario and the demonstration are interesting, then the audience can follow what is going on more easily, and will remember what has happened. They can use the story line as a trigger to remember exactly what features were demonstrated. For example, a prototype stock control system could follow the passage of a particular product through a factory, starting with the incoming components, moving on to quality control, then on to the factory floor where the components are assembled, and then finally into the warehouse. This scenario will be familiar to the audience, and will be easy for them to follow.

A prototype like this need not be entirely robust, and shortcuts can be taken as the presenter can avoid potential problems in the scenario. The disadvantage is that the details of the solution will not be noticed, and these may be important. In particular the audience generally concentrate on what is being displayed, and not on the commands that are being used.

Design considerations

The scenario needs to be carefully designed to avoid the prototype being misunderstood. In demonstrating to customers or users who are untrained or unfamiliar with the technology, they may concentrate on minor details of the system, and ignore the major issues. For example, if the stock control prototype displays a goods order form, they may notice comparatively trivial aspects like:

> 'the product code should have 12 not 8 characters'
> or 'the supplier address field is too short'.

They may completely ignore the fact that the order form can be sent electronically to the supplier, thus decreasing ordering delays and errors, and not mention that some suppliers actually have several invoice addresses instead of the single address assumed by the prototype.

So it is important to decide just *how* realistic a scenario should be. In the above example, it may be useful to show an order form with *all* of the possible fields, just to show it can be done, and then use simplified forms for the rest of the demonstration.

In contrast, some scenarios may need to deviate from reality in order to prove to the audience that a particular feature has been invoked. A good example of this is an electronic mail system, where the sending and retrieval of mail should be transparent to the user. However, this very transparency may mean that the audience doesn't believe that the system is actually using electronic mail.

By putting breakpoints into the scenario, and perhaps manually listing the contents of a directory, it can be shown that the items are indeed being mailed from system to system. Although one of the goals of a good system should be to hide complexity from the user, there may be situations where it is necessary to add extra steps in order to explain underlying activities which would normally be hidden.

Scenarios may also deviate from reality in order to demonstrate ideas that are not currently feasible, but which may be the subject of future developments.

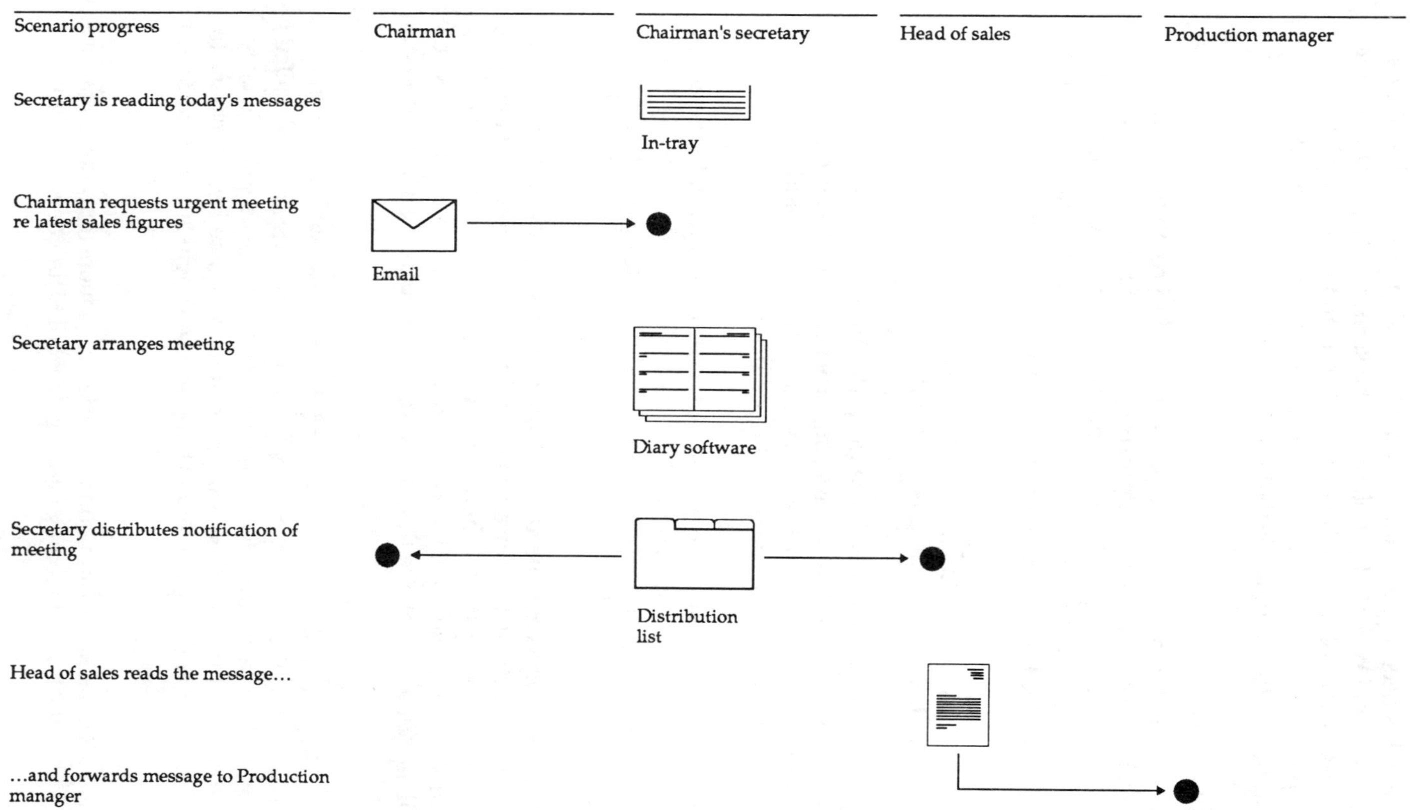

Figure 3.4 Scenario activity diagram

Documents

When presenting a scenario to an audience, it is very useful to have an overview document that describes exactly what is being demonstrated and why. For complex scenarios it may be necessary to draw a diagram that explains the sequence of events. Figure 3.4, which is taken from an actual scenario overview document, uses graphical symbols to represent the various activities.

Guidelines

The authors have found that the following points are worth considering in the design of a scenario:

- Scenarios should relate to the user's expected tasks, eg realistic problems of sufficient scope and complexity.
- Presenters should use a script to avoid missing out key points.
- The length of the demonstration can vary with the audience, but about 20 to 30 minutes is best.
- To avoid mistakes, little keyboard input should be done during the demonstration. Use pre-prepared files if necessary.
- Complex scenarios are best presented with one person driving the system, and one giving the presentation.
- There must be a clear description of what the system does and does not model; this can be included in an overview document for the audience.

3.5.2 Implementing the prototype

In theory, the activities of analysing problems, and of creating solutions to these problems, are clearly separated. However, in practice there is a gradual move from one activity to another, with solutions forming before all the detail of the analysis is complete.

The basic difference between this and the traditional approach to building systems is that when the prototype has been built, and is demonstrated as a potential solution, the users or customers often will say:

> 'That's not what I want – I want it like this...'.

The point is that problem analysis is hard to do in isolation from potential solutions, being too abstract. With a potential solution in front of them, the customers and users can tell immediately whether it is valid or not, whereas when presented with an abstract statement of the problem, and then an abstract solution, they find it much more difficult.

The strategy employed when building a prototype should recognise the fact that these two activities cannot be entirely separated. The activities involved during the creation of the prototype start with problem analysis, and include more and more solution creation with time. This process is shown in idealised form in Figure 3.5.

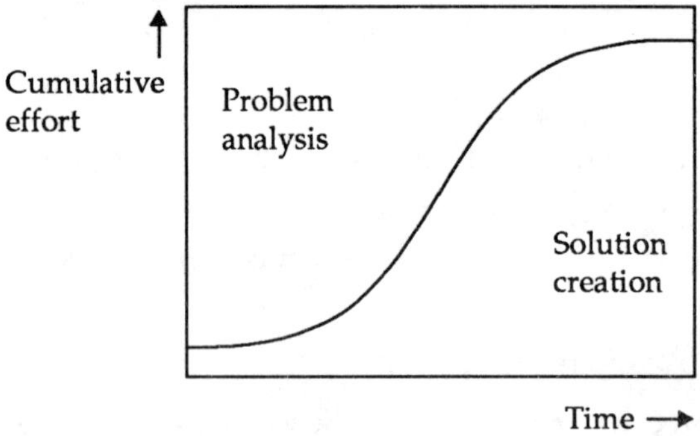

Figure 3.5 Problem analysis and solution creation
Note: This diagram is illustrative of the changing ratio between problem analysis and solution creation; the actual shape of the curve is not significant

Requirements analysis

It is important to start any project with a clearly defined set of goals. A good practical way of exploring the goals is to perform a requirements analysis. There are several methods for doing this; this section looks at CORE (COntrolled Requirements Expression), as described by Mullery (1979). Other methods have similar principles, but may use a different terminology.

Within any project various people must be identified as having certain responsibilities. These people are:

- the customer authority
- the several viewpoint authorities

The *customer authority* is the person who has the responsibility and authority of accepting the specification as being finished. This person will probably need to ask the advice of others, in particular the viewpoint authorities, as he or she may not have the necessary expertise to check the work, but their role involves taking this responsibility, and having the authority to sign off the document as being finished. The person taking on this role is usually the one providing the funding.

There will be various points of view regarding the problem. For some people there may be no problem at all, as the present system is satisfactory, but for others the existing system needs drastic changes. Each of these people has a valid viewpoint that must be taken into consideration. The various viewpoints are usually sources or sinks of information, for example the manager who receives a computer generated report, or the clerk who enters information from a handwritten form to a terminal.

Each of these people is sometimes referred to as a *stake holder*, in that they have some stake in the eventual outcome of a new system. For each point of view, a *viewpoint authority* is appointed. This person will represent all the others with the same point of view as themselves. The viewpoint authorities have the responsibility and authority to give the point of view of the people they represent. This does not mean that they should only give their opinion, but rather that they hold the authority to sign off a proposed solution as being valid for all the people that they represent.

Having defined the various viewpoint authorities, the analyst can then gather the information about the problem and start the process of requirements analysis. The viewpoint authorities can be the main source of information, but they are not the only source. However, if the viewpoint authorities have been chosen correctly, then they should form a sufficient set of people from which to gather information. The information gathered can now be used to form a solution.

Each of the viewpoint authorities must now be consulted to see if the solution is valid from their point of view. Each one of them has to agree that they, and the people they represent, are happy with the solution.

This is one of the traditional ways of performing the analysis and verifying the solution. The same method can be used as a basis for a prototyping strategy. The same process of analysis has to take place, and the same validation of the proposed solution. The only difference is that the proposed solution is a working prototype rather than a document.

Implementation

The implementation of a prototype usually starts as early as possible in a project, during the specification stages. Middle and late prototypes are also possible, but regardless of whether they are early, middle, or late, information still has to be collected about the problem before the prototype can be built.

The timing of the construction of the prototype is dependant upon the nature of the problem. If it is built too early, then not enough views will have been collected. If it has been built too late, then it will be too late to make major changes based on the reaction to the prototype. The correct balance must be found. A good rule of thumb is to start building after the first round of major viewpoints have been obtained, but before the details are refined.

An important decision is what features to include in the prototype and what to miss out. It is tempting to include the features that are well-understood, as these are the easiest ones to get right. This, of course, is the wrong thing to do. The features that are best understood do not need a prototype to explain them. The important things to examine are those features that are uncertain, so that the prototype can be used to understand the problem further.

The analysts may develop the prototype themselves, but it is quite likely that a development team will be used for this purpose. If this is the case, a close working relationship needs to be built up between the analysts and developers. The usual working relationship in a conventional software project is based around a formal specification document.

However, during the development of a prototype there are frequent changes in the requirements, and very little in the way of formal specifications. There needs to be daily, if not more frequent contact between the various parties, as there must be a regular exchange of views and of new information.

There also needs to be a good working relationship between developers and systems analysts, as their relationship is very informal. They need to trust each other. The developers have to be able to take daily criticism of their work. They have to be prepared to scrap large chunks of code which prove unnecessary when further analysis has been done. The analyst must be able to trust the programmer to interpret correctly verbal specifications and informal notes.

Testing

The degree to which testing is done on a prototype depends on the need for the prototype itself. Some prototypes, which are required as quickly as possible, or which may be thrown away after use, will not need to have such careful testing done as those that will ultimately evolve into a delivered product. Testing is one of the many simplifications that can be made for the purposes of building a prototype.

The development of a prototype should not, however, be used as an excuse for writing 'quick and dirty' code. The goals for the prototype should indicate the quality of coding and testing, and the prototype should be designed and implemented to meet these goals.

Human factors specialists, eg ergonomists and psychologists, may need to be involved with users in the testing of a prototype. People are easily affected by a test situation, and their behaviour and opinions may be biased in unexpected and unpredictable ways.

3.6 Experimenting with the prototype

The final part of the strategy is the process of experimentation. This determines whether the prototype has been successful, in which case it is accepted, or whether the scenario needs revising, or even if the prototype itself needs redesigning.

3.6.1 Exercising the prototype

If it is worth building the prototype, then it should be exercised in such a way that its ideas and features can be studied and evaluated. The process of exercising a prototype may involve:

- comparative experiments
- brainstorming
- demonstrations to customers and users
- use by the potential users

Comparative experiments

Comparative experiments can be used to compare different prototypes as potential solutions, or to compare a system and the prototype of its proposed replacement.

Brainstorming sessions

A brainstorming session is an informal presentation and discussion of a prototype, used to generate new ideas and features (Jordan et al, 1989). It is often used by the development teams to iron out problems before the prototypes are demonstrated.

Demonstrations

Demonstrations to different project participants may have widely differing aims, for example:

- for senior management, to help them make strategic decisions
- for customers, to decide on the requirements for a system
- for users, to discover problems in system behaviour and usability
- for developers, to solve a specific problem

Whatever the ultimate aims, the person presenting the prototype should make people aware of the benefits and limitations of the prototype. There is always a danger of raising expectations too high, and of people believing that the prototype is the *real* system, which in a way is the mark of a good system prototype. To balance this it must be stressed that although the prototype isn't the final system, it can be changed and enhanced if necessary.

Use by potential users

Another way to exercise a prototype is to give it to the potential users. This is an excellent way of finding problems. Users are very good at complaining about the things they don't like, and quite good at generating new ideas. The system must be robust enough to withstand unexpected inputs. The differences between the prototype and the eventual system must be made clear, otherwise the users may concentrate on criticising the features that are going to change.

Summary

Whichever method is chosen to exercise the prototype, the various viewpoint authorities must be consulted. Each must look at the prototype from their point of view and ask the question:

> 'Does this satisfy *my* requirements?'

At this point a collection of objections will have been raised from the various viewpoints. The prototype must be rebuilt to take into account these objections. The cycle must then be repeated. In the subsequent iterations it is probably not necessary to visit all the viewpoint authorities, but is is important that changes made by one person do not affect someone else who is subsequently not told.

The exercising of the prototype should check all or most of the following points:

- Can the users complete their given tasks?
- Do the users know when they have completed their tasks?
- Can the users correct mistakes and recover from them?
- Do the users have a model of the system compatible with the system itself?
- Is there a consistency between the tasks already carried out by the users and the ones they can perform with the prototype?
- Is the jargon used in the prototype compatible with the user's jargon?
- Can the least capable user complete the tasks?
- Does the most capable user find it too tedious?
- Is the time taken to complete the task acceptable?
- Is the effort required to complete the task acceptable?
- Are the users satisfied with the system?
- Does the user interface meet company style guidelines?

3.6.2 Evaluating the prototype

The evaluation process is a key step in prototyping, otherwise prototyping effort could be misused, misunderstood, or wasted. It provides feedback for the rest of the development process, and consequently needs the participation of all the relevant viewpoint authorities – users, customers, developers, etc.

The criteria for the evaluation must be stated before the evaluation process starts. The areas not covered by the prototype must also be stated, for example that the purpose is to evaluate the user interface, but not the system performance. Resources must be made available for the evaluation process, and training provided if necessary.

While the prototype is being evaluated, or after it has been, information must be gathered about the reactions of the users to the system. There are various items of information that can be gathered:

- users' opinions
- users' behaviour
- users' knowledge
- experts' opinions

Users' opinions

Users' opinions are gathered either while they are using the system, or afterwards. Opinions are a qualitative rather than a quantitative judgement on the system, and so are difficult to analyse, although it is often possible to spot trends. There are various ways to gather user opinions:

- record free flow of users' ideas as they are operating the prototype
- conduct structured interview
- conduct semi-structured interview
- conduct unstructured interview

Recording the free flow of opinions as the users operate the prototype has the advantage of tapping the opinions as they occur. Sometimes users have difficulty in expressing those opinions at the same time as they are learning something new.

Interviews conducted after the event can be much more systematic, but rely on the users remembering their feelings while they were operating the system. Interviews can be structured, in which the set of questions are preset, and always asked in the same order with the same words. They can be unstructured, with no preset questions, allowing for a free flow of opinions. They can be semi-structured, providing something in between. Structured interviews allow analysis of the data collected from large numbers of users, but tend to stop the free flow of ideas, whereas unstructured interviews have the reverse effect.

Users' behaviour

It may be useful to record the users' behaviour and activities when using the prototype, for example what functions they used, where they made mistakes, etc. The techniques for doing this are outside the scope of this book, but are covered in texts on human factors. See for example Salvendy (1987).

Users' knowledge

The purpose of the system is to aid the users in achieving some task, so a good test is to discover if the users *know* how to achieve the task. If they cannot, then the prototype has probably been badly designed.

The users must be given sufficient time to use the prototype, either after a training programme, or after their own experimentation. It is only after they know something of the system that their knowledge can be tested.

The users' knowledge of the way to achieve their task is tested very simply. They are given the system and asked, 'Please do such-and-such an operation'. No help must be given by the observer during this process.

It is important that the tasks chosen for the users to perform are related to those that they understand, and those that the system is set to achieve. A good example of a task to set them is:

> 'Find the address of Alison Brook from the database'.

A bad example of a task to set them is:

> 'Display the electronic mail menu on the screen'.

The former is related to a task understood by the user; the latter is related to the kind of system being operated.

Expert opinions

As well as gathering the opinion of users, the opinion of experts is also useful. Experts from a number of fields may be involved, for example:

- Experts in human behaviour.
- Experts on the design of user interfaces.
- Experts on the tasks that the users are to perform.
- Experts on the environment in which the system will be installed.
- Experts on ability level of the users.

The first two items on this list are very important, as the user interface is usually a critical part of most systems. Human factors experts or ergonomists may have to be hired specially, as these fields are highly specialised. Opinions may be gathered in the same ways as those of the users.

As well as the experts' opinion of the system itself, they may also be asked to give an opinion on the use of the system by the users themselves. This involves some kind of observation. There are a number of ways in which the information can be gathered:

- Direct observation of the use of the prototype.
- Recorded observation of the use of the prototype, eg by video camera.
- Observation of a computer log of the use of the system.

Direct observation or use of a video camera to record the use of the system can inhibit the users, but does give a clear indication of when the users find something difficult to understand. Recording the users' keystrokes or commands can be very useful in understanding how the system is used. It provides a set of quantitative data that can be analysed very easily for errors and common mistakes. Specialist advice should certainly be sought in the area of monitoring users, as it is all too easy to draw incorrect conclusions which relate to the nature of the observations themselves, rather than the actual task being monitored.

The evaluation plan

Before launching into a series of tests and interviews it is advisable to form an evaluation plan. This should state:

- The purpose of the evaluation.
- Who will use the system.
- How many people will use the system.
- What training they will need.
- What tasks they are to perform.
- What data will be gathered.
- How the data will be gathered.
- How the data are to be analysed.
- What the acceptance criteria are.

Outcome of the evaluation

The outcome of the evaluation process is a list of the major points discovered by the evaluation, for example:

- likes
- dislikes
- features
- problems

These may be ordered if necessary so that priority items can easily be identified, but the list is usually subjective.

Once the evaluation is complete, the prototype has to be accepted as it is, or rejected. If it is rejected it must go through a redesign. It may go through a series of progressively smaller changes until it is acceptable. Once accepted, the prototype must be signed-off by the customer.

The evaluation process is illustrated in Figure 3.6. The scenario may also need to be redesigned as a result of the evaluation process.

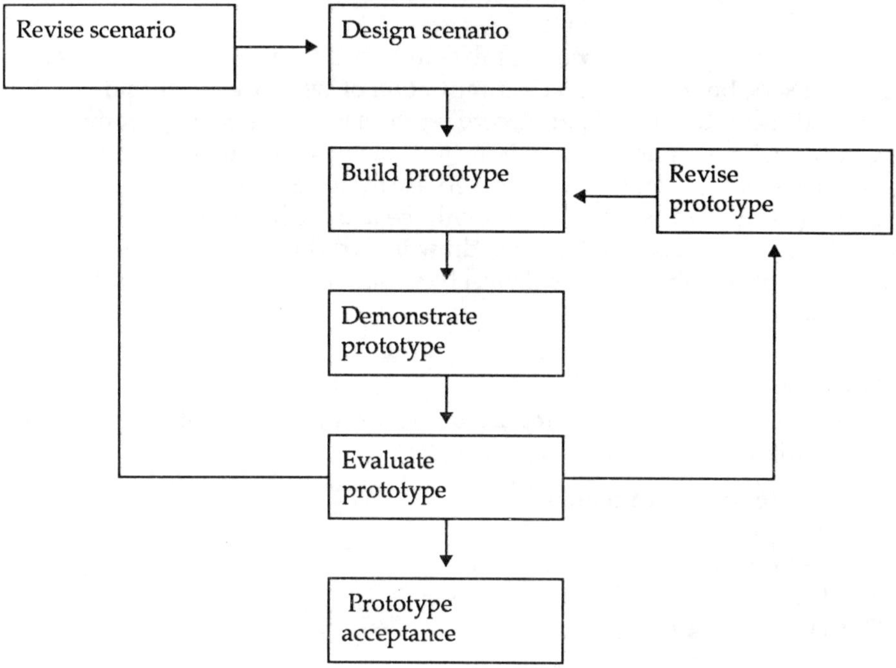

Figure 3.6 Evaluation of the prototype

Acceptance of a prototype means that the prototype has achieved the tasks for which it was originally developed. This may mean one of several things:

- The prototype is suitable as a deliverable item.
- The prototype can be thrown-away, and a conventional project development started.
- The prototype can be used as the basis for writing the system specification document.
- The prototype forms part of the system specification.

3.7 Conclusions

There is no set strategy for prototyping, but a sensible approach is to base the strategy on the need to resolve project risks. These risks might be of missing an important delivery date, or of the system not meeting strict performance constraints. Some people may argue that all this does is to push any development problems from the requirements analysis and specification stages, back even earlier to the risk identification and analysis. This is true to a certain extent, but the specification approach encourages people to concentrate on those areas that they best understand. Risk management forces people to think about the things that they *don't* understand, as these may be potential risks.

Prototyping is only one of several methods for reducing risks, but it does provide a good way of 'buying' information. Risks relate to knowledge; perfect knowledge of a situation means no risks. If failure is certain, the outcome is predictable. This is not to say that there are no problems; problems still exist, but their impact can be planned for. Complete knowledge of a system can only be gained by building the complete system, hence risk management is used to help select those areas of highest risk, where additional information is needed.

The strategy uses a cycle where risks are identified, analysed, and a prototyping response selected. There are some mathematical techniques available to assist in this, eg in the calculation of risk exposure and risk reduction leverage. Prototyping may also help in identifying further risks, and in quantifying known ones.

A key point here is that the cycle is repeated until the risks are resolved, or are reduced to a level that can be accepted. The cycle is driven by the need to *actively* avoid risks, rather than passively accept them. This is used as a basis for defining the reasons for prototyping, and for choosing the prototyping strategy.

If the maximum benefits are to be gained from the effort put into prototyping, it is important that prototypes are presented, exercised, and evaluated in the most effective way. The design of a prototyping scenario is particularly important, but in any presentation people must be made aware of the difference between a prototype as a model that will be thrown out later, or a partial implementation of something that will eventually form part of a delivered system.

People should be encouraged to comment on, and where relevant to test and use the prototype. This information can be used to direct the next cycle of prototyping, but at some time agreement must be reached that the prototyping has achieved the desired objectives.

This strategy is really only a general guide. It can and must be adapted to organisational working practices, and to the specific needs of each project. In this way the strategy can be used to guide a project towards achieving its goals.

Selected reading

Software risk management

Boehm, B W
Software risk management, IEEE Computer Society Press, Washington, DC, 1989

Charette, R N
Software engineering risk analysis and management, McGraw-Hill, 1989

Clapp, J A
Rapid prototyping for risk management, *Proceedings 11th International Computer Software and Applications Conference*, IEEE Computer Society Press, 1987, 17–22

4 Managing prototyping projects

Introduction

The management of software projects, or indeed any other type of project, has long been thought to be something of an art form. How else can completely different management styles produce results which vary from enormous success through to total failure? Like any art form, there are endless books and articles which promise to reveal the secrets of successful management.

In an attempt to improve their management of projects, many organisations have decided that a formal management strategy is essential. This strategy must always be followed. Those that do not believe in it are obviously not the right sort of people to be managers. However, this approach falls into the all too common trap – when a task is difficult and complex, a set of rules is proposed to solve the task.

The basic idea is sound. A set of rules can be very useful in such circumstances. But it must be realised that if a task is complex, the rules will almost certainly not be complete, and may in fact be wrong. Rules can be used to provide help and guidance, but a rigorous adherence to the rules will lead to trouble.

The earlier chapters of this book have discussed the problems of a software development strategy in some detail. To recap on this, the ideal strategy should be:

- A high-level framework for development, not a rigorous prescribed plan.
- A collection of useful ideas and tools for development.
- A starting point for designing a strategy tailored to the problem in hand.

Prototyping is one of the techniques that the authors believe is particularly important and powerful for software development. But it is not the only technique, and its use must be carefully managed. This chapter is about the management of software projects, with emphasis on balancing the informality of prototyping with the more formal controls needed to ensure that the project is completed on time and within budget.

The purpose of this chapter

The purpose of this chapter is to introduce the reader to the concepts and techniques necessary to manage a successful prototyping project, although they are equally applicable to any software project.

This chapter considers prototyping project management as being essentially the management of risk; identifying the major sources of risks, applying techniques (including prototyping) to control the risks, and monitoring the progress of the project. Good project managers are usually those that can balance the goals of a project against the risks of failure. Of course, project managers will still have to manage staff and attend meetings, but there are plenty of very good books on conventional management techniques, so these topics are not covered in detail (see selected reading).

General organisation

Section 4.1 expands the problem solving approach discussed in Chapter 1 to cover the managerial aspects of goals, and describes some practical techniques for managers to look at goals and solutions, for example critical success factors, and impact estimation.

The way that prototyping is introduced to an organisation is important for its future success. If it is not introduced correctly, the organisation may not gain the full benefits, and the use of prototyping may be abandoned. Section 4.2 looks at how prototyping impacts the development process, how to justify the use of prototyping within an organisation, and how to start up a prototyping project.

Section 4.3 explains basic aspects of project management, including staffing, team organisation, monitoring and control, and planning and estimating. Important techniques for minimising projects risks are also discussed.

Finally, section 4.4 examines the problems of prototyping, giving some hints on what to do to ensure success, and how to avoid failure. The section concludes with a set of guidelines for the project participants.

4.1 Managerial aspects of problem solving

This section discusses the problems of software management, and the management of prototyping projects. This leads on to an examination of the problem solving approach discussed in Chapter 1. The aim is to provide some simple techniques to enable managers to give a balanced assessment of the goals of a project, and of the proposed solutions. This is particularly important where the project manager has managerial, rather than technical, authority.

4.1.1 The problems of software management

Several areas contribute to the problems of managing software development projects, for example:

- The nature of software.
- The difficulty of specifying system requirements.
- The differences between software and traditional engineering projects.

The factors which contribute to the nature of software (complexity, accuracy, visibility, changeability), which were discussed in Chapter 1, have consequences for the management of software projects. The complexity means that it is very difficult to estimate the resources needed for a project. Although cost information is available from past software projects, the variations between projects and organisations are so wide that a great deal of skill is necessary in estimating. The need for accuracy means that sufficient time and resources must be allocated for testing. Because software is difficult to visualise it is hard to measure progress and quality. Changeability has two aspects:

1 Software reacts with, and changes, the environment.
2 Software systems and requirements are dynamic.

Since software systems are so varied, a new system reacts with and changes the real world. For example, an innovative product like the first spreadsheet created a new market, and almost immediately generated a new set of requirements for the product. This means that the needs of customers are dynamic, and systems must react to these changes. It is not wrong to alter the requirements in the middle of a project, it is inevitable, otherwise there is a risk of delivering an out-of-date product.

4.1.2 Managing prototyping projects

The problems outlined above apply to any software project, but they also have a particular importance for the management of prototyping projects. Complex project management and associated overheads must be avoided, otherwise the flexibility offered by prototyping is lost. Conversely, the increased flexibility offered by prototyping must also be controlled, otherwise there is too much freedom to do things wrong. It is all too easy to hide difficult problems in a prototyping project by saying 'It's just the prototype; the real system will be better'.

Prototyping, by its very nature, gives people the freedom to explore difficult or complex or uncertain parts of a project. The prototype that is developed may range from a single prototype which is ultimately thrown away, through to a series of prototypes, each one adding more features to the previous ones until the system is finished.

No single prototype can be run as a complete lifecycle development, with detailed requirements specification, functional specification, and design documents, otherwise there is no gain from prototyping. If a prototype is to be thrown out, it is clear that certain compromises can be made in developing that prototype, for example in performance or memory utilisation. If it is to become a part of a deliverable system, then the performance and memory utilisation must meet the stated objectives.

Whichever type of prototyping is used, it must be known what the aims of the project are, and how each prototype impacts these goals. The prototype is part of the problem solving process, so the project must always start by defining the problem to be solved.

These topics must be addressed by the project manager. Unfortunately, there are no simple solutions. This chapter aims to provide help for project managers by:

- Suggesting good ideas that have worked in the past.
- Noting those ideas that have caused problems or failures.
- Giving suggestions that may stimulate further ideas or techniques.

4.1.3 Understanding the goals

To recap on the discussion in Chapter 1 of project goals, there are three main aspects to the goals of a system:

1 Functional requirements
2 Quality requirements
3 Resource constraints

This is, however, only a part of the total picture. The system goals exist within the framework of the overall goals of the company or organisation. The system goals are a consequence of the organisational goals, for example the need for a system to solve a specific organisational problem, or to meet particular marketing requirements.

Organisational goals

Organisational goals tend to be objectives like profit, customer satisfaction, market share, or return on investment. Achieving these goals requires careful planning, as some goals may take many years to attain. The goals can be divided into:

- strategic goals
- tactical goals
- operational goals

Strategic goals are the long-term goals of the company, which will not be realised until several years in the future. They tend to be broad policy decisions, concerned with objectives and planning, rather than being activities directly concerned with control of the organisation. Strategic goals are set and monitored by the top-level management, who are ultimately responsible for ensuring that the goals are met. The major concerns at this level are the influences imposed by the external environment, for example market trends, or currency prices. Internal factors, like the daily operations of the company, are not significant.

Tactical goals are shorter-term goals, perhaps several months or a year away, rather than several years. They are the implementation of the strategic objectives and plans, and are set by the middle-level management. The emphasis for tactical goals shifts more towards internal factors, with more control activities.

Operational goals are concerned with day-to-day operations, like meeting delivery deadlines, or performing daily tasks. There is little planning done at this level, and the main emphasis is on controlling operations. Internal factors predominate; the external factors are not significant.

Managerial control of goals

The manager of a software project usually has little control of the organisational goals. It is up to the project manager to control the *project* goals to meet the organisational ones. Within the project, the factors that influence the system goals can be controlled to varying degrees. The functional requirements are not usually negotiable, for example a goal that the system *must* have fail-safe data storage is not likely to be open to change. However, quality requirements and constraints are often negotiable, as it is sometimes difficult to set sensible values at the start of a project, before the potential solutions and their costs have been evaluated.

Analysing goals

Even if the degree of control over the goals is limited, the starting point for any software project must be to analyse the goals. A good approach to this is to consider what the *critical success factors* are for a project (Rockart, 1979). A critical success factor (CSF) is a factor which, if ignored, can cause the collapse of the system as a whole. CSFs can aid the understanding of the key areas of a new project. Listing the project goals, and the CSFs needed to achieve these goals, can help in seeing how solutions impact these goals. Table 4.1 gives a simple example of the goals and the CSFs for a hypothetical project.

Goals	Critical success factors
Lower development costs	Clear system requirements Software tools Rapid prototyping
Higher software productivity	Training Productivity incentives Software tools
Easily maintained	Software coding standards
Easy to use products	User surveys User interface prototyping
High reliability	Modular development Code inspections
Easily extendible	Open architecture Software tools

Table 4.1 Examples of critical success factors

In this project, goals like 'lower development costs' and 'higher software productivity' are clear goals, with well defined CSFs. Failure to satisfy the CSFs would most likely lead to the goals not being met, and the project failing. In contrast, other goals like 'easily extendible' look rather weak, and 'high reliability', although a strong goal, does not have very good CSFs. This type of table immediately draws attention to the areas that need further investigation.

The next stage is to quantify the goals, so that the impact of the solutions on the goals can be estimated. The parameters of interest for each goal are:

- The technique used to measure the goal.
- The current level of achievement.
- The worst acceptable level.
- The best achievable level.
- The planned level.

All goals must lie somewhere on the line shown in Figure 4.1. For every goal, there is a level that is unacceptable in some way, and a level that is satisfactory.

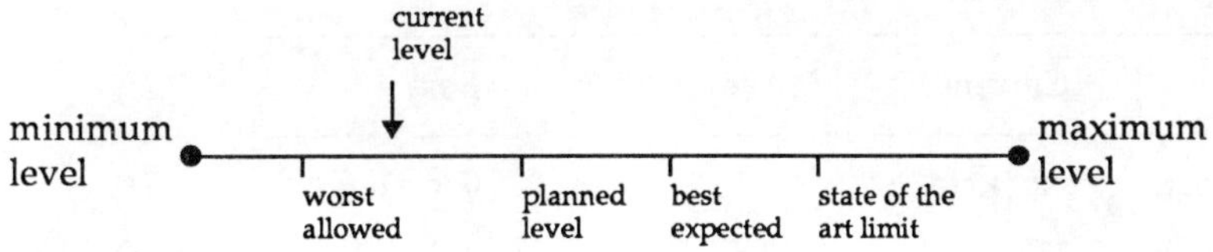

Figure 4.1 An example of the measurements that might be specified for a particular goal

A technique must be specified to enable the goals to be quantified in some way, so that the level of achievement of the goal can be measured. This will show how close the project is to meeting the planned level. For example, the goals listed in Table 4.1 can be measured by the methods listed in Table 4.2.

Goals	Measure
Development costs	Per cent deviation from planned costs
Software productivity	Lines of code per employee per month
Maintainability	Time to correct error once problem known
Ease of use	Time to learn selected tasks
Reliability	Errors/K lines of code/year
Extendibility	?

Table 4.2 Goals and their measurements

The table also highlights that fact that no measure has been identified for extendibility. Without some means of measuring this goal, there is no way to know if a particular solution meets this goal. It may also suggest that extendibility is not a meaningful goal.

The current level of achievement shows how the existing system, if there is one, meets the proposed goal. The planned level represents a realistic level to aim for, and lies between the worst acceptable and best expected levels. A level less than the worst level is *not* acceptable. The state-of-the-art limit lies above the best expected level, and may not be achievable without great difficulty.

The expected (rather than the planned) level of achievement may be given in the table if this is considered important. Table 4.3 illustrates the goals for a hypothetical project. The figures are for illustration only, and should not be regarded as indicative of current software practices.

Goals	Current	Worst	Best	Plan
Development costs	Not known	± 15 %	0 (on target)	± 5 %
Software productivity	150 ± 25	200	400	>300
Maintainability	3 – 5 days	4 hours	< 1 min	30 mins
Ease of use	> 5 days	1 to 2 days	2 hours	< 1 day
Reliability	Not measured	0.5 Kloc/year	0.02 Kloc/year	< 0.1 Kloc/ year

Table 4.3 Goals and their planned levels

Once the means of measuring the goals have been defined, the figures can be specified for each goal. As these are estimates, it is essential to give a measure of the uncertainly, eg 80 ± 20 per cent. If the figures are difficult to estimate, an attempt must still be made to specify a value, even if this means showing a very large uncertainty. Incorrect estimates can always be corrected at a later stage.

Estimating is very important, because without an estimate, it becomes impossible to apply any measure of control.

4.1.4 Evaluating solutions

When the project moves from the requirements analysis phase into the design phase, there is a need to find solutions, to estimate their impact on the goals, to quantify the proposed solutions, and to select the ones that best meet the goals.

This process is not one that can be solved formally. There is no such thing as an 'absolute' solution, although some solutions will undoubtedly meet the goals better than others, and the criteria for selecting the 'best available' solution may be defined. In many projects the situation is complicated by multiple solutions, each of which impacts on several goals, and each of which has its own associated risks.

Solution analysis

One of the simplest ways of analysing solutions is to draw a table of the goals, and the solutions proposed to meet each goal. Table 4.4 shows an example of this.

Goals	Solutions
Development costs	Software prototyping Code inspections
Software productivity	Structured coding Software prototyping Training
Maintainability	?
Ease of use	WIMP interface
Reliability	Code inspections

Table 4.4 Goal and solution mapping

The table maps solutions to goals, and gives an idea of the expected impact of the solutions on the goals. It shows those solutions that impact several goals, and those goals without a solution. In the above example, it is immediately obvious that maintainability needs a solution, and that software prototyping and code inspections have a powerful impact on the goals.

However, the impact of a particular solution is not quantified, nor does it show negative contributions, eg a positive solution to one goal might have negative effects on several others.

Impact estimation

In its simplest form impact estimation uses a table of the major project goals, giving the estimated impact of the solutions and strategies proposed for meeting these goals. This may indicate which solutions seem unrealistic, optimistic or even impossible, or perhaps show goals which do not yet have a solution.

Impact estimation helps to quantify the contributions of a solution to the goals. The estimates of each solution on the goals do not need to be particularly accurate, since the idea is to get a 'feel' for the relative impacts. The figures can be given uncertainly factors, as shown in Table 4.3, if necessary.

If the estimates are really difficult to derive, an alternative is to use a simple coding scheme, with symbols or numbers to represent the impact. For example, the impact could be coded as follows:

0 little or no impact
+ limited impact
++ significant impact
? unknown impact
– negative impact

Techniques like this, although very simple, should not be ignored because it is often much easier to notice anomalies visually, rather than from a table of figures.

Table 4.5 illustrates an impact analysis table for the example discussed above. Solution 1 is rapid prototyping, solution 2 is code inspection, and solution 3 is training. A figure of 100 represents maximum impact; 0 represents no measurable impact. This table does not give uncertainty estimates.

There is no reason why an impact estimation table should not include estimates for the subgoals as well, but this level of detail is not usually available, at least to any useful level of accuracy.

Goals	Impact estimates		
	Solution 1	Solution 2	Solution 3
Development costs	60	50	10
Software productivity	50	10	30
Maintainability	0	10	10
Ease of use	20	0	5
Reliability	30	70	10

Table 4.5 Impact estimation table (selected solutions)

Quantifying and choosing solutions

Once a proposed solution or set of solutions has been identified, the impact estimation table can be extended to show the impact on the stated goals. The sum across the table indicates how well this particular set of solutions meets a particular goal. The sum down the table indicates how well an individual solution meets all the goals.

This is shown in Table 4.6, which is sometimes called a multi-goal, multi-solution impact estimation table.

Goals	Impact estimates			
	Solution 1	Solution 2	Solution 3	Sum 1-3
Development costs	60	50	10	120
Software productivity	50	10	30	90
Maintainability	0	10	10	20
Ease of use	20	0	5	25
Reliability	30	70	10	110
Sum for all goals	160	140	65	

Table 4.6 Impact estimation table used for quantifying solutions

Selecting the 'best' solution can be done by summing the contributions for each solution to all the goals. The figures do not need to be weighted, since each goal is of equal importance, being a top-level goal. In Table 4.6, solution 3 is a much weaker solution than solutions 1 or 2, as shown by the low sum of its impact estimates. The table also shows that none of the proposed solutions really addresses the goals of maintainability, or ease of use.

4.2 Starting a prototyping project

If prototyping is to be adopted as a strategy, it is important to understand how it may impact the way that projects are run, and the changes that may be expected in the systems that are produced.

Knowledge of the advantages of prototyping is helpful in promoting the use of prototyping within an organisation, for example in giving presentations to senior managers. Simple guidelines are also given in this section for starting up a prototyping project.

4.2.1 Impacts on the development project

Prototyping is a relatively new strategy, and there is not the large body of information available that exists for the lifecycle strategy. Nevertheless, the current experiences of using prototyping in a production environment suggest that the following impacts may be expected:

- front-loading of development effort
- decreasing costs of development
- effort distribution
- schedule distribution
- productivity
- shift of emphasis to customers

The impacts will vary according to the functionality of the prototype, the use to which it is put, and the development strategy.

Front-loading of development effort

Because prototyping is often done at the earliest stage possible, before the requirements have been produced, this increases the costs of the early development. However, this tends to reduce the costs of the later stages, since it is more likely that the correct decisions will have been made, and so fewer changes will be necessary. Figure 4.2 shows the kind of effect that might be experienced.

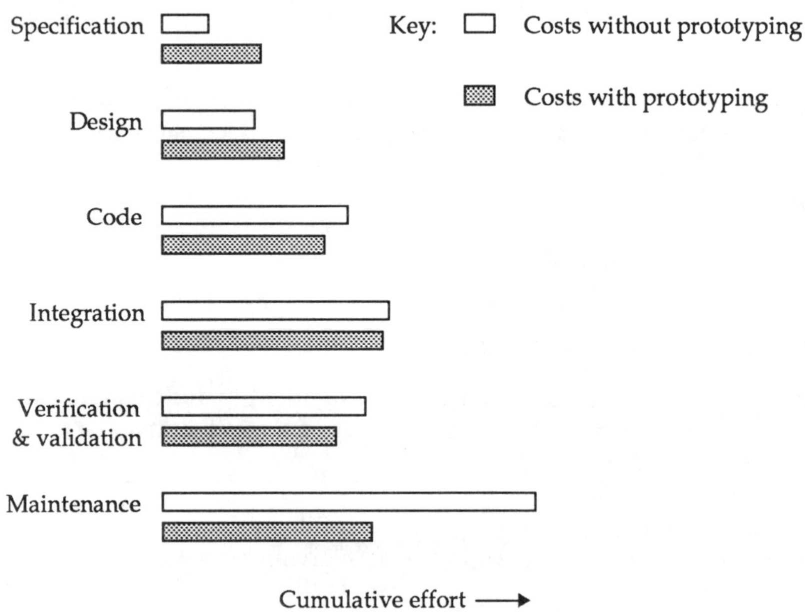

Figure 4.2 Development costs with and without prototyping

Decreasing costs of development

Front-end loading is always cost effective, since it is more likely that the customer's actual needs will be identified, and the system built the way the customer wants. 40 to 60 per cent of maintenance effort is expended on perfective maintenance, ie enhancements to the system, rather than on error correction, so building the right system is particularly cost effective.

Effort distribution

Prototyping allows the development effort to be directed according to need, rather than a uniform spread across all parts of the project. For example, the prototype may identify certain modules as being particularly high risk or difficult, so it would be worthwhile to apply extra effort to get them correct.

Schedule distribution

By building working prototypes early in the project, there is a change from the classic lifecycle model of top-down design/bottom-up development, to top-down development. This means that there is not the same concept of clearly defined lifecycle phases. In general, more effort is expended in specification and design, and less on integration and testing. Integration is on-going, rather than the traditional 'big-bang' approach at the end of the project. Testing time is reduced, since the design is better.

Productivity

Overall, higher productivity should be expected from prototyping. The main reason for this is that by the better focusing of the early project stages on the customer's requirements specification, time is saved in testing, re-working code, or enhancing the code under the guise of maintenance.

Shift of emphasis to customers and users

Prototyping puts less emphasis on getting detailed project plans and specifications right first time, which is rarely possible, and more emphasis on listening to customers, getting the users reaction to prototypes, and refining the prototypes to meet the requirements. Documentation is still needed in a prototyping project, but it is more flexible.

4.2.2 Impacts on the product

It is difficult to make firm statements on how prototyping impacts the system itself, since few statistics have been gathered on prototyping projects, and different organisations vary so widely in their ability. See for example Alavi (1984), Boehm et al (1984), Connell and Brice (1985), and Hekmatpour (1987) for further information.

The following discussion is based on a set of system parameters developed by Gilb (1988), which specify the key areas of a system. In some ways it is not entirely meaningful to discuss the effect of prototyping on a system, since any one factor can be chosen for improvement at the expense of another. For example, high performance can be traded for maintainability.

The system parameters which will be considered are as follows:

- What the system actually does (functionality).
- How complex the system is (complexity).
- How 'good' the system is (quality).

Note that the above list is almost certainly incomplete, as many more factors can be identified. Physical system parameters are missing, and quality is a complex concept which cannot be measured by a single parameter.

In considering the impacts on the system, a distinction must be made between a prototype that is used to gained information, and then thrown out, and a prototype that becomes part of a system, or is enhanced to become the system.

Functionality

There are no reasons why a product that uses prototyping at some stage in its development should have less functionality than one produced using a conventional strategy. All that can really be stated is that the prototype is far more likely to have the most *useful* functions. Obviously, a horizontal or vertical prototype will have limited functionality in comparison with the full system.

Complexity[1]

The complexity of a prototype will vary according to use. A throw-away prototype may be coded using a program generator, which may lead to quite complex code, or it may use a simple 4GL. There are no prima facie reasons why a prototyped product should be more complex, and hence more expensive to maintain, than a conventionally developed product.

Quality

It is meaningless to ask whether prototyping produces higher or lower quality products than conventional lifecycle developments, since any of the various quality factors can be optimised. What the prototype does offer is the information necessary to optimise quality factors. If optimum performance is needed, time-critical aspects of the system can be prototyped to get ball-park estimates. For usability, trials can be run with real customers on prototyped parts of the system to see how easy they are to learn. For marketability, the

[1] It is very difficult to measure complexity. There have been many suggestions over the years, for example the code volume, ie the number of lines of executable code, or the number of bytes of object code. However, these suggestions are simplistic and misleading, since they really measure the information content, and not the complexity. More sophisticated techniques measure, in some way, the number of decisions, which is far better.

concepts can be demonstrated to salesmen and potential users using a prototype user interface.

The key system feature which is essential to a quality product is really *conceptual integrity*. This is extremely important:

> 'Even though they have not taken centuries to build, most programming systems reflect conceptual disunity far worse than that of cathedrals. Usually this arises not from a serial succession of master designers, but from the separation of design into many tasks done by many men.
> I will contend that conceptual integrity is the most important consideration in system design. It is better to have a system omit certain anomalous features and improvements, but to reflect one set of design ideas, than to have one that contains many good but independent and uncoordinated ideas.' (Brooks, 1982)

There is no strategy which guarantees conceptual integrity; it is best achieved by a good design, which requires good designers. Prototyping, since it helps to clarify and refine ideas, goes a long way towards getting a good design, and thus a quality product.

4.2.3 Getting a commitment to prototyping

Prototyping is a relatively new software development strategy. The use of prototyping may have to be justified at several levels within an organisation. For example, the senior management must be convinced that it will enable them to meet their organisational goals, the developers must be convinced that it provides a good technical solution to their problems, and the accountants must be convinced that it will increase profits.

If an organisation is to be successful in adopting prototyping as a basic systems development strategy, a commitment must be obtained from key people in the organisation:

- The management, who set the aims and goals for prototyping, and control the finances necessary to establish it.
- The development team, who will use prototyping.
- The customer, who is the recipient of the results of prototyping.

This section provides guidance on obtaining this commitment.

Senior management

New and novel ideas must usually be sold to managers, unless there are very clear advantages. Selling some aspects of prototyping may be difficult; for example most managers will not like the idea of throwing code away.

The key selling points to management could be:

- The benefits to the company, eg in meeting goals, or producing good products.
- The technical advantages of prototyping, as described in Chapter 2.
- A way of minimising major financial commitments.
- The use of prototyping for risk management; a powerful concept for business people.

There are many advantages for the managers themselves. For example, they will gain in political credibility when a prototype can be demonstrated. This may be very significant for marginal, under-resourced, projects. A prototype can show delivered results even if sudden budget cuts or management changes affect the project. It gives the customer early results, particularly with evolutionary development, so the customer is happier. Conversely, if the development teams can't or don't produce anything useful, this problem is exposed as soon as possible. The involvement of potential users, as well as customers, early in the development process makes for a more successful product.

On the development side, the developers are confronted with the difficulties of customers and users, and the realities of the project, at an early stage. The prototype gives an early experience of estimating before the main development, so better estimates can be made. Project planning and organisation can also be improved. Building a prototype allows developers to become familiar with the technical methods used, and any tools and test data developed for a prototype will find use in later development. Once a prototype is built, the developers will gain confidence, and so will their managers.

Developers

The development teams probably already use many of the techniques of prototyping; writing 'quick and dirty' software to test an idea, or building a mock-up of a user interface to test the look and feel of a system.

Good technical solutions like prototyping will not need much to sell them to the developers. Prototyping is really just putting many of their established development techniques onto a firm foundation. It is, nevertheless, essential that the developers themselves are responsible for producing a customised prototyping strategy, albeit to meet the goals set by the management. Prototyping should not appear to be a strategy imposed by management.

Customers

Most customers will be keen to know that prototyping can produce visible results much sooner than a classic lifecycle strategy, and will enable them to define their requirements more accurately, and meet them earlier. It is necessary, though, to explain the difference between a prototype as an exemplar of a system, and a prototype as a version of a system. Failure to do this may mean that the customer is confused or annoyed by being told that an apparently working prototype is unsuitable as a product.

4.2.4 Starting up a prototyping project

This section discusses how a prototyping project can be started within an organisation, from the management rather than the technical perspective.

If prototyping is to be successfully introduced to an organisation several requirements must be met:

- The decision must be made to create a prototyping strategy.
- Clear aims and goals for prototyping must be set, and responsibilities defined.
- A commitment to prototyping must be obtained from customers, developers, and managers, especially from senior management.
- Funding must be made available at a corporate level.
- An appropriate organisation must be set up, with adequate staffing, and training courses should be established.
- A customised prototyping strategy and environment must be developed.
- Prototyping must be integrated with existing strategies.

This section describes in more detail how to achieve these requirements.

What are the aims?

A good start to any project is to have a clearly defined set of goals, and to make a distinction between the problem, and the solutions to adopt in meeting these goals. This is even more important for prototyping, since in general terms a prototyping project is harder to control than a classic lifecycle project.

It is necessary to consider *why* prototyping is to be used, and *what* should be expected from prototyping. In this way the correct decisions can be made, for example on the type of prototyping strategy to adopt, or even whether prototyping is appropriate to a particular project. Some projects, like real-time systems, may not benefit as much as others.

Although the technical aspects of prototyping are important, it is essential to establish the necessary skills and organisation to manage and sustain those projects that use a prototyping strategy. Even the most powerful development strategy may fail if it is not introduced carefully.

Getting a commitment to prototyping

The basic ideas for getting a commitment to prototyping have already been discussed in section 4.2.3. However, it must be emphasised that a high-level commitment must be sought from senior management, with prototyping a basic required philosophy, and clear levels of authority and responsibility established within the project teams. Without such a commitment the risk of failure is increased, since the organisational changes necessary to introduce prototyping are far-reaching, and may need authorisation at a high level.

Buy versus build

A radical approach to prototyping and to software development in general is to buy an off-the-shelf product, rather than to build one. This an often ignored and under-rated solution. Improvements in computer hardware power and advances in software mean that many sophisticated packages are now available that have wide applications. Brooks, in his excellent article 'No Silver Bullet', considers this:

> 'The most radical possible solution for constructing software is not to construct it at all.' (Brooks, 1987)

The advantages are many and varied:

- cost savings
- manpower savings
- range of capabilities
- earlier payback
- technology leverage and risk
- reliability and user engineering
- documentation, training, and user groups

There are some disadvantages to the buy rather than build concept, otherwise nobody would develop any software. In many cases the software products are not exactly what is wanted, and in some cases not all state-of-the-art software advertised for sale is actually usable; the final debugging has yet to be done by the unfortunate customers.

The primary disadvantage is that purchased software is difficult, if not impossible, to change, unless an expensive source code licence is obtained. Also, there is usually no control over upgrades and enhancements. In-house expertise is lost, since the knowledge that would have been gained in building the system is not available.

The key point about buy versus build is that people should consider alternative approaches; starting from scratch greatly increases the risk of development. Careful purchase of software can decrease this risk. The use of software tools like 4GLs or screen generators enables prototypes to be built quickly and cheaply.

Choosing and establishing a prototyping environment

The tools and techniques necessary to establish a suitable environment for prototyping are discussed in Chapter 6. In many cases their selection is out of the project manager's control because of top-level decisions or company policy. However, any tool, technique, or strategy is better than none, provided that it is acceptable, well-understood, and actually used.

A limited number of prototyping tools should be used for the first project. The power for prototyping of well-chosen software tools, such as 4GLs, should not be underestimated. Although it is in the nature of software developers to want to expand their knowledge by trying lots of new tools, it is far better to concentrate on a few well-known ones. A prototyping strategy should be customised for the particular organisational requirements, and a prototyping environment developed based on the project requirements. A prototyping environment cannot be established instantly; it must grow with the needs of the project, and with the skills gained in using the strategy.

Integration with existing strategies

It may be difficult to switch immediately to a complete prototyping strategy. Incremental or evolutionary development are a radical departure from the conventional lifecycle approach. It is far safer to start by adding a throw-away prototyping phase into a traditional lifecycle strategy. There is no need to integrate prototyping with the existing strategies; rather, the current strategy should evolve into a prototyping strategy.

Choosing a project

A suitable project is needed to start with, so that the chances of success are high. It would be wrong to start with something complex, like a real-time control system. The team size should be kept small, to avoid unnecessary paperwork and management overheads. A successful first project is extremely important. If the first attempt at prototyping fails, it may be difficult to justify its continued use.

Training

Success often depends on how new ideas are introduced, rather than on their technical merits. This implies that it is important to involve and educate people, with training made available, and to allow an active participation in prototyping planning. Training will usually require funding at a corporate level, because some managers may be reluctant to commit resources to establishing prototyping. It is important, therefore, that the managers themselves are also trained in the benefits and implications of prototyping.

What type of prototype?

Choosing the type of prototyping strategy to adopt depends on many factors. Primarily, it depends on the kind of project: how stable, how novel, and the degree of risk. Simple projects, with fixed requirements and no real technical difficulty, may not even need any prototyping.

If the project is unstable, prototyping *must* be done, because the requirements will certainly change. The only other approach is to wait until the requirements stabilise, provided that sufficient time is available. If the project is cancelled, then there is a chance that something will have been achieved. If the project stabilises, there is a choice of whether to continue prototyping, or to move to a conventional lifecycle development.

The different types of prototyping strategies each have their own particular areas of application, although these areas are not clear cut.

- Throw-away prototyping
  This is most appropriate for projects with a high degree of technical difficulty, to see if something is feasible, or if there is a need for metrics such as performance. Throw-away prototypes are usually 'quick and dirty', and best achieved using very high-level, non-production coding techniques. This is the best approach for a first try at prototyping.
- Incremental development
  Developing software in incremental steps is best for those projects with fairly stable requirements, which can have clearly defined deliverables. This gives a closer control of the project than an evolutionary development would, but with less flexibility. Incremental development avoids the 'big-bang' delivery of the classic lifecycle strategy.
- Evolutionary development
  This is ultimately the best technique for most projects, but is perhaps better reserved for those with experience in prototyping. Without a properly organised team, and software development tools such as a configuration management system, the project will suffer from lack of control and direction. Evolutionary development is not a good choice for the first prototyping project.

Establishing a strategy

Almost all software developers know that there is no such thing as a universal software development strategy. Most managers realise this as well; after all, there is no such thing as the universal business management strategy either. De Marco makes this point very clearly:

> 'Most managers know that a methodology can't hope to prescribe one Yellow Brick Road for all projects to follow. But they're quick to defend their methodologies with a statement like, "The project teams know that they have to tailor the methodology for the differences in each project." The higher you go in the management hierarchy, the more prevalent is the assumption that some common-sense tailoring of the methodology is expected at the beginning of each project. But at the lower levels, exactly the opposite attitude prevails: workers at the bottom of the hierarchy *know* that tailoring is discouraged or specifically prohibited by the methodology,' (de Marco, 1982)

Although it is impossible to have a universal strategy that will work unchanged for all projects, this does not mean that a new strategy should be developed for each new project. That would be far too expensive. A prototyping strategy *is* needed to allow the project to be managed, but it must be customised for each project. It is not possible to fit throw-away, incremental and evolutionary development within a single simple framework.

A suitable approach is to separate the task of building an outline strategy from the use of the strategy in a software development:

- One team develops the prototype environment and an outline strategy.
- The project teams customise these to the needs of each specific project.

This allows people to build up skills in constructing software tools, getting feedback from the project teams on what is really needed, while the developers can concentrate on the development process rather than the software environment. It also allows tools and standards to be developed to support the strategy.

4.3 Managing a prototyping project

The basis for managing and controlling any type of project is to have a project plan:

- To provide a basis for estimating resources.
- To allow progress to be measured.
- To allow deviations from the plan to be recognised as or before they happen.
- To give specified points for monitoring progress, setting deadlines, and performing reviews.

Most of the problems of managing prototyping projects arise because it is believed that since the project is being prototyped, plans aren't needed, at least for the prototypes. There may also be confusion over whether the prototype is thrown away or becomes the product. With evolutionary development the prototype may evolve into a product before it is ready.

4.3.1 Planning

Careful planning is essential for any project. In software development the plans are the responsibility of the project manager, although the actual preparation of the plans may be done at the team leader or software developer level. Many organisations have a set of standard plans which are required for all software projects, irrespective of the type of project, and they may not wish to change these plans to include prototyping. In any case the plans should always be adapted to the problem in hand.

Plans can take many different forms. A basic plan should include the following:

- Assumptions
  The *assumptions* are general project information, which it is *assumed* that everyone already knows, but frequently do not.
- Activities
  The *activities* are those activities needed to reach the stated goals, to the required quality levels.
- Dependencies
  Dependencies may either be between the activities themselves, or between the project and other projects. Dependencies are generally a bad thing, to be avoided if at all possible since they are outside of direct management control. The more dependencies the project has, the more difficult it is to manage. Dependencies should be kept off the critical path if possible.
- Resources
  The *resources* are the people, hardware, and software necessary for each activity and phase.

Conventional planning

Every project, including a prototyping project, should have a top-level plan, called a *project plan*. It is quite likely that a project will have more than one level of plan, of varying detail. Fortunately, only the project plan is needed to start with; the detailed plans can wait until more information is available.

Conventional phased planning runs something like this:

- Set the budgets, deadlines, and requirements.
- Plan the phases of the project.
- Manage the project through these phases.
- Deliver the final product.

Quite often the budgets and deadlines are set by senior management, usually for good reasons. For example, the ability of a company to take quick advantage of new technology, markets, and ideas, is vital for business success. The benefits of being the first to market with a new product are substantial. This implies that short-timescale projects are to be expected as a natural consequence of the way business decisions are made. The short life of many products means that the time to market is a major planning factor.

The consequences of this are that many conventional projects have artificially constrained timescales, within which a phased development is planned, often to an unrealistically high level of detail. Some project strategies subdivide the project phases into very short tasks, to a precision far greater than the accuracy of the plans and estimates.

Prototype planning

In contrast, a prototyping project can have a much simpler top-level plan consisting of:

- The project goals.
- The scope of the prototyping.
- An outline project plan.

The goals are those defined by the high-level management, and specify what the project should achieve, but not how to achieve it. The project manager must ensure that the goals are sensible, and are listed in priority order. If goals are unattainable, the project manager should make this known.

The scope of the prototyping is defined by the project manager, and should be designed to meet the above goals. For example, if the goals are early delivery and high reliability, then the project manager must consider incremental development as a possible approach.

The outline project plan is exactly as stated; a complete plan for the project, but without the high degree of detail usually associated with project plans. The planning is done by the project manager, using any of the customary planning techniques and tools. It must include the key planning items of assumptions, activities, dependencies, and resources. It does not include detailed, precise development plans, like:

> 'on Dec 14th at 09.30 start testing Module X'.

Each prototype is planned in more detail as a 'mini-project', which has the following stages:

- Set the goals, with respect to the outline plan.
- Define a mini-plan for the prototype.
- Build the prototype.
- Deliver to a real customer.

Figure 4.3 shows the relationship between the outline project plan, and the mini-plans for the prototypes.

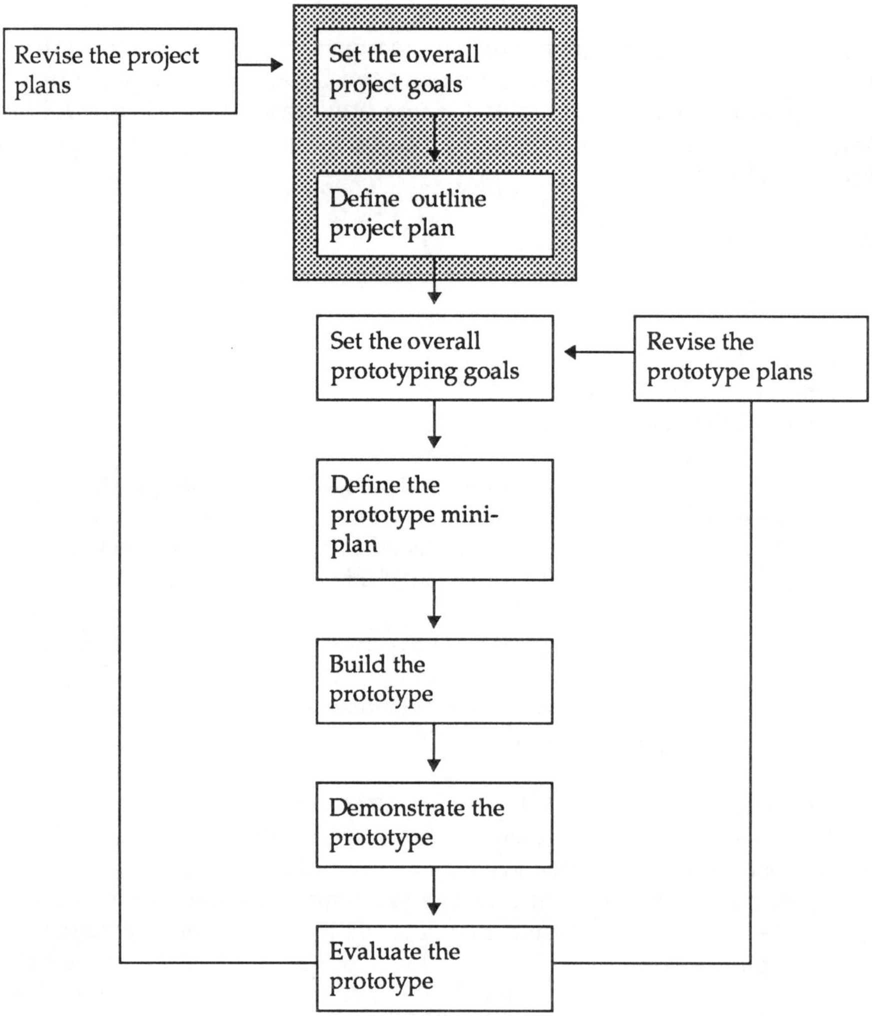

Figure 4.3 Outline project plans, and prototype mini-plans

The project manager is responsible for the prototype plans, and for ensuring that they can be achieved with the known resources. The developers are responsible for building the prototypes, and demonstrating them to the customer. The project manager must then interpret the responses and wishes of the customer, and adjust the plans accordingly.

Each mini-project will need signing off by the customer, agreeing that the prototype meets the stated goals. If not, the prototype will need to be revised. Information from the prototype may then be used to revise the outline project plan, changing estimates where appropriate.

This scheme allows for the variations between the different types of prototyping:

- For throw-away prototyping, the plan for the classic lifecycle phase is only done when feedback is available from the throw-away mini-project.
- For incremental development, each delivery is a mini-project, but there is little feedback to the top-level plan.
- For evolutionary development, each evolution is a mini-project, but the element of feedback into the top-level plan is far greater.

The basic differences in this feedback of information are shown overleaf in Figure 4.4.

In the conventional lifecycle model feedback only occurs once the product is built. Project planning and management controls only affect whether the product is built according to the project plan, and when complete the product is presented to the customer.

In the throw-away prototyping project the prototype is built first as a mini-project, and presented to the customer. The customer may then revise the project goals, or perhaps ask for the prototype to be refined, or for several more prototypes to be constructed. Once the customer is satisfied, the prototypes are thrown-out, and the project moves to a conventional development.

In incremental development there is no actual prototyping phase, but the product is incrementally grown, rather than being built in one go. Feedback to the user does not change the design, but it may affect which increment is built next, or whether it is built at all. Thus the system can change and grow in response to environmental factors, but only in a way prescribed by the project plans.

In evolutionary development the system has the freedom to grow and evolve as necessary. The project plan is only an outline plan at first, but as the prototype mini-projects are completed the plans can be changed and refined.

In reality, these distinctions between throw-away, incremental, and evolutionary development are never as clear cut as this, and the level of control and feedback of information should be adapted to a particular project.

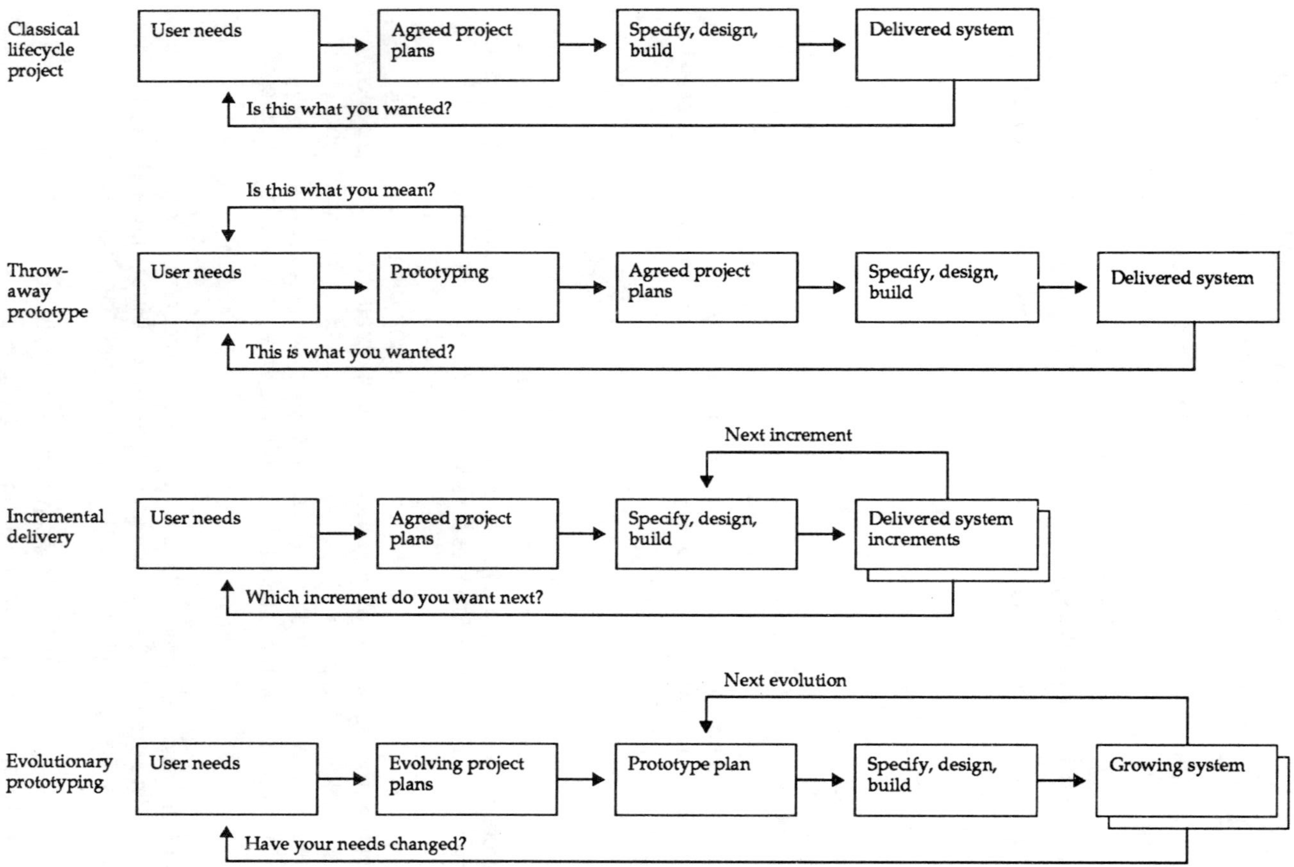

Figure 4.4 Project control and feedback

4.3.2 Plans for prototyping

This section looks at the types of plan and the information that is needed for software development and prototyping. Even if the standard plans do not give all the information described here, people should be aware of the missing information, and either take steps to include it in the planning, or at the very least note it down somewhere.

The planning steps that are described in this section are as follows:

- initial project statement
- formal project statement
- project plan
- risk analysis
- prototype plan

These are the top-level plans, and provide the information that is *essential* for using prototyping most effectively. The plans listed above may not even exist in some organisations. Few projects will have a separate document for each of these plans, and risk analysis is quite often ignored. In this case it is up to the developers to find out the missing information, even if it is recorded informally, and only used internally by the development teams. The plans can also be adapted to fit within an existing organisational framework, and *must* be tailored to a specific project.

Initial problem statement

This is produced by the customer. It is an informal statement of the problem, and the goals of the project. It is usually described in terms familiar to the customer, and is often incomplete and imprecise, although the customer may believe that it is sufficient for the requirements specification.

Formal problem statement

This is produced by the project manager, with input from both the customer, and the other project participants. It takes as its starting point the initial problem statement, and describes the project and the top-level goals using more precise terms. It is not the requirements specification, although it may be incorporated within a requirements specification, and is formal only in the sense that it is agreed between all relevant parties. The contents lists below should not be regarded as definitive, but they do provide a good starting point.

Project background:

- origin of project
- project mission statement (updated from the initial problem statement)
- relationship to the organisational goals
- other related projects

Project organisation:

- management structure
- responsibilities

Project goals, with an indication of priority:

- functional goals (top-level goals)
- quality goals (performance, reliability, etc.)
- constraints (resources, hardware, software, etc.)
- dependencies between the goals
- expected stability of the goals

Factors affecting the goals:

- project assumptions
- external factors (political, economic, organisational)
- internal factors (system environment)
- technology

Project plan

The project plan is the top-level system plan, which is produced by the project manager, and is based on the formal project statement. It should contain the project activities, their dependencies, the resources needed, and any assumptions made in the planning process.

Risk analysis

Risk analysis should be an integral part of a software development project, but unfortunately is rarely performed. The starting point for the analysis is the project plans.

Risk analysis is used to assess the top-level risks for each goal, for example:

- resources available versus resources needed
- schedule and budget factors (short timescales, restricted budgets)
- functional requirements versus the complexity and stability of the project

Prototype plan

The prototype plans take the output from the risk analysis, together with the project plans, and describe the most effective use of prototyping to meet the risks, and to achieve the project goals. The planning is still the responsibility of the project manager, but the details are usually defined by the team leaders and developers. A basic prototype plan should contain:

- goals for the prototype (expected aims and benefits)
- prototype development method (throw-away, incremental, evolutionary)
- prototype functionality (what will be prototyped)

- prototyping timescales (early, middle, late)
- prototype delivery (how it is tested, delivered, etc.)

Comparison of development methods

The strategy for prototype development should be carefully chosen, since this affects the level of detail needed in the planning. The different strategies are:

- Throw-away prototype planning
  Throw-away prototyping is the easiest type of prototyping project for planning, and the most suitable for inexperienced developers. The main consideration is that there should be a clear boundary between the prototype and the product, because this kind of prototype is unlikely to be built to production standards. The prototype must also be signed-off by the customer when complete; this is the agreement to throw the prototype away.

- Incremental development planning
  Incremental development demands a more detailed level of planning. There must be a clear and relatively stable set of requirements, and the development process must use good software engineering practices. The aim is for the early delivery of the most *useful* increments, so they must be ordered, taking into account their individual risks and benefits.

  The increments themselves should be well-structured, and their dependencies on other increments known. An exception plan must be produced to describe the actions to be taken if the project's requirements change.

- Evolutionary development planning
  Evolutionary development demands very good project management, and experienced developers (Nosek, 1984). It is most suitable for small project teams, as this reduces the possibilities for misunderstanding. Because the system is expected to change, the project needs to use software tools to speed up the development process, and must have a configuration management system to track the changes.

  Although the requirements may be changing, the project must always track these changes, and have a definition of the current top-level goals. Evolutionary development also demands a close involvement from the customer and user, since the evolutionary deliverables must be evaluated, and decisions made on how this changes the project.

4.3.3 Estimating

Estimating is an important activity. At the beginning of a software project the project manager must estimate the risks associated with the project, and estimate the resources necessary to complete the project. It might seem too difficult to do this at such an early stage but it is essential, otherwise it is impossible to make decisions, eg to set the project goals, budgets, and plans that must be approved by higher management. Managers cannot make sensible decisions without estimating (Mills and Dyson, 1990).

The critical factor is that there should be confidence in the estimates. This does not mean that they have to be highly accurate, only that where the estimates are not very clear, the degree of uncertainty is specified. If there is high uncertainty, for example that a particular technique may not work, then the management must be made aware of this, and of the possible consequences.

There are three basic techniques for making estimates:

1 Experience of past projects.
2 Standard estimating techniques, eg those developed by Boehm (1981).
3 Modelling the current project by building prototypes.

Once estimates have been made, for example the likelihood of a particular solution meeting the goals, then techniques such as impact analysis can be used to evaluate them.

With conventional phased planning it is essential to estimate the costs and resources needed to complete the project plans to the necessary level of detail. Many published techniques are available to aid the estimating process, for example the COCOMO model of Boehm (1981).

Unfortunately, the effectiveness of estimating models varies according to the data collected to produce the model, the widely differing types of project they are applied to, the experience of the staff, and many other factors. No analytical technique can ever include all the factors that influence project costs. Most models will give an idea of the scale of the costs, but will not be sufficiently accurate for detailed planning. The models described in the literature are *static* prediction models, which are not transportable, and are only valid for the organisation in which they were developed.

But real projects live within a dynamic environment where the goals change with time; where people's concepts and ideas change with time; and where environmental factors interact in a complex and unpredictable way. Obviously there are some projects for which prediction models can work well, but these are usually the simpler and smaller projects where accurate estimates are not so critical, rather than the larger, more complex projects where they are.

To achieve a useful degree of accuracy it is essential to develop a cost model locally, based on the experience of previous projects. This will take into account all the factors within the development environment that will be missed by using someone else's model. Inaccurate data is much worse than no data at all:

> 'Most software engineering technologies are inherently *qualitative*. They address questions like, What requirement? What design? What approach to coding and testing? But the problems of software development are not exclusively qualitative. There is, as well, a host of *quantitative* problems: How much time? How much money? How much risk? For a typical software development manager, the quantitative unknowns are usually the more troubling and the more urgent. Failure in a quantitative sense can lead to utter chaos. Successful management of a project's quantitative parameters leads to control.' (De Marco, 1982)

However, this cost model must have suitable data as input, derived from previous projects. This suggests that a department should be set up within the organisation to capture this data, otherwise it will be lost. The data may then be used to support or refute a particular cost model, and the model modified accordingly.

The older the projects for which data are available, the less useful that data will be, since techniques and tools may have advanced, and people will have learned from their mistakes, and become more skilled. This means that the most accurate prediction of costs is the current project. The closer the project is to the delivery date, the closer the estimated value will be to the out-turn value. At project completion, by whatever criteria completion is determined, the two should agree. The better the estimating, the faster the convergence.

The traditional lifecycle model makes estimating difficult, especially if a good cost model based on past projects is not available. But even if a good model is available, then making estimates from project phase to project phase is still difficult, since there is no fixed relationship between the known costs of one phase, and the estimated costs of the next. For example, knowing the cost of producing the requirements specification does not give an accurate measure of the costs of the functional specification, or of the design, coding, and testing stages.

If a prototyping strategy is to be used, then the estimating can be done as follows:

1 Use locally derived cost models to get estimates for the project plan.
2 Use the actual costs of the prototype(s) to revise the estimates.

The estimates will be more realistic once the prototype is actually built. Throw-away prototyping is probably the least accurate for establishing an estimate, since there is still a conventional lifecycle to follow once the prototypes are thrown out. Nonetheless, the prototyping phase will give an early indication of significant cost deviations. Incremental development will provide more precise estimates, since the project is split into easily quantifiable chunks, and development can be stopped if the costs get too high, hopefully leaving a useful system to deliver. Evolutionary development can provide the most accurate estimates, since the estimates are constantly revised with each delivery cycle.

Design to cost

In engineering projects a completely different approach to estimating is often used, called *design to cost.* This fixes the costs, leaving the developer to build the best possible system within these constraints. Software projects routinely estimate the costs, but this is always difficult even with good information, so incorrect estimates and time/cost overruns are common.

If costs or time or any other resources are critical, achieving them must be made a basic goal of the project. Using a design-to-cost strategy has several consequences for the way system development is done:

- Since the costs are fixed, a conventional lifecycle approach can't be used.
- The project must have incremental or evolutionary deliveries.
- Priorities must be set for these deliveries.

Using a conventional lifecycle approach increases the risk of not completing the project before the time or money runs out. Unfortunately, the final stages of a lifecycle project, ie the testing, integration, and system validation stages, are the most critical. Leaving them partially complete may mean either that the product cannot be finished, or is of poor quality.

With throw-away prototyping the cost estimates are more accurate, so the risk of failure is decreased. The best approach, though, would be to use incremental or evolutionary development. Since integration and testing and validation are done continuously throughout the project with these strategies, stopping the development early still leaves a viable product. This does assume that the deliveries have a priority order, and that the most important ones to the customer are delivered first.

4.3.4 Organisation and staffing

Organising and staffing a prototyping project is really no different from a conventional lifecycle development. There is no simple, correct method. Various methods work for different companies, people, and projects.

What differences does prototyping make, though? The flexibility of prototyping does not fit as well into a rigid organisational structure as, say, a strictly phased traditional lifecycle development. Prototyping requires the feedback of information from many people: customers, users, other developers, and testers. Prototyping also requires some control to avoid confusion.

Team organisation

The organisation of any software development project depends on how the key project roles are allocated. These are:

- Project manager
  – responsible to higher-level management for the project
  – gets the necessary resources
  – gets qualified teams together
  – sets project goals (unless already defined)
  – sets projects plans, organisational structure (unless already defined)
  – ensures that plans, schedules, etc. are met
- Technical leader
  – design authority, makes technical decisions
  – responsible for solutions rather than goals
  – responsible for the conceptual integrity

Many organisations would regard the project manager's role as the most important within a project. However, the technical leader is often more important, since with a poor technical leader there is less hope of producing a quality product, even with excellent project management.

These roles can be performed by the same person, although this is rare, or by different people. The most well-known arrangements are those described by Brooks in his book 'The mythical man-month':

- Project manager is also the technical leader.
  This is the *Chief Programmer Team* concept (Baker, 1972). The project manager is also the chief designer and implementor. In some cases the manager may 'subcontract' work to other team members, and will also require additional resources such as a backup programmer and administrative librarian. The productivity and quality of such projects is very high, but it requires exceptional staff.

  If it is difficult to get good managers, and good technical people, then a combination of both is extremely rare. Unfortunately, the chief programmer concept does not scale up. Because of the double responsibilities the team needs to be limited to a maximum of 5 to 7 people. This is a high risk, high payoff strategy.

- Project manager is an administrative manager with technical authority.
  The project manager has overall authority for both the project and the outline design, but the detailed design is done by the team members. This still requires a high level of technical competence. A larger team can now be supported, with both administrative and technical assistance for the project manager. This is a lower risk, lower payoff strategy, for larger projects.

- Project manager is administrative manager.
  This is perhaps the most common, traditional form of project management. The project manager has no technical authority, although is responsible for the technical solutions meeting the required goals. Detailed technical design work is done by other team members. Usually the team has a technical leader or *Chief Technician*, responsible for the conceptual integrity of the design. This is the lowest risk and lowest payoff strategy.

Of course, in reality the roles are blurred, and there is a continuous spread from the extreme chief programmer team concept to the conventional management/ technical split. Most projects will need more than one team, which further complicates things.

Team size

In most cases small is beautiful! A large team *always* means a large product, even if this is not what is required. With evolutionary or incremental development the project stages can be kept quite small, so there is no need for a single large team, as several teams can work on different stages.

Unfortunately, although small teams can be highly productive, they are vulnerable to the loss of staff, since every person is vital. Poor quality staff cannot be allowed in a small team, since there is nowhere for them to hide.

Team selection

Individuals vary greatly in their programming performance. A difference, according to ability, of between 1 : 3 to 1 : 5 is not uncommon (Boehm, 1981). This can easily give a variation of 1 : 10 between teams, unless the teams are very small. Different organisations vary just as widely in ability. For team selection, it only needs one or two people with low productivity to affect greatly the combined performance of the team.

With such a wide spread of abilities it is essential to match staff to jobs, and not the reverse. Although prototyping does provide a form of damage limitation, poor quality staff will produce a poor quality product, and no organisational method can avoid this.

Summary

The comments above apply to any software development project. The introduction of prototyping does not really change any of the concepts, although it may increase the confidence and productivity of the less good staff, since it gives a chance for their skills to grow, rather than them being 'thrown in at the deep end'.

4.3.5 Monitoring and control

Once a project has started, the project manager is responsible for monitoring the project, and controlling the activities to meet the project plan. The only way to do this is to set regular milestones, which can be used to measure progress.

A major problem with software development is that it is difficult to measure completeness. This leads to the '95 per cent finished' syndrome, where the project seems to be on target, until nearly finished, and then progress slows dramatically. The last 5 per cent of a project is always very difficult to complete. Figure 4.5 illustrates this effect.

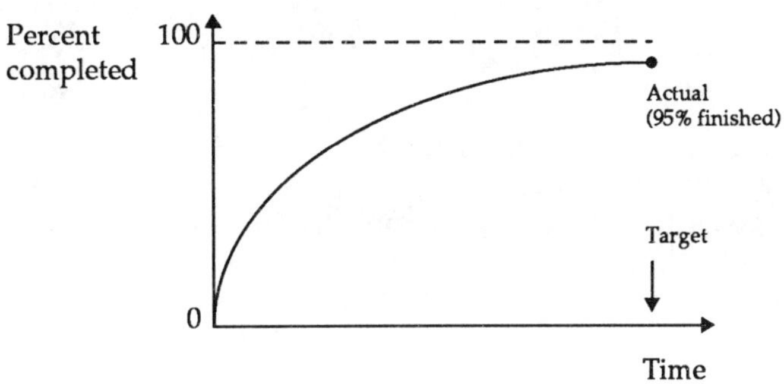

Figure 4.5 The 95 per cent finished syndrome

Why is this? There are several reasons, but primarily it is because in the classic lifecycle approach the final phases are the most difficult, with the most people involved. It may also be that the monitoring of the project is incorrect. In many projects the manager controls the project by monitoring the manpower and non-manpower costs. Each person accounts for their time by booking to one or more defined tasks. The project manager then measures the progress by how much time has been booked to each task; a task with 70 per cent of its resources already spent is then assumed to be 70 per cent complete.

Unfortunately, there is no correlation between the resources booked to a task, and how complete that task is. Tasks may be mis-estimated, or unexpectedly hard. People do not always account for their time accurately, often booking to the wrong budget for political reasons, or because the allocation for their particular task has been used up. The easiest tasks usually get done first anyway.

There is a natural tendency towards the end of a long project for people to get increasingly disillusioned with booking their time, especially if they see that the project is not meeting targets, or that their inputs are being ignored. The traditional lifecycle model also makes booking difficult, as the activities cross phase boundaries, and do not often meet the sometimes arbitrary milestone dates.

The only real way to measure progress in a software project is whether a task is complete or not. The resources taken to complete a task only matter as input to the estimation for subsequent tasks. This requires a sensible granularity of tasks, to gain from the deadline effect[2].

With prototyping, the granularity can be based on delivered prototypes. For throw-away prototyping it is the delivery to the customer for evaluation. For incremental and evolutionary development it is the actual prototyping steps.

4.4 Coping with problems

Prototyping does not allow a 12 month project to be completed in 6 months; no software development strategy can do that. If it is really necessary to complete a project in 6 months, the goals must be reduced accordingly. This is fine if the goals are well-defined and don't change. If they do change, a conventional lifecycle project has no time to react. This is where prototyping is most effective. But of course impossible projects do exist, and problems will always occur.

Projects of any kind fail for many reasons, but usually because they fall into one or even both of the following categories:

- poorly understood systems
- very complex systems

Systems may be poorly understood for many reasons; perhaps because of poor communications between developer and customer; a lack of agreement between them; or even unrealistic expectations on the part of the customer. If the expectations are too high, the developers may attempt to solve too many problems with one system. Problems may occur from not knowing all the requirements, or, much more serious, from not understanding them.

Even systems that are well-understood may be trying to solve a problem that is too complex for the timescale. Many systems fall into this category, for example: very large systems, systems with tight performance constraints, systems based on new technology, real-time systems, and distributed systems.

---

[2] The deadline effect is the increase in productivity which is usually observed when a delivery deadline is close. The effect is not as pronounced if too many deadlines are set, as people rapidly become disillusioned

The problem of complexity should, however, be put into perspective:

> 'Although large, advanced and sophisticated programming efforts are more spectacular, we must not forget that quite a lot of machine time and programmer's energy is really spent on small, down-to-earth projects and the present efforts to make computing facilities more directly accessible to the individual user will only reinforce this tendency.' (Dijkstra, 1982)

4.4.1 Why prototyping projects may fail

Prototyping projects, like any other, may fail because of their complexity or a lack of understanding, but they may also fail because of the way that prototyping is used:

- A lack of commitment to prototyping.
- Problems in managing prototyping projects.
- Poor system implementation due to a lack of prototyping in critical areas.
- The use of a prototype too early, as a product.
- The wrong choice of project for prototyping.
- The wrong choice of prototyping strategy.

Getting a commitment to prototyping

Most projects do not fail because they are too difficult. If the managers, customers, and developers are not committed to prototyping, the strategy will probably not work. Without the proper training it will be misunderstood, and when it fails to solve everyone's problems, blamed and abandoned.

Problems in managing prototyping projects

Management problems can affect any type of project, not just those using prototyping. Therefore, for inexperienced developers the flexibility offered by prototyping needs careful control.

Poor system implementation

The system may be poorly implemented due to a misunderstanding of the reasons for prototyping. If the prototype ignores goals that are critical to the success of the project, for example high performance or high reliability, then it will not be surprising if the product fails to perform as expected. Scaling a prototype into a product without a re-design can also cause many problems.

Using a prototype too early

In any prototyping project there must be a clear understanding of the use of the prototype. A throw-away prototype must be discarded, as it is unlikely to be of product quality. A prototype that evolves into a product must have a cut-off point which defines a certain minimum level of functionality, otherwise it may be used too soon.

Choosing the wrong project

Choosing the wrong type of project to prototype can be very serious. In fairly general terms, application areas can be ranked into those of a high risk of failure, and those of a lower risk:

- lower-risk application areas
  - dynamic systems
  - transaction-processing systems
  - systems with an interactive user interface
- higher-risk application areas
  - very large or complex systems, eg a DBMS
  - systems with little or no user interface
  - real-time systems
  - distributed systems
  - communications systems
  - number crunching systems

Two points must be made clear about this:

1 The perception of risk depends on experience.
2 A high-risk project has more need of prototyping than a low risk project.

An inexperienced development team would be unwise to start with an application in the higher-risk category, although this is not to say that they would be unsuccessful, but that their lack of experience may mean that they do not get the most benefit from prototyping.

Of course, the more difficult, higher-risk projects are precisely the ones where prototyping *should* be used, since they cannot be simplified or speeded up by adding more resources. In this case it is even more critical than usual to get the basic requirements specification and functional specification correct.

Remember that many problems are due to attempting to over-achieve in projects, and by trying to push too close to the state of the art, or indeed to the ability of the developers. The costs of pushing systems to the state of the art limit increases very quickly to impossibly high levels.

However most customers will be happy with the 90 per cent solution, provided that the project is on time and within budget. The problem is finding the most *useful* 90 per cent, which prototyping can help identify.

Choosing the prototyping strategy

The choice of prototyping strategy depends on the nature of the project, and the experience of the development teams. There is not really a simple right or wrong choice, but there must be a balance between familiarity with the strategy, and the risk associated with the particular project.

4.4.2 Management guidelines to avoid failure

It is impossible to define a set of guidelines, which, if followed, will guarantee that a project is successful. Defining guidelines is also unrealistic as projects and people vary so widely. All a manager can do is to provide the best environment for the development teams to work in, and to give good management support. The developers must be insulated from the daily problems that can afflict a project, like budget cuts or staff shortages, for as long as possible.

The people involved should perform their respective roles in a professional manner. The following lists are intended to indicate what might reasonably be expected of them.

Senior management

- Provide support for the project.
- Provide an adequate level of funding.
- Set realistic strategic goals.
- Don't become involved in day-to-day project issues.

Senior managers are responsible for setting organisational and strategic goals. Any involvement with the project should be through the customer, and only if the project adversely impacts these goals.

Customers

- Define the goals of the project but not the solutions.
- Set an adequate budget and realistic timescales.
- Identify and order the deliverable items.
- Provide feedback on the prototype and system demonstrations.
- Introduce potential users and specialists to give feedback and ideas.
- Sign-off the deliverable items.

It is the customer who must set the project goals; the customer must be informed if the goals are really solutions. An adequate budget is expected, and the timescales must be realistic for meeting the project goals. This does not exclude the possibility of a short timescale, only that the timescales must match the goals.

The deliverable items must be identified and listed in order, with help from the project manager if necessary. Finally, all deliverable items, including prototypes, must be formally accepted by the customer.

Project manager

- Define the goals of prototyping.
- Estimate the risks.
- Set up training schemes.
- Set up the development teams.
- Use a top-down planning approach.
- Demand an early delivery of useful systems.
- Demand demonstrations to the customer.
- Evaluate the reaction of the customers, and modify the goals and plans accordingly.

If possible, the project manager should choose the first project to use prototyping. The prototyping goals must be defined, perhaps using critical success factors, and the project risks must be estimated. These provide the basis for top-down planning. Detailed plans must not be prepared without input from prototypes. The planning must be sensible; for example, if the budgets are cut, the goals must be reduced. It is far better to reduce the goals than to leave out the prototyping stages.

Training will be necessary if prototyping is new to the organisation, and this should include courses for managers as well as the developers. Once the development teams have been set up and the development is under way, the aim is to get a useful system as soon as possible. This system must be demonstrated to the customer, and the project goals and plans modified according to their reaction.

Developers

- Provide the solutions to meet the project goals.
- Use an open systems architecture.
- Develop a prototyping strategy.
- Develop SCM and rapid prototyping tools and environments.
- Develop the deliverable items.
- Collect metrics throughout the project.

The developers are responsible for finding the solutions to meet the project goals. Unless there are other requirements, the system should have an open architecture, so that it is easily extendible, and can be developed in small units.

The environment, tools and strategy are the developers responsibility, working within guidelines set by the management. It may be possible to set up a special team, separate from the development teams, to do this work. As the project components are constructed and delivered, measurements must be taken so that the strategy and tools can be refined, and to see if the results meet the plans.

Users

- Provide feedback to the developers.
- Become involved in formal *and* informal testing.
- Should test and use the system for themselves.

It may be necessary to define various roles for the users, eg operator, supervisor, manager. The degree to which the users are involved in the operation and testing of the prototype may vary according to their role, but their main responsibility is to provide feedback on how the prototype can be used for realistic tasks. If users are actively involved they may provide valuable suggestions for improvements, since as end-users they have an obvious interest in the usability of the completed system.

4.5 Conclusions

In the same way that there are no easy solutions to software development, there are none for project management. Prototyping may help in building useful systems, but it doesn't make the management of such projects any easier. In fact, if the developers are inexperienced, it may be more difficult. There will always have to be a trade-off between flexibility and control in managing projects, but the balance doesn't have to be fixed. It may vary according to the chosen prototyping strategy, and the goals of the project.

Although this advice may seem vague, there are some formal techniques available to the project manager. Critical success factors, and impact analysis and estimation, are particularly valuable because they help in the key steps of analysing goals and potential solutions. They also emphasise the importance of gathering and using measurements.

The management of a prototyping project is largely based on traditional practices of setting objectives, planning a project to meet these objectives, and monitoring and controlling the course of the project to achieve them. The basic idea is to have two types of plan – a project plan, and a simple prototyping plan. The results of analysing the prototype may mean that the prototyping plan must be revised; if necessary the project plans might also be changed. The degree to which the plans are revised distinguishes between throw-away prototyping, and incremental and evolutionary development.

However, software management is not something that can be learned from a textbook, even this one. It is learned by experience; by planning projects, coping with sudden changes, and managing the crises that can happen all too frequently. Not all projects will succeed. Some will fail because they are too difficult for the level of experience of the people involved; others will fail because they are badly managed.

Projects often fail because of their complexity, and a lack of understanding. One of the fundamental problems for a manager is the difficulty of communicating ideas between the people involved in a project. Large projects often fail not because they are too difficult technically, although they may be, but because of the difficulty of communicating the abstract concepts that define a project. Informal documents are singularly inappropriate for this; precise, unambiguous documents cannot be written in English.

People learn from all these projects. For every project that fails, they learn to estimate the risks better once they have experienced them first hand. If a project is known to be of a high risk, it must be planned accordingly. The worse thing that can be done as a manager is to ignore these risks. Risks are a fundamental feature of software development; if they are ignored, sooner or later they will catch you out.

Prototyping allows the risks to be better understood. Each prototype that is built teaches people something about the system being developed; when potentially difficult areas are discovered, the plans can be adjusted accordingly. People *learn* how to solve the problems by exploring them with prototypes.

Selected reading

Software project management

De Marco, T
Controlling software projects, Yourdon Press, 1982

Gilb, T and Finzi, S
Principles of software engineering management, Addison-Wesley, 1988

Conventional project management

Cleland, D I and King, W R (eds)
Project management handbook, Van Nostrand Reinhold, 2nd edition, 1988

Davidson Frame, J
Managing projects in organisations: How to make the best use of time, techniques, and people, Jossey-Bass Publishers, 1988

Lock, D
Project management, Gower, 4th edition, 1989

5 Guidelines for prototyping

Introduction

This chapter introduces guidelines and ideas for prototyping software. No textbook on prototyping can provide a methodology that can be applied to *every* type of software system; systems vary far too widely for this to be practical. What this chapter does do is to examine several types of system, and discuss some possible approaches to prototyping.

One of the problems of trying to do this is that any classification of software projects suffers from considerable imprecision. A database system may well be a large-scale system, with critical performance constraints, and have a user interface. Furthermore, the potential applications of prototyping in software development are many and varied. The projects discussed in this chapter only illustrate a few of the possibilities.

By studying these examples, in conjunction with the prototyping strategy discussed in Chapter 3, the guidelines given in this chapter may suggest or stimulate appropriate ideas.

The purpose of this chapter

This chapter is a practitioner's guide to prototyping. The aim is to provide software developers with sufficient information to use prototyping in a wide variety of problem situations, and in different types of software project. It is also intended for managers who may need a more technical view of prototyping, and an appreciation of how prototyping can be applied to a particular problem domain.

General organisation

The sections in this chapter contain guidelines for prototyping specific types of system, like distributed systems, and for specific aspects of a system, like the performance or the user interface. They don't cover all the possible uses of prototyping in systems development, but are a collection of the more interesting ones. There is a degree of overlap with Chapter 6, prototyping tools and techniques, and it may be necessary to refer to both chapters in order to understand fully the concepts.

The following information is provided for each of the subject areas:

- An outline of the area under discussion, with references to standard texts.
- Why it is important to prototype, eg known problems, types of risk.
- The aims of prototyping and the expected benefits.
- Hints on how to perform the prototyping – and what not to do.
- References to Chapter 6 for useful tools and techniques

It is not possible give a definitive description of how to apply prototyping, but nevertheless these sections should provide useful ideas. At the end of each section there is a summary of the role of prototyping in that area. It is included to provide an overview for developers, and to assist in comparing different techniques.

5.1 Database systems

Prototyping can be very useful in designing, building, and using database systems. The nature of a database means that there is a separation between the logical design of the database, and the physical implementation of the database. Prototyping can help in the logical design process, to ensure that the database meets the requirements of the users, or the needs of the application programs that will use it. In the physical implementation, prototyping can assist in specific problem areas, such as performance. Prototyping can also help in the development of application programs *using* the database.

5.1.1 Definition of a database system

A database is an integrated collection of data items, which is accessed and managed by a database management system (DBMS). The DBMS allows users and application programs to access the data efficiently, and provides facilities for defining and managing the database. A database can be distinguished from a filing system because it provides an abstract view of the data, and hides the details of how the data items are stored and retrieved. It allows users to define a data model, without having to worry about the complexities of the physical representation of the data.

5.1.2 Why is prototyping important?

The data belonging to an individual or an organisation are often of paramount importance, far more important than the application programs that use this data. If the data are lost, the costs to re-generate the data can be enormous. The trend in application systems is towards more open systems that are data-oriented, which emphasises the key role of data.

In many cases software development is still application-oriented. These systems are often closed, state-determined systems, which can be designed by functional decomposition. However, this only really works well if the requirements are well-understood and relatively fixed. Requirements that are not static will cause great problems. The prototypes for such systems are mostly used in the requirements specification, or for specific system problems, such as performance.

In contrast, open systems are more flexible, since it is far easier for them to change and adapt to dynamic information requirements. The lifetime of data in open systems exceeds that of the system, since data are usually integrated into other systems, rather than being thrown out. The data are not fixed and static, but are always changing and growing.

In systems where data from a wide variety of sources must be collected, integrated, processed, and shared, the *need* for this data is defined by the information requirements for the system; conversely, the *availability* of the data impacts on the information requirements. So it is difficult to fix either the data or the information requirements at the start of the development, and even if they are fixed it is very likely that they will both change during the development.

Appleton (1988) lists the following reasons for data prototyping:

- to validate information requirements
- to discover an optimum structure for the metadata (data about data)
- to provide for bottom-up integration of shared data
- to define macros that compute or derive new data from stored data
- to validate domains
- to evaluate update and retrieval efficiency
- to improve physical database design
- to anticipate changes
- to facilitate implementation and acceptance

The purpose of the prototyping is to discover the information requirements, to structure the data so that it can be stored and accessed, and to integrate any shared data.

5.1.3 Use of prototyping

Since the use of prototyping is so wide-ranging, two main aspects will be discussed:

1 Database prototyping
2 DBMS application prototyping

The scope of database and DBMS application prototyping is shown in Figure 5.1.

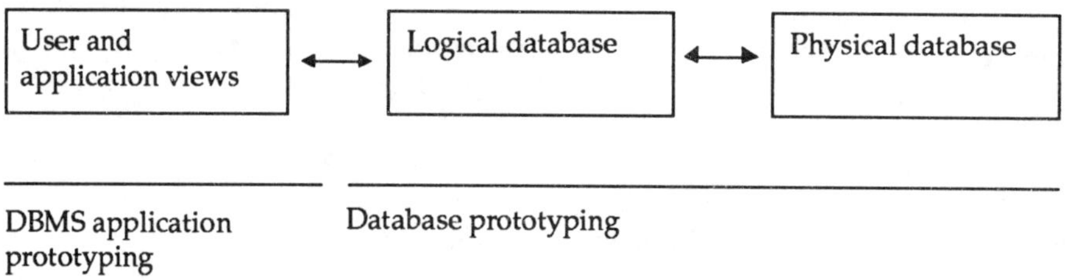

Figure 5.1 Prototyping and database levels of abstraction

Database prototyping is used to discover the information requirements, and to construct a data model. Once basic data models are available, it is possible to refine the models, and to prototype the DBMS applications.

However, it is not possible to consider these areas in isolation, since the behaviour of the DBMS application depends on the correct design and implementation of the database, and the database must be designed to meet the requirements of the DBMS application.

Database prototyping

In prototyping a database the concerns are that the data items contain the necessary basic information, that the relationships between data items are correct and meaningful, and that the constraints on the data are defined. These go together to make a data model. But apart from the data model, it is also necessary to know if the model can support the transactions that need to use the data. At this stage of prototyping, the implementation details are not of concern.

Once the initial data analysis has been performed, it is important to consider the transactions which will use the data model:

- Are all the current transactions supported by the data model?
- Are there future transactions which may need to be modelled?
- Are there parts of the data model which are not needed by any of the transactions?

These questions can be answered by building a prototype of the database. A very effective way of prototyping is to use a 4GL. Some 4GLs even have graphical design tools which can allow a database to be generated from an Entity-Relationship diagram[1].

The 4GL can be used to model the database, and will allow the model to be tested using sample data. Those 4GLs with a screen formatter can be used to build sample end-user screens, and thus to prototype the complete application.

DBMS application prototyping

DBMS prototyping is concerned with more quantitative factors such as performance, storage requirements, transaction processing times, and the mapping of the data model onto the DBMS schema. Once the database has been implemented on the DBMS, the problem becomes one of application prototyping, ie the behaviour of the application programs that use the DBMS.

The database prototype ignores a great many implementation details that would be of importance in a real database system:

- normalisation of the data model
- performance considerations
- optimisation of the internal schema
- transaction processing times

These factors must be considered in moving from the database prototype to the DBMS application. There are several analytic techniques that can be useful here, in conjunction with prototyping:

- statistical models
- simulations
- queuing theory

If sufficient information has previously been collected from the operation of related systems, then statistical models can be used. A typical application

---

[1] An Entity-Relationship or E-R diagram is a logical data model that uses entities (an item of interest, eg a person), sets of entities (eg all the people in an office), and the relationships between entities (eg which people are managed by what person).

would be in modelling the demand distribution for the database, ie whether data accesses follow a uniform, normal, poisson, or some other distribution. This information is necessary if performance predictions are needed. Queuing theory can also be useful here, for example in estimating transaction processing times.

If there is no source of data to predict the behaviour of a new system, then simulation and modelling can be used to estimate the parameters of interest.

There are no special techniques for prototyping a database application program. The techniques described in the following sections can all be applied to various aspects of the application. For example, performance prototyping, real-time systems prototyping, and user interface prototyping.

5.1.4 Summary

The role of prototyping in database systems varies greatly between the database prototype, and the DBMS application prototype.

- Functionality
  The modelling of the data and the transactions using the data must be developed with sufficient depth and breadth to be able to prototype the complete database. The DBMS application prototype must be sufficiently detailed to investigate or measure implementation factors such as performance.
- Strategy
  A database prototype is generally thrown-away once its purpose has been achieved, but it may evolve. The DBMS application prototype may use any strategy depending on the type of application.
- Problem solving technique
  The purpose of the database prototype is to test the data model to see if it supports the required transactions, and so it is largely experimental. The DBMS application prototype is also experimental, and may evolve over time.
- Tools and techniques
  4GLs are particularly useful for database prototyping. Graphical systems may be used for data model and data flow diagrams. The DBMS application prototype may use a wide range of tools, including an analyst workbench.
- When
  The database must be prototyped before any application prototyping can start.

5.2 Distributed systems

In recent years there has been a rapid increase in the use of communications and distributed systems. The driving force behind this is in the large number of communications-based applications now available that allow users to share information and other resources. Examples of distributed systems are:

- shared printers
- file servers
- electronic mail systems
- directory services
- remote data base access
- electronic funds transfer
- electronic data interchange

These distributed systems are based on communications software, known as *protocol stacks*. A protocol stack uses the concept of a set of layers sitting one on top of the other, each layer handling a particular part of a complex protocol.

Books on communications systems often give a very simplified view of the world of distributed systems. There is a tendency to describe the communication between only two points in a distributed system. The communication protocols between any two points, or even in a small subnetwork, are often simple enough to be covered in this manner.

In reality, a complete system will consist of many different networks, each with their own set of protocols. Bridges, routers, and gateways will have to be placed between them all so that they can work together. Many of the network protocols will have to work with other quite different protocols.

When creating a new distributed system, there are a number of potential problem areas that may need to be prototyped (Cieslak et al, 1989; Dupuy et al, 1990):

- interworking problems
- new application protocols
- user interface

Interworking problems are to do with different communications systems working together. At the very least, interworking needs to be tested before the system is built.

When a new application is built, the protocol that is conveyed in the application layer will usually be new. For example, suppose an application is required to send a message to a fire station giving details of an emergency. The details to be sent will need to include an address or location, the type of emergency (fire, petrol spillage, child with head stuck between railings, etc.), and possibly other information. All this will have to be encoded in some way, and this encoding is part of the protocol. The protocol will have to be designed, and possibly tested.

Any new application will need a user interface. This is covered in section 5.6 on prototyping user interfaces.

5.2.1 Introduction to communications and distributed systems

This is a very brief introduction to communications and distributed systems. It is not intended to be comprehensive, and it only provides an outline of the terminology, and the concept of layered protocols. There are many good textbooks on this topic. See for example Coulouris and Dollimore (1988), or Tanenbaum (1981).

Communications software is divided into a series of layers. Each layer provides a level of service that is used by the layers above it. The top layer is the application itself, for example the file transfer application. The bottom layer has a connection to the physical network, for example a length of cable. The lower layers are usually implemented in hardware or firmware. Figure 5.2 shows the basic structure of a protocol stack.

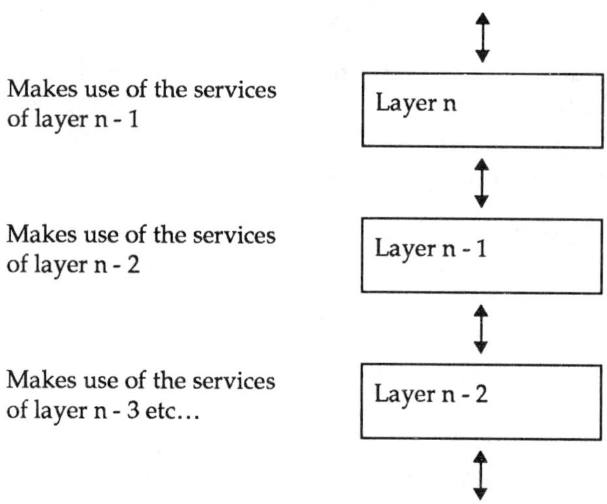

Figure 5.2 Structure of layered protocol software

Each layer 'talks' to the equivalent layer in another computer, and no other. That is, each layer at level n encodes and decodes the same bit patterns as the remote layer at level n, and interprets them in the same way. The structure of the bit patterns employed, and the sequencing of them, are known as the *protocol.*

The international standards bodies have defined various protocols in a seven-layer model. The top layer, layer 7, is the application. The bottom two or three layers are the network, for example a token ring. There are also a number of widely used proprietary protocols, for example IBM's SNA, and DEC's DECnet.

Very simple systems may use only one set of protocols, but realistically it is difficult to build a distributed system without including a mixture of both standard and proprietary protocols. For example, an electronic mail system could use:

- A network filing system (proprietary) over a token ring (standard) to send mail from a PC to a minicomputer.
- X.400 (a standard electronic mail protocol) may be used to send the mail over X.25 (standard) to another minicomputer on the same site.
- The mail may then be transformed in a proprietary X.400 to Unix mail gateway.
- The mail is then sent over TCP/IP (de facto standard) over an Appletalk network (proprietary) to a workstation.

This is not an atypical example, and is included to show that in a distributed system there is a great variety of protocols employed.

5.2.2 Prototyping to test interworking

One of the complexities of a distributed system is that of interworking between a set of different protocols. Most of the communications software and hardware will be available as off-the-shelf items. The main tasks of the system developers are to build the system-specific parts, and to integrate the bought-in parts.

Creating the prototype

The main function of the prototype is to test the interworking of the communications modules. This can only be done when the protocols involved have been specified. The protocols used are a major architectural feature of the system, and so may be defined as early as the requirements stage. Indeed, many operational requirements documents include details of the protocols that are needed. In any case, the complete set of protocols must be available by the time the high-level design is finished. It is at this stage that interworking experiments can be performed in order to verify the design.

The prototype itself should contain any protocol stacks that are going to be used, so much of the integration work of the developers will have to be solved at this point.

Exercising the prototype

The completed prototype should allow the exercising of all aspects of the protocol from end-to-end. That is, all communication links should be working at the same time. The user interface, or other application-specific parts, may be omitted, or be implemented with greatly reduced functionality.

It is not sufficient to test each part of the system in isolation, and then hope that they will work together. Interworking is only fully tested when everything is running at the same time.

Each function to be tested should be invoked with the system running, and the result checked to see if the appropriate response has been made. A more complex set of tests can be carried out to test error recovery. The most common errors in a distributed system arise when one part of the system goes down. The functions should be tested with different parts of the system taken down, to see if the system recovers from the problem in a graceful way. Each part of the system can be taken out in turn, for example by killing a process, unplugging a network cable, or switching a machine off.

The sort of unacceptable responses to look out for are:

- the application hanging, ie not responding to user commands
- the application reporting success when the system has failed
- infinite loops between machines
- duplication of messages
- data being corrupted
- data disappearing

It is sometimes useful to test the performance of a distributed system with a prototype. Section 5.4 on performance prototyping gives more details of this.

5.2.3 Prototyping application protocols

An application protocol consists of a set of protocol data units, and a handshaking procedure. The protocol data units are the information units that have to be passed between the machines. The handshaking procedure is the statement of what data units are allowed to go in what order. For example, an acknowledgement can only be sent after something to acknowledge.

After a protocol has been designed it needs to be tested to make sure that sufficient information is being passed between the machines, and that the flow of control between the machines is correct.

When building the prototype, as much of the protocol software as possible should be implemented. It is important to include all the error handling parts of the software, as these are some of the most difficult to get right in a distributed system.

If the interworking prototype has been built as well, then the protocol prototype can be built on top of it. If it has not, then some substitute for the network is needed as part of the prototype. There are two options:

- use of a different communications package
- use of a simulated network

The communications package that underlies the application could be replaced by another one. For example, if the specification calls for the use of a file transfer protocol, then it may be easier to try the prototype with a network filing system instead. The substituted protocol may perform exactly the same functions; for example, if the specification calls for the international standard transport protocol TC0, then it may be easier to use the more commonly available transport protocol TCP.

It is sometimes easier to create a simulated network on a single computer, than to use the real thing. To simulate a network, a multiprocess machine must be used. The network is simulated using an interprocess communications package. In order to simulate a protocol data unit being sent from one machine to another, the data unit must be sent from one process to another. This is an effective way of simulating a network, but can only be used for the higher layers, as the interprocess communications cannot introduce the random noise and timing problems of a real network.

5.2.4 Summary

- Functionality
  Usually part of the system must be prototyped in depth to test the design.

- Strategy
  The software is sometimes thrown away, as it is just used to test the design. It is sometimes kept to be used as part of the development, as it may be produced to production code standards.

- Problem solving technique
  The software is being developed to test the design of the system.

- Tools and techniques
  Communications packages and interprocess communications packages are particularly useful.
- When
  Prototyping should begin as early as possible, to test the design.

5.3 Large-scale systems

Many people would consider that prototyping is really only suitable for a small-scale software project, and indeed it is true that many small projects have used prototyping very successfully. But as system size increases, so does the system complexity and the risk of failure. Although the application of prototyping to a large project will not be easy, most large projects are going to be difficult anyway, and the cost of their failure will be high, so any technique that might help should be considered.

5.3.1 Definition of a large-scale system

It is not possible to give an exact definition of how large is a large-scale project, since it depends on the organisation and previous experience. New techniques in software development mean that what was once considered large is now routine. The degree of difficulty of a large-scale system relates more to the size and complexity of the problem being solved than to the final size of the code, although code size can be a good indicator.

The definition used in this section is that a large-scale system is one that exceeds the span of control of a single manager. The system is predominantly a software system, although some hardware development may be involved. Because of the size of the project, a structured development process must be used to control the development effort. A large project often needs a multi-level design process, eg high-level design, detailed design, module design, and is invariably of a high cost.

Large-scale systems often have special characteristics, by the nature of the problems that need such a solution strategy:

- They are long-lived. Because of the cost of producing the system, it is not practical to replace it with a totally new system. The costs are only recouped over a long period.
- As a consequence of the expense of replacement, the system is modified continually during its lifetime, as the requirements change.
- Some systems may have to function correctly at almost any cost, and have real-time constraints, eg avionics control systems.

- There are many people involved in the development, from tens to hundreds. As a good working estimate, any project development with more than twenty people can be considered a large-scale development.
- The system needs up-to-date and consistent documentation, stored in a project database, and configuration management and version control.

The systems development process must partition the system into independent modules, in order to reduce the complexity. But the larger the system, the more reliable its modules must be just to get a working system. Reliable large systems must be built from *very* reliable modules.

5.3.2 Why is prototyping important?

Some authors state that prototyping is not any good for a large system, but prototyping is *more* important as the system size, and hence the risk, increases. Figure 5.3 illustrates how the relative cost to fix a system error increases with the project size, and also with the elapsed time from the start of the project.

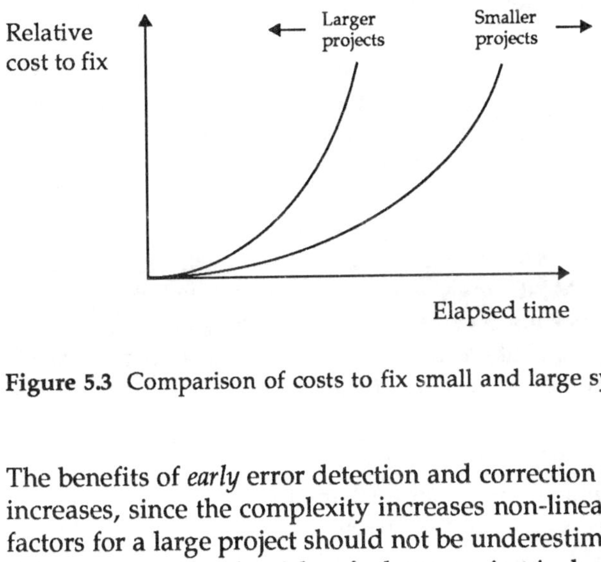

Figure 5.3 Comparison of costs to fix small and large systems

The benefits of *early* error detection and correction increase as the project size increases, since the complexity increases non-linearly with size[2]. The risk factors for a large project should not be underestimated. For example, the driving factors for the risks of a large project include:

[2] The number of interconnections between system modules can be taken as a simple measure of complexity. If a system has n modules, then the maximum number of interconnections is $n(n-1)/2$. Thus a system with 5 modules has a maximum of 10 interconnections, and a system with 50 modules a maximum of 1225, ie well over 100 times more.

- stability of the organisation and funding
- stability of the requirements
- complexity of the requirements
- size of system
- maintainability goals
- performance goals
- reliability goals

Almost any one of these factors is sufficient reason to consider the use of prototyping; taken together prototyping becomes almost essential for a large-scale systems development.

5.3.3 Use of prototyping

There is no specific strategy for prototyping large systems. Prototypes can be usefully employed for several aspects of a large system; to assist in the requirements analysis, to estimate the system performance, prototyping at the module level, etc. It is likely to be difficult to build a useful prototype for the whole of a large-scale system, and it may be better to apply prototyping to specific problem areas, or at the module level.

Incremental prototyping may be possible if the system is well-structured. Some large-scale systems, such as transaction-processing systems, may actually have quite a simple structure despite being large. Evolutionary development in a large system demands a high level of project control and organisation.

Since large-scale systems are so difficult and expensive, it is extremely unlikely that the developers will have much freedom in the design of the systems development strategy. Most organisations will have developed their own in-house strategies. This does not mean that prototyping has no place in such a project, only that it is more likely to be used for specific problem areas, rather than be used as an overall development strategy.

Requirements for prototyping large-scale systems

The requirements for prototyping a large-scale system are really no different to those for prototyping any other kind of system, except that the risks of failure are much higher if they cannot be met. Also, while these are *necessary* requirements, they are unfortunately not *sufficient* to guarantee success. The major requirements are that the prototypes must be:

- easy to change
- easy to understand
- traceable to the requirements specification
- able to model the system environment

Large and complex systems are hard to understand, and the customer must be satisfied that the requirements are correct. This means that any prototypes must be easy to understand, and easy to change to reflect any changes in the requirements. Version control is important, since it may be necessary to go back to a previous prototype, and the code must have good modularity.

The prototypes need to be traceable to the system requirements, since a single prototype is unlikely to encompass the whole of the system requirements, at least at a useful level of detail. So it must be possible to match up a prototype to specific statements in the requirements documentation.

Finally, the critical components of a large system tend to be at the lower levels of the system, but these are difficult to prototype in isolation from the rest of the system. There is thus a need to model the system environment, at least partially, to allow subsystem prototyping.

5.3.4 Summary

- Functionality
  The prototyping of a large system may vary in functionality according to the problems needing to be addressed.
- Strategy
  It is most likely that the prototypes will be thrown-out, since incremental or evolutionary development may be difficult to organise. However, subsystem prototypes may be developed using any strategy.
- Problem solving technique
  Any of the problem solving techniques may be employed.
- Tools and techniques
  A wide range of tools and techniques may be used. An analyst workbench, project database, configuration management system, or any tool to help manage and control documents, and software versions, are important.
- When
  Prototyping should be started as early as possible in the development, as the larger the system, the more expensive the errors will be to fix later on.

5.4 Performance

Performance is to do with the utilisation of some limited resource, which causes a bottle-neck in the system. It is often thought of as being only a problem of limited processor performance, as this is a major bottle-neck in many systems. However, there are a number of other limited system resources, and the principles can equally well be applied to any of them.

Table 5.1 shows some of the main performance constraints in computer systems, and examples of applications where the problem might occur. Systems may also have specific constraints, for example due to the choice of an inefficient algorithm, or by being operated outside their normal limits.

Bottle-neck	Example system
Processor time	Compiler
Main memory	Spreadsheet
Network	Network file server
Disk	DBMS

Table 5.1 Computer system bottle-necks

Not only is performance dependent on the use of a limited resource, but it is also concerned with the perceived speed of the system by the user. Table 5.2 shows the main performance aspects as seen by the users.

System attribute	System module
Response time	User interface
Data throughput	Information processor
End-to-end speed	Communications link

Table 5.2 Performance as seen by the user

For example, in an electronic mail system the performance problems may be concerned with:

- The time between sending a message and its delivery.
- The response time of the user interface after giving a 'send' command.
- The total volume of traffic the message system can handle.
- Efficient use of the network, as it may be shared with other applications.
- The amount of processor time used to encode the communication protocols.
- The use of memory on the PC where the message is created.
- The number of times the message has to be transferred between disk and memory.

A good specification document will have statements concerning performance. For example, the following statement might be found in a specification of an electronic mail system:

> 'The mail server must be able to handle 20 incoming messages per minute, each message averaging 2,000 characters, and with up to 5 recipients. 95 per cent of these messages must be correctly delivered within 1 hour of submission'.

The performance of a system is a problem that must be carefully considered in the design. Much of the literature on performance concerns the measurement of existing systems, but a far more difficult problem is how to estimate performance during the design stage.

5.4.1 Why is prototyping important?

The top ten risks to software development projects were discussed in Chapter 1. Only two out of the ten are technical risks, and one of those concerns performance. Performance is, therefore, a major technical problem that needs to be well thought out at the design stage. If the system has lower performance than is acceptable to the users, the whole of the system development effort has been wasted.

A specification should state some sort of performance criteria, but unfortunately many specifications omit this. There is often an assumption that the developers will do the 'right thing' and produce a system that has a reasonable performance. If the relationship between the analyst and the development team is a good one, then this is sometimes sufficient. However, it does give the developers an escape route.

The analysts who are writing the specification are often reluctant to set values for performance figures, and for good reason. For example, if they state that the message server will be able to handle 20 messages per minute, and this turns out to be easy to achieve, then the developers will not bother to spend much time improving the throughput any further, even if a few days work could double the performance.

On the other hand, if the specification says 40 messages per minute, and this turns out to be particularly hard, then the developers may spend a disproportionate amount of time improving the performance. The real requirement may be that the throughput of messages should be as high as possible *without* putting too much effort into the development. However, such a statement is rarely put into a specification.

Figure 5.4 shows the cost of attempting to improve system performance. The law of diminishing returns applies to all systems, thus the trend of the curve remains the same whatever system is being built. Most customers want the best performance for the least cost.

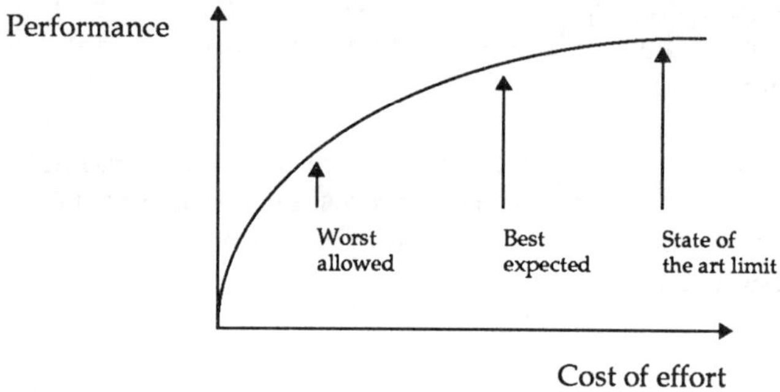

Figure 5.4 Effort versus performance trade-off

The traditional approach is to specify the performance at the start of the project and then measure it at the end to see if the criteria have been met. A better approach is to negotiate the performance figures throughout the development stages. The ideal state of affairs is when the development team can get a good idea of the likely performance costs during the design, or even the specification stage. This can be achieved by using a prototype.

Performance prototyping usually occurs during the middle and late stages of the lifecycle. In order to create the prototype, the high-level design must be complete. That is, all the major modules and their functionality must be specified. At this stage a prototype can be built in order to estimate the eventual performance of the system.

Another reason for prototyping is that of testing various design options. Performance estimates may be made for each option, and these can be used as a basis for selecting the best design.

There are other ways of estimating performance. These are based on analytic methods. Naturally, the decision to build a prototype will depend on the relative costs, and the importance of performance.

The literature on performance engineering often describes the measurement of the performance of an existing system. This is done, typically, in order to make the choice between various systems on offer. Prototyping is used to estimate performance before a system is built.

5.4.2 Modelling for performance estimation

In order to estimate the performance of a system, a model must be created. There are two basic types of system model:

- Analytic simulation
  Analytic simulation involves the creation of a mathematical model of a system. The behaviour of the system is described by a set of equations.
- Simulation by prototype
  A simulation of the system can be performed by creating a software model. This model is, of course, the prototype. Having generated the model, some performance measurements can be made directly on it. If the prototype is an accurate one as far as performance goes, then the measurements can be taken to be precise. The prototype may not be that accurate, in which case some analytic work may be needed as well.

The most cost effective way of estimating performance will usually be a combination of analytic and prototype modelling. For example, the whole system may be modelled analytically to discover the likely bottle-necks. Then the software that is the cause of the bottle-neck could be prototyped in order to get some accurate performance figures. These figures can then be used in the analytic model in order to estimate the performance of the whole system.

5.4.3 Strategy

This subsection defines a prototyping strategy that can be used when estimating the performance of a system. The method is as follows:

- Design the system
  Only the high-level design need be done; the detail of the exact interfaces between all the modules can be ignored unless any of them are likely to cause a performance problem. It may be necessary to come up with more than one design in order to compare them.
- Find the bottle-necks
  Examine the system design, either using common sense, or an analytic method to discover the bottle-necks in the system. The bottle-necks are all the points where the critical resources are used to their capacity.
- Build the actual system component, or build a model of system
  There are two alternatives for this step:

  1. Build the actual system component being tested, or possibly build the most used path through it. If errors are not included in the test data, and the least used paths through the software are ignored, the basic code can be developed very quickly.
  2. Build a simulation of all the components specified in the design.

The step chosen will depend on how accurately the results are to be calculated. If the results need to be very accurate, then the actual components, or at least the most important part of them, need to be built. If the accuracy of the results are not so important, then it may be more cost effective to build a simulation of the system.

- Build a test harness for the system
  This is a program that runs the system without the full user interface. It simply accepts data from a file, and treats that as the input data.
- Develop a set of test data
  If only part of a system component has been built, then the data used to test the system must be chosen with care so as not to crash the system.
- Measure performance
  The performance is measured by running the test harness and monitoring the system using an appropriate tool.
- Use an analytic method to estimate performance
  Based on the measured results, use an analytic method to estimate the performance of the whole system.
- Consult the customer on the results
  If the results are unacceptably poor:
  - possibly use a software monitor to discover the bottle-neck in the system
  - redesign the system
  - repeat the process. This time it may be possible to reuse some of the code in the existing prototype
- Throw the prototype away
  The prototype should be thrown away because someone may want to use it for the actual system!

5.4.4 Summary

- Functionality
  One part of the system must be developed with sufficient depth to be able to measure or estimate the performance.
- Strategy
  The prototype is generally thrown away once its purpose has been achieved.
- Problem solving technique
  The purpose of the prototype is to test the design to see if performance requirements are going to be met.
- Tools and techniques
  Accounting data, program timers, software monitors, hardware monitors, benchmarking, and analytical analysis are all useful in performance prototyping.

- When
  The performance prototyping can only take place once the high-level design has been completed.

5.5 Real-time systems

As discussed earlier, large-scale systems often have specific real-time constraints. Conversely, real-time systems are often large systems as well, and share many of their problems. They also lie at the boundaries of currently achievable systems, the most difficult ones tending towards the limits of the state of the art. This section does not attempt to do more than outline a few ideas for prototyping in real-time systems.

5.5.1 Definition of a real-time system

Real-time systems are systems which have real-time constraints, for example a bound on the response time of a process, or on the time between invocations of an activity. Systems in which the constraints must be satisfied under *all* operating conditions are called *hard* real-time systems. Hard real-time systems are those which, because of the nature of their tasks, must always respond within their constraints, for example an air traffic control system.

Examples of real-time systems are:

- industrial process control systems
- missile guidance systems
- patient-monitoring systems
- operating systems

The term *embedded systems* is commonly used to describe hard real-time systems with absolute performance requirements.

The characteristics of a real-time system can be quite varied, but the following features are typical:

- A complex external environment, usually unintelligent.
- The environment interacts with the system.
- The system has multiple modes or states.
- Concurrent processing of multiple simultaneous inputs is performed.
- The system has specific performance requirements, which may be critical.
- High reliability is needed.
- The system is highly complex.
- It is very hard to test, and often cannot be tested in an operational environment.

5.5.2 Why is prototyping important?

Real-time systems are frequently large programs, which because of their cost will have a long lifetime, often longer than the average turnover time of the staff that work on them. Also, because of the way that real-time systems interact with their environment, and the complexity of this environment, the requirements are difficult to specify precisely and in a way that is easy to understand.

Since the system is closely coupled to its environment, changes in the nature of the environment will be reflected in changing system requirements. It is difficult to estimate the impact of these changes without modelling the environment.

Most real-time applications also have strict resource constraints, like the physical size of the system, or environmental conditions like temperature. These are clearly critical for a real-time system.

5.5.3 Use of prototyping

Prototyping may be used for specific applications in a real-time system, such as:

- feasibility of requirements
- performance prototyping
- model-level prototyping

Real-time systems often tend towards the limits of technology, so high risk areas need to be identified, as early as possible in the development.

The complexity of real-time systems, and the way that the system interacts with and sometimes changes the external environment, mean that high-level system modelling is very difficult. There are various ways of modelling a real-time system, from different perspectives:

- Operational modelling – the user view, from external input to final system response.
- Requirements modelling – the customer view of what the system is required to do.
- Implementation modelling – the developer view of how the system is implemented, the physical system design.
- Environment modelling – the overall view of the system environment.

Figure 5.5 shows how these models relate to the system and the environment.

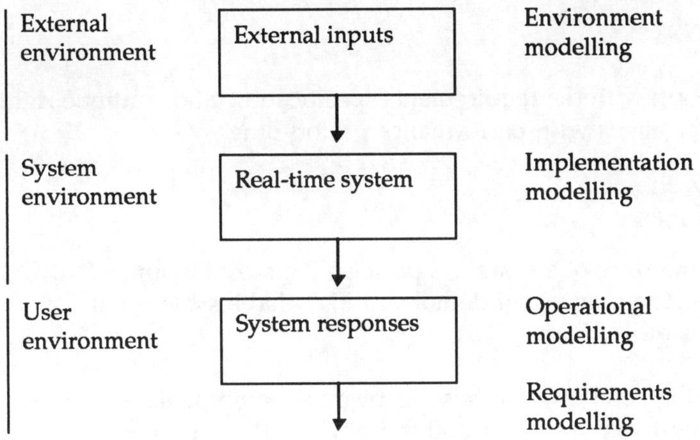

Figure 5.5 Real-time system models

The environment is an important source of changes, so this model helps to anticipate changes, to establish environmental constraints, to decompose the interface between the system and the environment, and to test the system interacting with a model of the environment.

Although it is impossible to describe a complete strategy for prototyping real-time systems, a possible scenario is as follows:

- build requirements model to establish the system requirements
- build environment model
- define boundary between environment and system
- build operational model of system interacting with the environment model
- build implementation models as appropriate

5.5.4 Summary

- Functionality
  The prototype must be developed in sufficient detail to identify high-risk areas.
- Strategy
  The prototype is usually thrown out once its goals have been achieved.
- Problem solving technique
  The purpose of the prototype is to investigate the system requirements to identify high risk areas, and to explore potential solutions.

- Tools and techniques
  The tools and techniques specified for performance analysis may also be useful here.
- When
  Prototyping can begin with the requirements specification, and continue right through to the final stages with performance prototyping.

5.6 User interfaces

Prototyping the user interface of a system is perhaps the most obvious of all prototyping activities. The purpose of demonstrating what a system will eventually look like is quite clear.

It is important to distinguish between those software developments where the eventual users of the system are known, and those where they are not.

Users of the system are known
This is the case when a system is being developed for a specific purpose, to be run on one or a limited number of sites. The system has a known customer, who has probably commissioned the work. For example, a stock control system for a particular factory might fall into this category.

A major characteristic of this sort of system as far as the user interface is concerned is that most, or all, of the users can be consulted directly. A very precise task description can be given for the jobs they have to do.

Users of the system are not known
The other situation is where the users of the system are not known, eg where software is being developed to be sold as a general commodity. It is not usually developed with a specific customer in mind, and has to have money invested in it. Word processors fall into this category.

A characteristic of this sort of system, contrary to the first type, is that the users cannot be consulted so easily. A representative population has to be found. There is a danger that this selection might not be representative as it should be, and subsequent changes to correct problems in the software will have an adverse effect on the sales. No task description can cover all the tasks that the users have.

This latter type of development, although it is harder because of the imprecise nature of the task description, can be treated in very much the same way as the former. The main difference is that a representative sample of users must be used as the basis for all the work. It is important that they are truly representative. They certainly should not be the developers and designers of the system, as these people use computers all the time and have a very different perspective. Indeed, they are probably the most unrepresentative group that could be found.

5.6.1 User interface concepts

The user interface is that part of the system that the user interacts with. In most systems the user interface goes a lot deeper than just a screen layout. As a system is being used, the users develop a mental model of what is going on behind the scenes. This conceptual model is different to the one that the system designer has, being from a different viewpoint. A conceptual model cannot be forced upon a user, but a good system design can lead people towards developing a useful model. The best models allow people to predict how the system will behave in a particular situation, and to understand the actions needed to perform a particular task.

A user interface prototype can have a number of different purposes:

- As a specification of a user interface.
- As a tool for exploring the options available.
- As a tool for checking that the users are able to perform their tasks.

The study of the interaction between human beings and computers is known as *human factors*. It is not simply a study of user interfaces, but stems from a combination of computing, psychology, ergonomics, and design. It may be advisable to use the expertise of specialists in this field when building a system with a critical user interface.

5.6.2 Task analysis

The purpose of building a system is to perform a particular task, so it is vitally important that the nature of the task is analysed. This is not an analysis of the tasks performed by the users of a system, but of the *purpose* of the system as a whole. The system as a whole consists of the hardware, the software, the environment, and the users.

Task analysis may be considered as consisting of three processes:

1. Task elicitation
2. Task representation
3. Generic representation

Task elicitation

Task elicitation is the process of answering the question:

> 'What is to be done, and how well is it to be done?'

The answer should not consist of a list of commands that the users can give to the system, but relates to the job they are actually doing. Once these tasks have been listed, they can, if necessary, be analysed to produce a list of subtasks. For example, in a word processor, the tasks might be to enter a document, store it, and print it out in a revised form. The subtasks might be to delete a character, to select a print command from a menu, or select a document from disk.

Task representation

Task representation is the process of recording the information gained during task elicitation, in such a way that it can be checked as being accurate with the people who gave the information. It may not be appropriate to generate standard charts, such as data flow diagrams, if they cannot be understood by the users. The representation must state what is to be done, as well as how well it is to be done. Each individual viewpoint can be represented separately at this stage.

Generic representation

Generic representation is the process of combining all the information collected. The information must be checked for consistency and completeness, and the completed representation should be checked with the users.

The generic representation of the tasks performed should state what the system as a whole does, and then break that down into a set of subtasks. For example, the system being analysed may be a factory, with the overall task being to produce goods at a cost effective price. The subsystems might be the incoming stores, the factory floor, and the warehouse, each with its own task. The system can eventually be broken down into the task of each individual in the factory.

Only when the tasks are analysed can the system be designed. This generic representation will enable a check to be made to see if the prototype matches the task. For example, the task of the goods inward clerk might be described as that of checking that the goods delivered have actually been ordered, accepting the delivery, and recording the fact that they have been delivered.

When the prototype is complete, the goods inwards clerk can be asked to perform these tasks on the prototype.

5.6.3 User interface architecture

Systems which contain a user interface are best designed with an architecture that separates the details of the user interface from the tasks that the system is to perform. A well-defined interface between these two modules is a key architectural component in such a system. This interface is shown in Figure 5.6.

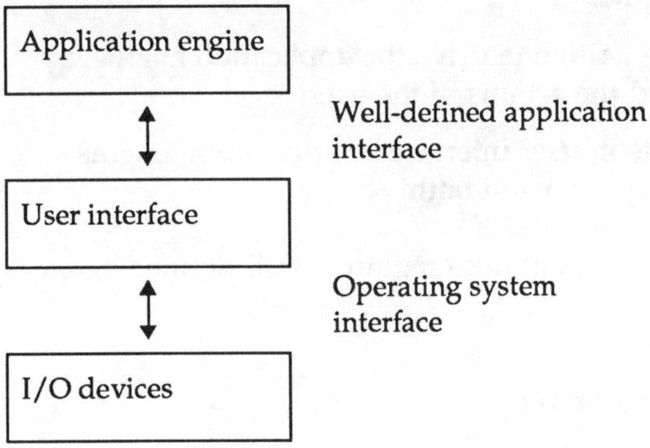

Figure 5.6 Simple user interface architecture

The application engine module performs the jobs that the user wants to do. If the application is a word processor, it manipulates word processor files. If it is a stock control system, it manipulates the database.

The user interface module performs the following tasks:

- Operates the devices through the operating system interface.
- Accepts commands and data from the user.
- Performs simple validation on the input from the user.
- Passes the commands onto the application engine module.
- Accepts information from the application engine module.
- Passes the information onto the user.

The interface between the application engine and the user interface module should bear a close relationship to the commands that the user gives. For example, if there is a user command to print a mail message on the printer, then the application engine should have a similar procedure, such as `PrintMailMessage`.

Thus the user interface module has no knowledge of the purpose of the application engine. It is restricted to validating the syntax of the commands, and has no knowledge of their meaning. Likewise, the application engine has no knowledge of the style of the user interface.

The model of keeping the user interface and the application engine separate, with a clear interface between them, is a good architectural principle as this means that:

- Migration to different forms of user interface is easy.
- There are no hidden side effects caused by modifying either the user interface or the application engine.
- A regression test harness can be written to drive the application engine, by simulating the user interface and the actions of the user.
- Staff can be trained as specialists in user interface or application engine design, without having to be a specialist in both.

This technique requires no special tools, but does require a well-defined architecture.

5.6.4 Building the user interface prototype

In order to decide the features to be put into the prototype, it is important to understand why it is being built, and how it is going to be exercised. If the purpose is a specification of the user interface, then the screen layouts and the user commands need to be accurately built, but very little functionality needs to be underneath them.

If it is mainly exploratory in nature, then the features chosen should only include those that are being designed. These may be the overall functions of the system, the order of appearance of messages on the screen, the look and feel of the user interface, or something else.

If the prototype is being built to check that the functionality is correct, then the full functionality should be there, but the details of the screen layout need not be accurate. Common sense should be used to determine exactly how much to build.

The tools that are used will depend largely on what is available, and what is known by the development staff (Lee, 1990). Fourth generation languages are probably the best tools for a lot of jobs. Hypertext systems are also very useful. If the prototype is being used as a specification, then the tool used may have to be the same as the one to be used in the finished product.

If the prototype is to be given to users to experiment with, then it needs to be built robustly. If it is to be demonstrated by a trained presenter, then it can be built without so many safeguards against erratic user behaviour. If the prototype is to be modified on the fly in front of the users, in response to suggestions, then a tool is needed that allows very fast modification.

Overall, building the prototype simply requires common sense. The main pitfall to avoid is starting without thinking out why it is being built, who is going to use it, and how it is to be used.

5.6.5 Exercising the user interface prototype

Any method of exercising the prototype must involve the users. These can be either the people who are going to use the system, or a representative sample. The users can be active, and allowed hands-on experience, or passive, where the system is simply demonstrated to them.

If the users are active far more information can be gained from the experiment, as it will mirror the system as it is used in real life. For example, if there is a system message which is ambiguous, the active users will sometimes make the wrong assumptions about what it means, and this will become clear as they use the system. The passive users will not demonstrate this ambiguity, as they will follow the demonstrators in what they are doing. The passive users will never realise that the ambiguity is there.

5.6.6 Summary

- Functionality
  The purpose of the prototype is only to demonstrate the user interface, and so this is strictly horizontal prototyping.
- Strategy
  The user interface prototype can be used to check or demonstrate a user interface, in which case it may be thrown away, or the user interface could evolve.
- Problem solving technique
  Any technique may be employed:
  – to specify or demonstrate the system (explanatory)
  – to test which user interface is best for the users (experimental)
  – to try out various ideas in user interface design (exploratory)
  – to evolve the best user interface for the job (evolutionary)
- Tools and techniques
  Graphical systems may save time in user interface development.
- When
  The user interface prototype is normally built during the requirements analysis or functional specification.

Selected reading

Database systems

Date, C J
An introduction to database systems, volume 1, Addison-Wesley, 5th edition, 1990

Korth, H F and Silberschatz, A
Database system concepts, McGraw-Hill, 1986

Distributed systems

Coulouris, G F and Dollimore, J
Distributed systems: concepts and designs, Addison-Wesley, 1988

Halsall, F
Data communications, computer networks and OSI, Addison-Wesley, 2nd edition, 1988

Tanenbaum, A S
Computer networks, Prentice-Hall International, London, 1981

Performance

Smith, C U
Performance engineering of software systems, Addison-Wesley, 1990

Real-time systems

Allworth, S T and Zobel, R N
Introduction to real-time software design, Macmillan, 2nd edition, 1987

Burns, A and Wellings, A
Real-time systems and their programming languages, Addison-Wesley, 1989

Luqi and Berzins, V
Rapidly prototyping real-time systems, *IEEE Software*, Vol 5, No 5, September 1988, 25–36

User interfaces

Cockton, G (ed)
Engineering for Human-Computer Interaction, North-Holland, 1990

Myers, B A
Creating user interfaces by demonstration, Academic Press, 1988

Pfaff, G E (ed)
User interface management systems, Springer-Verlag, 1985

6 Prototyping tools and techniques

Introduction

There are many different types of tool used in the software development process, for example:

- analysis tools – project planners, decision support systems
- document tools – word processors, spreadsheets, graphics packages
- administrative tools – configuration management systems, planning tools
- reusable tools – software tools, libraries, object classes
- language tools – compilers, language interpreters
- miscellaneous tools – operating systems, command interpreters, loaders, linkers

Most software developers will use the majority of these tools at some time, and even a simple software project will use several. The use of tools is so essential in the production of software that it is impossible to think of building *any* system starting with just a bare machine.

When creating a software prototype, the need for tools is also critical. The tools themselves are largely the same as those in the normal developer's toolkit, but the emphasis on *which* tools are used may change. In any development, some tools are more useful than others. For example, a user interface library may be *useful* in the production of an application, but a compiler is *essential*. In prototyping, the user interface becomes far more important, and there is now an emphasis on producing code quickly.

When choosing the tools for prototyping there may be a wider range available than is first realised. For example, a prototype may be built on a machine other than the one for which it is targeted, thus all the tools on that machine are available for the developer to use.

It is critical that the developers understand *why* they are producing the prototype, in order that they may choose the most appropriate set of tools for the job in hand. For example, a prototype built to demonstrate the user interface needs good graphical tools, whereas a prototype built to test the efficiency of a system needs to use the same tools as the target system, at least for the parts being tested.

The purpose of this chapter

The purpose of this chapter is to describe some of the tools that can be used in prototyping, and the techniques for using them. As has already been stated, these are the same tools and techniques that should be used in any software development. There are no tools specifically for prototyping; any tools that are useful in software development will be useful for prototyping.

The tools and techniques discussed in this chapter have been chosen because they are particularly important in prototyping, even if they just increase software productivity. This chapter aims to give a view of a wide range of tools, and to show how each may be applied in various prototyping projects, in order to start the developer off in the right direction. It is not comprehensive, nor can it be as prototyping is a philosophy for software development, and is not characterised by the use of specific tools or strategies.

General organisation

Section 6.1 looks at Computer-Aided Software Engineering (CASE) tools; the generic name for tools used in software engineering, and discusses how the tools should be selected, evaluated, and used.

The next sections, 6.2 to 6.6, discuss specific tools and techniques. They have been chosen to represent a wide range of topics, and to illustrate the statement made earlier than many different tools and techniques can be used in prototyping. The following information is provided for each topic:

- An outline of the tool or technique under discussion, with references to standard texts.
- How the tool or technique can be used in prototyping.
- Benefits and limitations.
- Example areas of application.

Section 6.2 looks at formal executable specifications, ie specification languages that can be interpreted and run. There is great interest in formal methods in software development, and this section describes the fundamental concepts.

Section 6.3 looks at the different types of programming language. While many projects may have restrictions on the choice of a language for the product, a throw-away prototype may use a more specialised language for speed and ease of use.

Section 6.4 gives an overview of some of the tools and techniques that can be used in estimating system performance.

Section 6.5 covers graphical systems, ie those systems that use graphics or produce graphical applications. These have obvious applications in user interface prototyping.

Section 6.6 examines the concepts of configuration management, a topic which is sometimes neglected in software projects, but which is essential for prototyping projects, especially those using incremental or evolutionary development.

This chapter should be read in conjunction with Chapter 3, developing a prototype, and Chapter 5, guidelines for prototyping, to provide a complete overview of the tools and techniques that can be used for prototyping in a specific application area. Chapter 7 contains several case studies which discuss the use of prototyping within actual software development projects.

6.1 CASE tools

CASE (Computer-Aided Software Engineering) tools are software tools which provide support for the software development process (Smith and Oman, 1990). The aim of CASE is to improve the productivity of the development process. This can be done by raising the efficiency of the development process, in terms of reduced time and cost, and by improving the effectiveness of the final system, in terms of meeting the development goals. CASE tools are applicable to any systems development, but are particularly useful in prototyping.

The range of CASE tools is very wide; for example:

- data and activity models
- screen and report generators
- fourth generation languages
- application generators
- program design tools

Many products sold by vendors are termed CASE tools, but unfortunately the term has been blurred by inappropriate usage. An important point about CASE tools, which distinguishes them from the more general term 'software tools', is that they should produce output which is capable of being used *directly* in building the target system.

Tools which produce output which has to be re-written before it can be used are not true CASE tools. For example, a drawing package for designing data flow diagrams (DFDs) can be considered a CASE tool if it can transform the DFDs into skeleton software modules which become part of the target system, otherwise it is just a useful software design tool.

IPSEs

It is important to distinguish between the terms CASE and IPSE (Integrated Project Support Environment). An IPSE is a tool which provides support for *all* of the systems development process, in a completely integrated and automated fashion. However, this is not really feasible yet, due largely to the enormous complexity of the development process. In contrast, CASE provides a more realistic view – a collection of tools which may be integrated, and which automate some parts (but not all) of the software lifecycle.

CASE and prototyping

CASE tools, such as fourth generation languages, make it possible to develop software rapidly, and hence facilitate prototyping. Because prototyping is being used, it doesn't mean that traditional methods should be discarded. There is still a need to produce specifications and designs, and it is much more important to have software tools to support the development process. This could mean the use of an individual tool for a specific activity, or an analyst workbench, or a full-blown IPSE. The more powerful the tools, the more effective prototyping can be, and the greater the reason to use prototyping.

6.1.1 Analyst workbenches

A term which may cause some confusion is a *workbench*. Workbenches are integrated sets of CASE tools for particular development activities, for example:

- analyst workbenches
- programmer's workbenches
- project management workbenches

Analyst workbenches are CASE tools which support systems analysis and design. They are particularly important since they support structured methods and techniques for the critical early phases of a project.

Problems of analysis and design

The process of systems analysis and design involves many separate activities. Starting from a description of the required system, the analyst must interview potential users, structure the data, model the data flows and activities, etc. Some of the information given to the analyst may be in error, the data flows may not be described correctly, different users may not agree with each other, different data items may be given the same name. Unless the system is so small that the analysis can be easily understood by one person, it is almost impossible to prevent inconsistencies and inaccuracies.

To try to avoid this many analysts use a specific strategy. By following the rules of the strategy, errors can be reduced. For example, by following a prescribed set of rules, an Entity-Relationship diagram can be converted to a set of tables for input to a relational database, or a data flow diagram can be converted into skeleton code modules. But if these processes are performed manually, mistakes will occur from time to time. Furthermore, no strategy covers *all* of the systems development process. Often, the difficult parts of a system don't quite fit into any strategy.

The goal of the analyst workbench concept is to avoid these problems by giving support to the tasks of analysis and design. A workbench could be used to draw analysis diagrams, cross-checking different diagrams, and updating all the relevant parts when alterations are made. In this chapter the term *design object* will be used to refer to components of the specification and design; these consist of all the kinds of object generated during the analysis, eg data items, diagrams, data flows, plans, user manuals, test cases, etc.

Components of an analyst workbench

The degree of support offered varies quite widely, but the ideal analyst workbench should provide the following features:

- Support for the most popular analysis diagrams, eg data flow diagrams.
- A graphical user interface, with a diagram editor.
- A data dictionary or database for storing design objects.
- Some means of validating the design objects, and specifying the rules.
- Some means of producing textual output, eg forms or a report writer.
- Facilities to support sharing between analysts.

Few analyst workbenches provide support for the design process; most concentrate on the far easier task of supporting the various types of diagram used in the analysis process, of which there are many:

- data model diagrams, eg Entity-Relationship or Bachman
- data flow diagrams, eg Yourdon/De Marco or Gane and Sarson
- activity-decomposition diagrams
- activity dependency diagrams

- state-transition diagrams
- process specification diagrams, eg action diagrams, structured English, or mini-specs

Of these, data model diagrams and data flow diagrams are by far the most popular. However, certain types of system development may need other kinds of diagram. State-transition diagrams are particularly important in real-time systems development.

Data dictionaries

A data dictionary (DD) is a database which contains data about data, called *meta-data*. In a relational DBMS, a DD is used to store the information that is needed to maintain the database, for example:

- names of the data items
- descriptions of the data items
- validation rules for the data items
- names of the database tables (the relations)
- constraints for the tables
- names of the authorised users

Data dictionaries may be passive or active. Passive DDs maintain their information separately from the database, and must be updated manually. Active DDs are automatically kept in step with the database, and the DBMS always consults the DD at run-time for the necessary definitions, etc. Consequently, an active DD is closely integrated with the DBMS.

A DD by itself does not automate the tasks of checking that the database updates are performed correctly; it is merely used to store the information needed to *perform* all the necessary checks.

In the context of an analyst workbench, an active DD is used to store the design objects, and is the basis for several commercial products.

Project databases

Conventional DBMSs and DDs are optimised for traditional data processing applications. Although they can be used in an analyst workbench, they are not the complete solution to the problem of storing design objects.

Specialised DBMSs have been developed for specific applications, such as computer-aided design (CAD) systems. They have been developed to meet the need to store data describing a design, allowing multiple designers to work on different designs, or even to work on different versions of the same design.

This is exactly the same problem which is addressed by an analyst workbench. These specialised databases are variously called design databases, engineering databases, or project databases. The term *project database* will be used in this book. Project databases have applications to any project which has the following characteristics:

- A large number of design objects, of various kinds and sizes.
- Design objects are interrrelated in a complex manner.
- Many possible *views* of a design object, eg from high-level diagrams to low-level descriptions.
- May have several *versions* of a particular design object, eg a released version, and a version being modified.
- Multiple users may access the database concurrently.

Due to the way that a CAD system user interface is driven interactively, usually from a graphics terminal, the database transactions tend to be very much longer than for an application-driven business transaction, of the order of hours or days, rather than seconds. This causes severe complications for concurrency control and recovery, so new transaction models are being developed to help solve these problems.

The development of project databases is still very much a research activity, but they are particularly important for the future of analyst workbenches.

6.1.2 Fourth generation languages

Third generation languages (3GLs) like C or Ada are *procedural* languages, where the programmer has to specify *how* a particular task is to be accomplished. In contrast, fourth generation languages (4GLs) are *non-procedural* languages, where the programmer only has to specify *what* is to be accomplished.

The difference is that whereas a 3GL has low-level, detailed constructs, a 4GL has higher-level, more general constructs, and is more oriented towards specific applications. For example, a database query language, a screen generator, or a report writer can all be considered as 4GLs, as their output requirements can be described in a non-procedural way.

There are many advantages in using a 4GL for prototyping, instead of using a conventional language:

- Application generation is much faster.
- Applications have fewer errors and are easier to change.
- Debugging and maintenance are reduced.
- A 4GL is problem-oriented, rather than solution-oriented.

The last point is important. The 4GL removes much of the tedious, error-prone coding that is part of a 3GL application. Programmers can concentrate on developing solutions to their problem, rather than on the detailed mechanism of the solutions.

Integrated 4GL environments

Many database systems now offer an integrated 4GL environment, which supports the complete development process. A typical environment might contain the following components:

- An active data dictionary.
- A relational DBMS.
- A 4GL for database maintenance and querying.
- An application generation language.
- A report writer package.
- A screen generator package.

Some 4GL environments also include more specific components, such as financial analysis tools or spreadsheets.

6.1.3 Introduction and use of CASE tools

Although there are great benefits to be gained from the use of CASE tools, they are not always given the correct support, and are often used by developers on an ad hoc basis. This section explains how CASE tools and techniques should be introduced and used in an organisation.

Selection and evaluation

It is not realistic to give more than general guidance, since so much depends on the kind of project normally attempted, the size of the organisation, and the experience of the staff. As a rule, it is better to build on what is known, and add tools for specific purposes, or adapt the software tools already provided by the operating system. A cost-benefit analysis should be performed, although it is impossible to quantify the benefits of a particular tool, since so much depends on how it is used. However, it should be possible to estimate the productivity gains and expected improvements in product quality.

Support

CASE tools need to be supported independently of the projects that use them, preferably by a CASE team. Although it is not always possible to fund the development and enhancement of a CASE environment separately, this is the ideal approach, as it allows the CASE team the freedom to develop the best CASE tools, which can then be applied to a wide-range of projects, and thus gain the maximum benefits for the organisation. If the tools development is funded from *within* a project, it is at risk when funds are short.

The development of a CASE environment is complex, since not only are the requirements open-ended, but as the development proceeds they will almost certainly change. The following points should be considered:

- Software tools should be integrated so that they work together.
- The tools should use an open architecture, with standard interfaces.
- A phased development should be used, adding new tools to a basic toolset.

Integration and maintenance

The use of CASE tools should, if at all possible, be integrated into the development strategy. For each stage of the strategy, the input and outputs should be defined so that the correct tool can be chosen for the appropriate tasks. It is useful to try out the CASE tools on a pilot project.

CASE tools also need to be maintained, eg fixing bugs, or responding to requests from the users for enhancements. A tool may need to be changed completely if the development strategy changes. A useful approach is to monitor which areas of the development project are highest risk, in terms of their degree of difficulty and availability of tool support.

Training and documentation

It is important to provide adequate documentation and training in the use of the CASE tools, especially as tools are often customised for specific tasks. A list of the developers and their expertise in particular tools is useful, since it is often far better to get advice directly rather than to have to read the documentation.

6.1.4 Summary

CASE tools, which support the software development process, are important in prototyping because they increase the speed of development. However, they may also reduce the number of errors introduced during the development process, by supporting system analysis and design tools. They may provide tools, such as project databases, which help control the different versions of a prototype; these will be useful for incremental or evolutionary development.

6.2 Formal methods

There has been increasing academic and commercial interest in writing specifications with formal, mathematical precision, although their adoption has been slow. As evidence of this interest, see Computer, IEEE Software, and IEEE Transactions on Software Engineering for September, 1990.

Most specifications are still written in a natural language such as English. When a specification is written in a precise language, it is possible, with the correct tools, to execute the specification. Thus the specification can be treated as a very high level language. Currently, there are few implementations of such languages, and those that do exist tend to be too inefficient to be used in a product. Clearly, an executable specification can be treated as a prototype.

This section examines the background to this topic, in particular the importance of formal specifications. It looks at the possible strategies that can be used in developing executable specifications. It also examines the critical questions that need to be asked before embarking on the use of this strategy.

6.2.1 Formal specification

Specification is the act of describing something as precisely as possible:

> 'To define and set the standard for the target system, a requirements specification should be precise, unambiguous, internally consistent, sufficiently complete, minimal (so that the target system is not over constrained), formally manipulable (if verification will be used to accept/reject an implementation), and testable (if acceptance testing will be used).' (Zave, 1986)

The most precise science that we have is mathematics, thus it is to this subject that we look for a description of software.

Programming languages can be described in mathematical terms. For example, the mathematical concept of a *set* is that of a well defined collection of objects. This is the same as the programming concept of *type.* A type may be considered to be a set of all the values that a variable of that type can hold. For example, the boolean type can be considered to be the set {TRUE, FALSE}, and the set of sixteen-bit signed integers can be considered to be a subset of the natural numbers in the range {– 32768 ...+ 32767}, assuming a 2's complement representation.

Having defined the data that the programs manipulate in terms of set theory, the actionable part of the language can be described in terms of functions. For example, the concatenation of two strings can be defined as a mathematical function. This function takes a member of the set which is the cartesian product of the string set, and produces a string:

concatenate: string x string –> string

The result can be precisely and unambiguously defined with mathematical precision.

The programming concept of a function can be represented mathematically, as can other programming constructs such as loops and if-then-else statements, eg a loop can be represented by a recursive function. There is a well-known theorem of computer science that states that functional programming languages, eg pure LISP, have equivalent power to imperative programming languages, eg C. This is proved by showing that both these languages have precisely the same power as a Turing machine[1]. Thus all the data structures in a program can be represented by sets, and all the algorithms can be represented by functions:

Data Structures + Algorithms = Programs
Sets + Functions = Mathematics

The mathematical definition of sets and functions is precise, and forms the heart of most modern mathematics. The theory of sets and functions is well known and well understood. It is therefore a suitable basis for defining programming languages. When a programming language is defined mathematically, an individual program written in that language can also be defined mathematically. This formal description of the behaviour of a program is a precise specification.

The process of formal specification starts by creating a mathematical description of the software, and then creating the program from this. There are specification languages which have sufficient precision to do this, eg Z and Lotos. Unfortunately, few programming languages are defined with the same precision, and so there is a gap in formality between the specification and the resulting program.

The mathematical specification of a system specifies the functionality precisely. However, some aspects of the system cannot be defined mathematically in a useful way:

- Performance
  It is possible to define the performance of a system mathematically, but this is no help in the design of the system.
- Reliability and robustness
  Reliability and robustness can be defined mathematically, but it is usually impossible to prove mathematically that a system meets that specification.
- Hardware
  Target hardware can be defined mathematically, but such definitions are not commonly provided by the manufacturers.
- External software modules
  Most software relies on other modules of software outside the developers' control, eg a compiler or an operating system.

---

[1] A Turing machine is a theoretical computer with minimal functionality. No computer has more functional power than a Turing machine, although most are a good deal more efficient.

- Conformance to standards
  There are moves within some standards organisations to set up formal definitions for standard protocols and interfaces, but these are not available yet. Part of the problem is that most standards were designed without using formal techniques.

Why use formal specifications?

There are some cases where formal specification together with formal verification are particularly important. The most notable of these is the one-off program, eg a program in an embedded system that has only one chance of success, and no chance of being tested. For example, the software controlling a spacecraft must be correct; if it is not there is a high risk of a mission critical failure. The cost of a rerun due to a software bug is to launch a new spacecraft.

Other cases where the cost of failure is high arise when security and safety are at risk. For example, the software controlling an industrial robot has a safety risk associated with it. A software bug may mean that the robot is not going where it should – this is an obvious safety risk.

An attitude that is taken by those who profess formalism in software specification is that one should not consider software programs which contain errors to have *bugs* in them; one should consider the software to be *wrong*. If a software program does not match its specification, then it is in error and should be corrected.

The goal of formal software specification is to produce a system with zero errors. The only way to check whether a program is wrong is to verify its correctness formally. There is a lot to be said for this argument. The only counter-argument seems to be based on the time taken to perform the proof, the uncertainty as to whether the proof is itself correct, and the lack of staff with enough mathematical training to be able to do the job.

6.2.2 Executable specifications

If an interpreter is available to run the specification directly, without refining it into a program, then we have an *executable specification*. This is a very high-level language. A specification can be either *implicit* or *explicit*.

Implicit specifications

The usual type of system specification is an implicit specification. It states what the system must do, but does not state how it could be done, and thus gives no indication if it is possible. For example, it could state that a program has to sort a file by some key. This can be specified informally as follows:

Sort Program Specification

Input:
A file of records, with one field nominated as the key.

Output:
A file of records, with the following constraints:

1 There is a one-to-one correspondence between the records in the input file, and the records in the output file.

2 Each input record is exactly the same as its corresponding output record.

3 Given any two records in the output file, the key of the one that occurs second is always greater than or equal to that of the first.

This is a specification, in that it tells us what the output is, given any input, but it is *implicit* in that it gives no indication of how the program can be written. However, it is known that there are a number of well-documented algorithms to solve this problem, and that it is therefore possible to write such a program.

Suppose that a further constraint is added to the specification:

4 If the number of records in the file is doubled, then the time taken to perform the sort will be no more than doubled.

The specification now states that the sorting time is to increase by O(n), ie the sort time is directly proportional to the number of records[2]. This is a perfectly valid statement to make, but, alas, there is no known algorithm to achieve it. The fastest known algorithms are O(n $\log_2$ (n)), and are thus slower than required.

So it is possible to write an implicit specification without knowing an algorithm to implement it; indeed, there may not be such an algorithm. Nevertheless, the specification can still be written, precisely and unambiguously, and therefore with mathematical precision.

Explicit specification

Conversely, an explicit specification must not only state what is to be done, but also state *how* it can be done. In the sort program example, the specification

---

[2] The order notation O() is an indication of how the efficiency of an algorithm increases with the size of data. 'n' is used to indicate the number of data items. For example, O(n) means that doubling n will approximately double the time taken to perform the task; O(n^2) means that doubling n will approximately quadruple the time, tripling n will multiply the time taken by nine, and so on.

would also have to indicate an algorithm. This does not mean that the specification states how it *should* be done, but rather shows that it *can* be done. The designer may choose another method for the implementation, provided that it is equivalent to the specification.

Formal verification

To verify a system formally, one must take the system and prove that it is equivalent to its specification. The specification must be formal, ie written with mathematical precision. Explicit specifications can be proved by a process of *transformation;* implicit specifications are proved by a process of *refinement.*

Transformation

An explicit specification contains a statement of how the program could work. The specification must be transformed into another, equivalent specification. This transformation has to be performed in a series of stages, each of which can be proved using a set of theorems which are defined for the specification language. Thus it can be proved that the first specification is functionally equivalent to the second. This process of transformation is repeated until the code for the final product is achieved.

An example of a transformation theorem, written very informally might be:

```
if X then        is equivalent to:    Y := X
    A                                 if Y then
else                                      A
    B                                 endif
endif                                 if not Y then
                                          B
                                      endif
```

where Y is a variable not used elsewhere in the program.

Refinement

If the specification is implicit, then there is no statement of how it could be done. To prove the equivalence of a specification and a system, one must produce an explicit specification which is equivalent to the implicit one. The proof of equivalence between these two versions of the specification must be done in an ad hoc but precise way. There can be no standard way of proving the equivalence, but what proof is done must be precise.

Once an equivalent explicit specification has been produced, then the process of transformation can be carried out to prove the specification equivalent to the system. The process of proving a program equivalent to its specification is demonstrated in Figure 6.1.

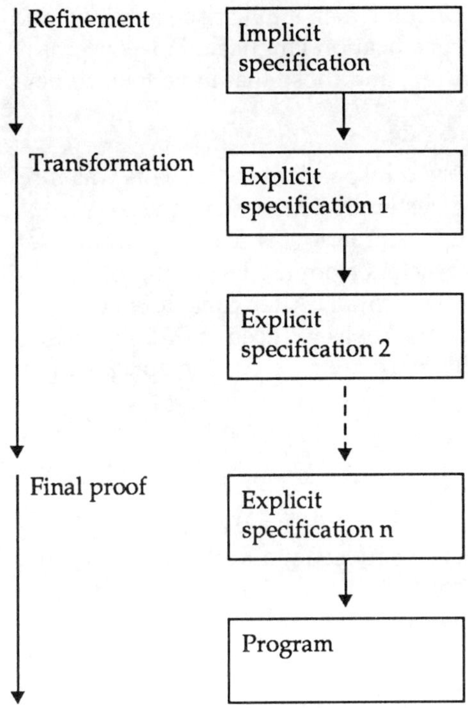

Figure 6.1 The process of proof

One of the difficulties with either form of proof is that the programming language must be defined with sufficient rigour. Some languages have the mathematical basis with which one can do this, but many do not. It is noticeable that the functional languages tend to be defined with more rigour than the imperative ones, as they are often based directly on the mathematical concept of functions. Some languages are now defined mathematically from their initial conception, and this allows for programs to be proved equivalent to their specifications. One such example is the language Occam, which was developed for the transputer.

The proof from specification language to programming language is made a lot easier if:

- The specification language uses the same terms as the programming language or...
- ...the programming language uses the same terms as the specification language.

Often, specification languages are written in terms of sets and functions, and programming languages are written in terms of imperative statements.

To write an executable specification one must have an explicit specification and a suitable interpreter or compiler for the specification language. Few systems for executing specifications have been written, and those that have tend to be inefficient.

An example of a simple benchmark is reported by Sanders (1989). This was for an executable specification of an operating system function, which was designed to write to a file. The task of the benchmark was that of writing five characters, with an offset of a hundred characters from the beginning of the file. The executable specification took 341.51 seconds. After considerable transformation, the time for the same benchmark was reduced to 0.26 seconds. Even the latter time is far too high for this particular executable specification to be used in a product.

6.2.3 Using executable specifications

Clearly, if one has an executable specification, it can be used as a rapid prototype as there is a certain correspondence between it and the target system. However, as listed in section 6.2.1, some characteristics of the target system cannot be prototyped, notably the performance.

The 'Me too' methodology

'Me too' is a both a methodology and an executable specification language. A detailed description can be found in Alexander (1987). The methodology has a very simple evolutionary cycle, as illustrated in Figure 6.2.

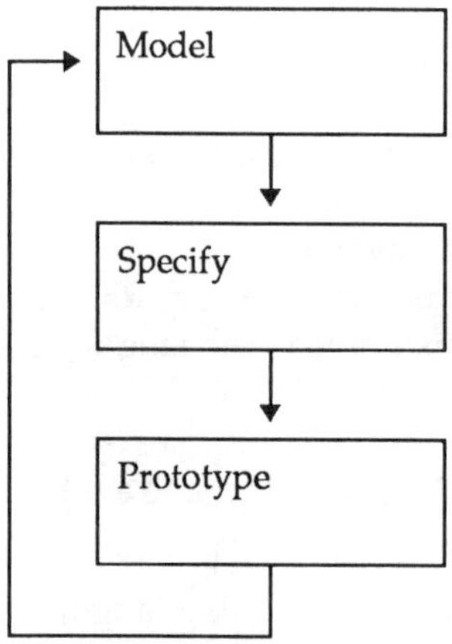

Figure 6.2 'Me too' methodology

The stages are as follows:

- Model stage
  In the first stage an abstract data model is made of the system. This defines a set of abstract objects, and the functions that can be applied to them. For example, to define a word processor, the abstract objects might be *document, search string, character*, and so on. The functions to be implemented might be *open* (for a document), *search* (on a document with a search string), *delete* (on a character), and so on.
- Specification stage
  The abstract objects and functions are then coded in the 'Me too' specification language. This converts the informal model into a formal specification. Note that 'Me too' is an explicit specification language.
- Prototype stage
  The formal specification is now executed using the 'Me too' interpreter. This tests the specification and design for validity.

When the prototype is tested, it is possible that the result is not exactly what is wanted, and so the cycle loops back to the beginning and the system is remodelled. This process is repeated several times until the prototype is satisfactory.

A final step, which is not always mentioned in the literature, is the transformation of the finished prototype into the target system. This will add the functional parts of the system that couldn't be defined in the 'Me too' language.

A variation on this theme is to define an implicit specification between the modelling and the specification stages. A refinement is then needed before the 'Me too' specification is built.

Verification and validation

As discussed in Chapter 2, verification is the act of testing the final system against the functional specification to verify that they correspond. Validation is the act of checking the final system to see if the goals of the system have been met.

Unfortunately, it is impossible to define the goals mathematically, and therefore the requirements specification, of which the goals form a part, cannot be precisely defined. Verification can be performed mathematically using a formal proof, but validation must be done by using a prototype.

Tools and techniques

Access is needed to certain tools and techniques to use executable specifications:

- Specification language interpreter
  Clearly the most important tool is an interpreter or compiler for the specification language itself. Currently there are few of these systems, and those that do exist run fairly inefficiently.
- Configuration management tools
  It is vital to retain the correspondence between various versions of the system. This is even more important than in informal software development. To prove that a specification is equivalent to a program, it is necessary to derive a series of equivalent specifications and programs, and to be able to prove that each is equivalent to the next. Thus a configuration management tool is needed, not only to keep track of different versions, but also to keep track of which ones are equivalent (also see the next section).
- Formal quality assurance procedures
  Formal quality assurance involves formally reviewing each document and program in the development. When formal proofs are used, it is important that these are checked for correctness. Sanders (1989) states that it is normal for only some of the proofs of equivalence to be carried out in full; the others are only written out in full if requested in the formal quality review.

6.2.4 Use in prototyping

The supporters of the use of formal specifications often express their views very strongly. This is partly due to the sheer elegance of being able to treat programs and specifications with mathematical precision. There is also a very valid view that a program that does not conform to its specification should not be considered as a program with one or two bugs, but as a program that is wrong. Therefore all programs should be formally verified.

Clearly, the use of formal specifications is required when there are safety, reliability, or security implications, or when the program will just be run once, but why have these techniques not been more widely adopted? This may be largely for the following reasons:

- The effort required to learn to use formal specification techniques is high.
- The effort required to perform the proof is high.
- There are few staff available with the necessary training.
- The specification is not understood by the customer (but this can be alleviated by the use of rapid prototyping).

The manager of a project should perform the necessary risk analysis to see if it is worthwhile using formal specification techniques. Under most circumstances, if these techniques are used, then rapid prototyping should be used in conjunction with them (Henderson, 1986).

6.3 Programming languages

The choice of programming language has a great effect on systems development. The expressive power of a language strongly influences the design of a solution to a problem. Languages with limited semantic expressiveness make it difficult to solve complex problems; languages with a complicated syntax make writing programs slow. This section looks at conventional programming languages, object-oriented languages, and languages for specialised tasks.

6.3.1 Conventional languages

Many commercial software projects are written in a language which is an organisational standard, and the choice of language is outside the control of the developers. However, if a new project is being proposed, and there is a possibility of choosing the programming language, then the following points should be considered:

- The experience of the developers is very important; conversely, as staff turnover is usually high (an average of 18 months is typical), the language should be one that is well known.
- The language should allow for good modern programming practices, eg data abstraction, and modularity.
- Many languages have extensive libraries, either with the language, or available commercially.

There are, of course, languages for specialised applications, and while these may not be suitable for a product, they can be ideal for rapid prototyping. These are discussed further in section 6.3.3.

Syntax-directed editors

A syntax-directed editor is an editor which has a knowledge of the syntax of a particular programming language. The user is only allowed to input well-formed language statements, thus removing almost all compile-time errors. Many such editors provide 'templates' for common language statements, such as if-then-else, leaving blanks to be filled in. There are many benefits to this approach:

- increased speed of learning a new language
- greatly reduced coding and debugging time
- standardised language formatting
- powerful text manipulation facilities

The advantages of a syntax-directed editor are applicable to any type of software development, but are obviously particularly important in rapid prototyping.

6.3.2 Object-oriented languages

Object-oriented languages are seen by many as a way to break through the software crisis, as they encourage software reuse in a most natural way. Smalltalk is the archetypal object-oriented language, and is the main ancestor of all the others. It embodies all of the object-oriented features in their purest form, which gave rise to many of the early Smalltalk implementations having a poor performance. Later versions of the system are much more efficient. Smalltalk provides a complete programming environment, and so is difficult to integrate with the underlying operating system.

More recent object-oriented languages, such as C++, tend to be much more efficient, and well-integrated with the existing environment. However, in order to do this they have had to make a compromise between the pure object-oriented paradigm, and the pragmatism of the third generation languages. C++ is now used as a commercial tool for producing systems and application software.

There are a number of features of object-oriented languages that make them suitable for rapid prototyping. The distinguishing features of object-oriented languages are:

- object model
- data abstraction
- encapsulation
- polymorphism
- inheritance

Object model

The metaphor that is the basis of the object model is that of *message passing* between objects. Everything in the system is considered an object. Objects are entities, chosen to represent the problem under consideration. They have a private memory, and so can retain data and state information. Each object also has a set of operations, and so can perform computations. All objects are uniform; there are no first-class objects.

Computations are invoked by sending *messages* between objects. A message is a request for an object to perform an operation. In a conventional programming language an operation is invoked by calling a named procedure, and supplying it with the data to act on. If the wrong data are supplied, the wrong results will often be returned. In an object-oriented language the message *selects* an operation, which an object performs by using its own procedures, called *methods*. There is no mechanism for operating on data directly. Message sending is uniform, in the sense that no other mechanism is available, and also in that one message is very much like any other.

The objects contain the data, and the methods that they can apply to this data. If an object cannot act on a message, because it doesn't hold the appropriate methods, the message can be passed on to another object. Objects may also send their own messages to other objects, requesting that they perform an operation. Figure 6.3 shows the conceptual model for an object.

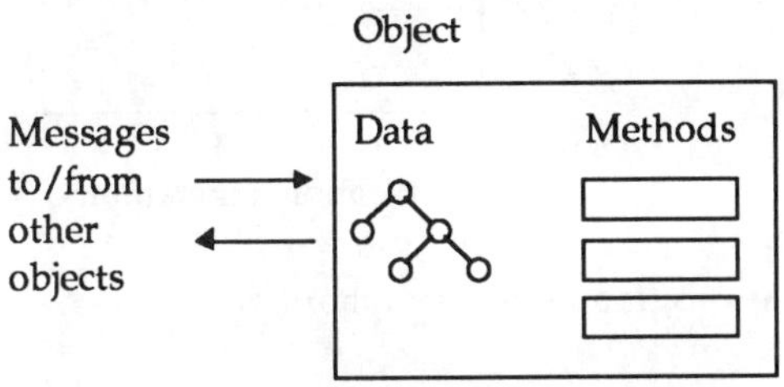

Figure 6.3 Conceptual model of an object

Objects may be grouped together into *classes*, with a class object describing their common features. New objects are created by requesting the appropriate class object to generate a new object. Since objects are uniform, a class is just like any other object, and each object is an instance of a class[3].

Data abstraction

Objects provide data abstraction, as only selected properties are made visible to the outside world, and their internal representations are hidden. The object model has a great advantage over conventional languages in that low-level implementation details are not visible. Thus the way objects are used to model complex systems is very similar to the way that people understand these systems – by grouping ideas and concepts into simpler, more abstract units.

Encapsulation

Encapsulation means that the objects contain both the data, and the methods that they can apply to this data. For example, the data type *string* may be considered a particular class of object. It has data – the characters in the string; and a set of methods – the functions that can be applied to the string, like

---

[3] There is an argument as to whether classes are a necessary part of the object model. An alternative approach called *prototyping* (no connection with rapid prototyping) allows new objects to be created by cloning a 'prototypical' object.

printing. To print the string, the message 'print' is sent to the string object. The non-object-oriented metaphor is to call a print function with the string as a parameter. In C, for example, the `printf` function allows the printing of integers, strings, long integers, and other built-in data types. Figure 6.4 illustrates the different programming metaphors.

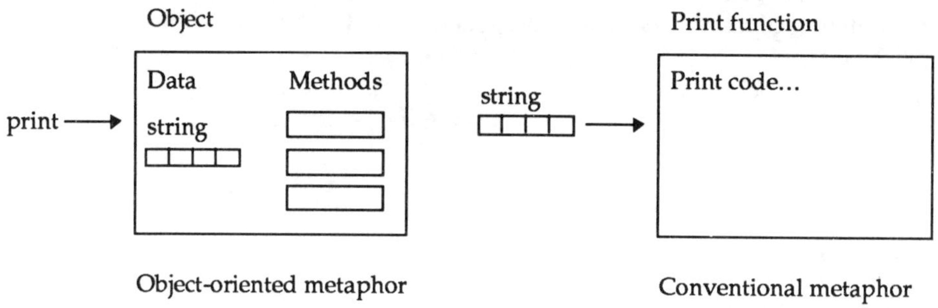

Figure 6.4 Object-oriented and conventional programming metaphors

Whichever mechanism is used to invoke printing, the details of how to perform the printing must be specified in both object-oriented and conventional languages. However, the code that initiates the printing is very different. In the non-object-oriented case, a selection must be made of the appropriate print function to call. In the object-oriented case, the print message is sent to the object *whatever type it is*, thus the structure and range of records can be extended without changing the calling code. Changing the implementation of the print function within the object has no effect on any program that uses printing.

This can speed up software development as the developer who has the task of modifying a particular object class need not worry about the possibility of hidden side effects elsewhere. In evolutionary development, the software is constantly being modified, and encapsulation gives the programmer peace of mind when changing code. Encapsulation is a very useful in the development process, particularly as it protects the maintainers of a system from introducing errors into other developers' code.

Polymorphism

The ability of a function or subroutine to accept parameters of any data type is called *polymorphism*. This allows generic code to be written, since one routine can handle many different data types. In an object-oriented language polymorphism is available as a consequence of the way that all operations are invoked by messaging.

Inheritance

Inheritance is a feature that allows the developer to create a new class of object from an existing one by inheriting the behaviour, and then modifying or adding to it. This ability makes it very easy to take existing systems, or libraries of generic classes, and create new object classes based on the existing ones. This is software reuse at its most useful. How often do we want to create a system that is almost but not quite like an existing one?

Use of object-oriented languages

One of the places where it seems most natural to use object-oriented languages is in the development of user interfaces. For example, a library of object classes can be developed that provide a basic windowing capability, where each window is an object. The base of this hierarchy is a simple window with no features. Further object classes can be added that contain title bars, scroll bars, and editors. The developer can simply create a new class, inheriting the objects from the library, and adding or removing the features as appropriate.

Object-oriented languages provide a natural way to reuse software, and a clean way of avoiding unwanted side effects when modifying code. They are therefore a very natural tool for all types of prototyping. It should be borne in mind, however, that a change to using object-oriented languages does not just require retraining of staff in a new language, it also requires system designers to relearn the design process.

Perhaps the most important aspect of an object-oriented language is that the object metaphor allows programmers to develop code in an evolutionary way. The first versions of a program can use the standard object classes, as defined by the language. Successive evolutions can enhance the program by defining new object methods to over-ride existing ones, and finally by defining new object classes. This ability to 'sketch out' a program, in increasing detail, is missing from conventional languages. It is this that makes object-oriented languages so powerful for prototyping.

6.3.3 Specialised languages

There are many languages available to the software developer. Most establishments will only use a few because of the time needed to train staff, and the consequent problems of having many languages around to maintain. The languages that are used tend to reflect the type of programming that goes on in an organisation. They are often general purpose languages for which staff can easily be found, eg C, Modula-2, Ada, or COBOL.

There are also many other specialised languages. The creation of a new language, together with its implementation, is about the right size of task for a doctorate, so maybe this is the reason for the great number of experimental languages produced! Among these are a number of excellent commercial languages, which do not fall into the 'general purpose' category. These can often be used for prototyping if the job in hand is easily solved using the language's specialism.

Two language tools available on Unix systems are lex[4] and yacc[5]. These are used to create compilers, and are widely used in the creation of new languages. They are, in fact, language interpreters in their own right.

lex is used for lexical analysis; the lex 'language' allows the programmer to specify the lexical atoms in the new language, and the lex tool produces a C program that performs the lexical analysis.

yacc is used for syntax analysis; the yacc 'language' allows the programmer to specify the syntax of the new language in terms of the lexical atoms, and the yacc tool produces a compiler for the new language. The code generation or interpretation has to be embedded in the yacc program.

These are very useful tools for creating command line interpreters, or for building special tools for a particular job, as well as creating whole new languages.

6.3.4 Reusable software

Building prototypes, or any other kind of software, would be greatly speeded up if programs could be constructed from existing components. The difficulty of this simple idea is that the effort required to find and assemble relevant components may exceed that needed to construct the system from scratch.

For example, there are 88 system calls listed in the Unix system V.3 programmers' reference manual (AT&T, 1987). In addition to this there are 425 subroutines in the accompanying libraries. To be able to use these libraries efficiently and quickly requires the developers to have a good working knowledge of them. With such a wide range of subroutines to choose from, experienced people are needed who know their way around the libraries.

Libraries and toolsets

The difference between a library and a toolset (or toolkit) is not a precise one. Libraries are collections of modules for specific software tasks. Toolsets contain tools which can be used for more general tasks, and which may be combined to build more powerful tools.

---

[4] Lexical analyser (Lesk and Schmidt)

[5] Yet Another Compiler Compiler (Johnson)

Libraries

A simple approach to software reuse is to use a software library which contains a collection of components. This approach can be very effective, provided that two conditions are met:

1. The user of the library is familiar with the components.
2. The components are sufficiently flexible to be useful in a range of applications.

The components of a library are procedures which can be called from an application program, and can be linked into the application. Most computing environments will have access to several libraries:

- operating system calls
- libraries packaged with the operating system
- commercial libraries
- in-house libraries

An organisation should build up its own library of utilities. For example, a company that produces applications may have a house style for its user interface. This can be coded up as a library which is used consistently throughout the business. Businesses which are managed wisely and have good designers will build up large sets of libraries to avoid re-implementing software.

The limiting factor to a software library is that without a really good classification scheme or index, or expert knowledge, it can be difficult to find the relevant component. A library is not much use if it takes a long time to find the information.

Toolsets

The concept of a toolset is that by writing generic modules for particular software abstractions, efficient use can be made of development effort. It is the mark of a good designer when a system contains well abstracted modules. The extent to which one can keep on developing toolsets is debatable. For example Tracz (1988) states that somewhat less than one hundred reusable abstractions exist in most problem domains. Typical abstractions include:

- WIMP user interface
- databases
- stacks, queues, and trees
- interprocess communications
- transport channel between computers
- numerical integration
- file transfer between computers

Most conventional languages do not support generic tools. In contrast, object-oriented languages like Smalltalk, because they use messages to invoke operations, allow generic tools to be written easily. They support code reuse because the class inheritance concept allows new objects to inherit the properties of existing objects. Smalltalk also provides a hierarchical browser, which allows relevant classes of object to be found quickly.

The Unix software tools use a different but highly effective approach. Since the tools take their input from a standard input file, and write their results to a standard output file, it is simple to connect tools together to perform complex operations on the input data.

Example – Unix command interpreter

Most operating systems are supplied with a command interpreter which gives the developer direct access to the system calls without actually having to write programs. Command interpreters can have a number of features that make them useful for creating prototypes:

- A series of commands can be stored in a file. This allows the user to treat a file of commands just like any other program.
- They contain the necessary control structures to write programs, such as if statements and while loops.
- They make calls directly to the operating system, so the power of the operating system is made available to the user directly. Instead of having to write and compile code to access the operating system, there are commands that will do this on the users behalf.
- Existing programs may be invoked. Editors, viewers, sort programs and other programs may form part of the code.

Unix has a number of very flexible command interpreters, of which the best known are the C-shell and the Bourne shell. Apart from the items listed previously, there are a number of other useful features of the Unix shells that make it easy to build up commands:

- Pipes
  Piping the output of one command into the input of another is a very useful feature. For example, the command:

  ```
  who | grep fred
  ```

  will take the command `who`, which lists the users currently logged into the system, and feeds it as an input file into the command `grep`, which performs a search on a file. The parameter `fred` is used by `grep` as a string to search for. Thus the effect of this command is to see if there is a user called `fred` currently logged onto the system.

- In-line commands
  A command can be placed 'in-line', that is the command can be placed in a position that would normally be held by a parameter to a second command. The in-line command is evaluated first, and its output is treated as the value of the parameter for the second command. For example,

  ```
  grep 'whoami' namefile
  ```

  will first execute the command `whoami`, which finds the user's login-id. It then uses that as a parameter to `grep` as it searches the file `namefile`. The result is a command that prints out any line in `namefile` that contains the user's login-id.

- Redirecting output
  The output of commands is usually directed to the screen, but can be directed into a file instead. For example,

  ```
  whoami >> logfile ; date >> logfile
  ```

  appends the user's login-id from `whoami` to the `logfile`. It then appends the date to the `logfile` using the `date` command. Thus a command has been created to make an entry in a log file.

There are other features in the Unix shells that make them useful as tools to build programs. The examples given above are simple one-line programs that would require a considerable amount of code in a third generation language.

These few simple examples show how it is possible to create quite complex commands from existing ones. These can be produced very quickly as they are so short, and so the command interpreter is a very useful tool for rapid prototyping.

System modification

One of the simplest, but still very effective, methods of rapid prototyping is in modifying existing systems. If software is available that performs some or all of what is required, it may be easier to modify this code than to start from scratch. Of course, if a program is modified without too much thought, it is all to easy to end up with badly designed program which is only suitable for a throw-away prototype.

Having said this, it can be a very efficient use of programmer time. The authors were once asked to produce a set of examples of novel office automation tools within a short period of time. It was felt that it was insufficient to write a paper describing our ideas, and would be better to produce a simple prototype.

A machine was available with which we were totally unfamiliar, but it did contain some example code that was quite close to what we wanted to do. Five days were spent modifying this code, and five or six demonstrations were produced, each of which was grossly inefficient and had a lot of code that was not used, but which served as a demonstration of our ideas far better than a paper document would have done.

6.3.5 Use in prototyping

The use of programming languages in prototyping may seem obvious, but the choice of the correct language may prove to be the difference between success and failure. There are a very wide range of languages, some of which are highly specific to particular problem domains. These may be very effective for a throw-away prototype, but many specialised languages are completely unsuitable for a full systems development. Conversely, traditional development languages, like C, Modula-2, or Ada, may not be the fastest for writing code. What counts most of all is the experience of the developers – the differences in performance between programmers in an organisation is very wide – and the software development environment.

6.4 System performance

As described in Chapter 5, prototypes can used to estimate system performance. There are various tools and techniques that will help this process, and this section provides a brief overview of some of them. See also Nichols (1990).

6.4.1 Accounting data analysis

Most multi-user systems collect accounting data which can then be analysed. This data is normally collected for the purpose of things like charging customers, or allocating costs between departments. The tools available include:

- operation logs – from system daemons
- billing information, eg seconds of processor time used by a user

This information is very cheap to collect as the software is usually present in the system. Sometimes there is software provided to analyse the data as well.

6.4.2 Stop watch

The simplest way of measurement is by timing the process. This can be done with a stop watch if the time for the process is long enough. If the time for the process is very short, a driver program may have to be written that runs the process many times sequentially. Many operating systems come with a software tool for measuring the time taken for a particular process to run.

When measuring the time taken for a process it is important to distinguish between:

- processor time
- program time
- elapsed time

Processor time is the time the processor is engaged in the application. Program time is the time the program takes to run by itself, ie the processor time plus any idle time waiting for external devices, such as disk drives. Elapsed time is the actual time from the start to the finish of the running of the application. This includes the time the processor takes while it is engaged in running processes for other users.

Sometimes the timings will not be consistent, as the conditions are not always identical. Several measurements should be taken and then analysed statistically. Depending upon the purpose of the measurement, either the maximum, minimum, or average of these timings should be used. Measurements may vary throughout the day, as the load varies. If a measurement is to be taken on a non-loaded system, it may be appropriate to take it at night[6].

6.4.3 Timing analyser

A timing analyser uses the instruction set execution times to calculate how long each path of a program will take, and finds the longest path through the program. This is important for real-time systems which may have a critical timing constraints.

6.4.4 Software monitors

A software monitor is a system that samples the use of a running program to see what it is doing. There are two varieties:

1 Time-driven monitors
2 Event-driven monitors

Time-driven monitors

Time-driven monitors are run by an external process which interrupts the monitored process at regular intervals. The program counter is examined to see which procedure is being run. The data collected, when analysed, will reveal which parts of the program are being used most often.

[6] When taking measurements at night, be wary of certain times when the night time processes all start up. For example, at 2am, all the overnight jobs might launch automatically causing a surge in the processor usage.

Event-driven monitors

Event-driven monitors put extra statements in the program which count how many times the program executes a particular statement. These are sometimes known as *software profilers* or *execution profilers*. For example, an option in the Unix C compiler puts the extra statements in the program. During the running of the program a data file is created. A program is available to analyse the data, which produces a table that gives:

- percentage time in each procedure
- number of calls to each procedure
- average time taken per procedure call
- name of procedure

Another package will give an analysis at the level of each line of a program. An annotated listing is produced stating how many times each line was run.

The summary data can be useful in determining which procedures, or lines of code, are used most often, and therefore which ones should be optimised. In a prototype care must be taken to interpret the data correctly; the differences between the prototype and the system it is modelling should be considered[7].

6.4.5 Hardware monitors

Probes are available to measure the activity of the hardware. For the software engineer, one of the most useful hardware monitors is the *protocol analyser*. This is connected to a network line, and the analyser displays the protocol data units (PDUs) that are being sent. The number and size of PDUs can be recorded and used as a measurement of performance.

6.4.6 Benchmarking

A benchmark is a standard set of data items which are regarded, in some way, as typical of the data that the program might come across under normal conditions. The benchmark must be representative of the things that are being measured. For example, if the disk activity is being measured, the benchmark should contain data designed to cause a lot of disk activity.

---

[7] An early example of the use of a software monitor was on a processor intensive program on a CDC 6600. Visual inspection of the code showed no inefficiencies. Using a software monitor showed that 20 per cent of total processor usage was taken up by one line of the program. This proved to contain a square root function. Further examination of the data and of the surrounding code showed that the variable that had its square root taken always had the value 2 at this point. The actual value of the square root of 2 was put in as a constant, with the result that the performance improvement freed one hour of CPU time per day.

In order to test several designs, prototypes can be built and each one run against the same benchmark. Thus a direct comparison can be made. Subsequent changes to the software can be compared against the same benchmark.

6.4.7 Use in prototyping

The tools and techniques described above can be used in any systems development project to measure or estimate performance, and are not just limited to prototyping projects.

6.5 Graphical systems

Graphical systems have many uses, in particular in the production of user interfaces. User interfaces often take up a very large part of the code of an application. This is generally because the software has to react in a proper manner to anything that the user may do, and so much of the user interface is dedicated to catching errors. The variety of possible user actions that must be coped with is enormous, so user interface code tends to be quite large.

The user interface is perhaps the most important part of a system that can be prototyped, because it provides the user's view of the system. A prototype can also be used as the specification for the user interface. Graphical systems are, therefore, a very important prototyping tool. It is important that the system produces a good representation of the user interface, and that the code can be written quickly, cheaply, and easily (Lewis et al, 1989).

Some graphical systems have more than just user interface capabilities. For example, fourth generation languages typically have not only a user interface system, but also a database, and a language that can be used with the database. Some hypertext systems have sophisticated languages supporting a user interface tool.

6.5.1 Screen generators

Screen generators allow the production of screens, which can form part of the user interface. Forms and report generators can be used on a standard 80 x 25 character terminal. On a more modern bit map screen, windows, icons, pull-down menus, and pointing devices may also be used.

The input to a screen generator tool is a set of commands, either in a special language for describing user interfaces, or input interactively through a graphical user interface. The language has to be interpreted by a special compiler, whereas the graphical interface can generate its output on the fly. Various types of output may be produced by a screen generator tool:

- Interpreted code
  Interpreted code requires a run-time system to be provided with the product. There may be efficiency problems, both in terms of speed of execution and amount of memory used. Many such systems have poor provision for linking the code with other software applications, relying on their own inbuilt logic to provide the application engine. If there is a method of linking to other modules, it is specific to the particular system being used. The run-time system often needs a licence to run. This may prove prohibitively expensive if the system is to be duplicated en masse.
- Executable code
  Executable code is usually provided as a set of procedures which must be linked with the application engine software.
- Source code
  Source code has to be compiled and linked with the application engine software. It has the advantage of being portable, but requires a compatible compiler. A problem with source code is that the developers are often tempted to fiddle with the code in order to 'improve it'.

Building a screen

The sequence of actions involved in producing a user interface screen are typically as follows:

- definition – specify the screen layout
- creation – using a user interface language, or interactively on screen
- generation – interpreted, executable, or source code
- link – with an application program
- run – either the executable code, or the interpreted code which uses a run-time system

6.5.2 Forms and reports

Forms and report generators lie at the heart of many data processing systems. Most common types of screen generator will produce forms and reports. A form is simply a screen that allows the user to enter data in a structured way. It contains a set of fields which allow data of particular formats to be entered. Simple syntax checking is often provided, eg for numeric or character data, the range of numeric data, or the length of data fields. A form could have the following items on it:

- fixed text, eg headings, that cannot be changed by the user
- blank fields – data that may be filled in by the user
- modifiable fields – data supplied that may be changed by the user
- fixed fields – data supplied that may not be changed by the user
- commands that can be applied, eg cancel, confirm, or help

The simplest form is the menu; this consists mostly of fixed text and has a single field that indicates the choice that is to be made. Some forms may be much more complex, with several fields, and links to one or more other forms.

A report generator takes data from a database or file, produces a report, and displays it in a form with fixed fields. The report could be anything from a single record, to a set of statistics about the contents of a file. Report generators have their roots in commercial languages like COBOL and RPG.

6.5.3 Windows-based interfaces

Modern computer systems use a bit-mapped display screen to present graphical and textual information to a user. These often have a WIMP interface (Windows, Icons, Mouse, Pull-down/Pop-up menus), where information is selected from a window or a menu by using a pointing device such as a mouse.

Just as there are systems that allow the building of forms and reports with relative ease, there are also systems that simplify the programming of windows interfaces. One such example is the Interviews library. This is a public domain library that provides an easy way to build a windows-based application on a terminal that uses the X Window System.

6.5.4 Hypertext

A document, such as this book, is designed to be read from beginning to end. However, the physical form of a book allows the user (ie the reader) to perform many other actions as well. These include the ability to:

- Mark particular pages with a piece of paper inserted between the pages.
- Flip, backwards or forwards, to a given page number.
- Use the index, contents, list of figures, etc. to determine where to flip to.
- Scan through the book by leafing through the pages quickly.
- Skim the information in the book by speed reading.

Computer-based document systems usually provide facilities to move forwards and backwards through the text, and to do string searching. Although satisfactory for small documents, such systems are unsuitable for documents of several hundred pages. Hypertext was originally developed to provide the facilities necessary to read large documents on screen.

The main feature of hypertext is that the text is no longer considered as linear (Nielsen, 1990). Conceptually, it may have links from one part of a document to several other places. These could be used to link a paragraph where a reference to another paper was made, to the full reference for that paper (which is usually held in the references section), and then back again. If the reference itself is held in the same computer system, then it can be displayed in full.

Thus the users are provided with the facilities to perform the equivalent of putting a page marker at their current position, flipping to the references at the back, and finally returning to their original position. This is illustrated in Figure 6.5.

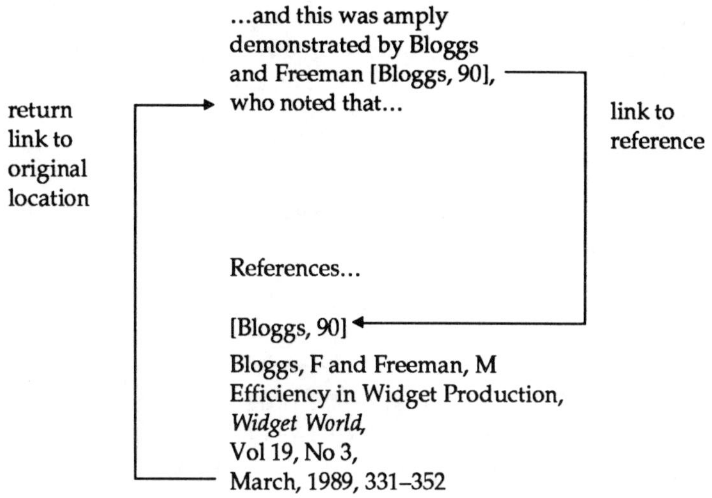

Figure 6.5 Hypertext link to a reference section, and back again

Although the concept of document links was originally designed to enable the user to read large documents on screen, they have since been extended to allow all sorts of other applications to be built.

Two different conceptual approaches have been made to the problem of linking to different parts of a document:

- Freetext-based systems
  Freetext-based systems treat the document as a long stream of text, in a similar way to a normal word processor. Special characters or diagrams in the text can trigger a jump to another part of the document, as shown in Figure 6.5 above. One such system is called 'Guide', which was developed at the University of Canterbury in Kent, and sold as a commercial product.

- Page-based systems
  Page-based systems treat the document as a series of discrete pages, sometimes referred to as paragraphs or cards, each of which typically fits on one screen. The links go from one card to another, rather than from one character to another as in the freetext-based systems. These cards may or may not have an order; if they do, it is provided by links from each card to

its successor and predecessor. The most successful products using this system are Hypercard (Goodman, 1987), and its competitor Supercard.

Hypertext documents

A 'normal' document can be considered as a set of paragraphs linked in sequential order. A hypertext document does not necessarily have a linear order. For example, after reading a particular paragraph, the reader may be given a choice of three different paragraphs to choose next.

This simple concept of a document with a set of links is the basis for all hypertext systems. Many hypertext systems also provide additional facilities. Perhaps the most powerful is the ability to associate a card with a simple programming language, called a *script*. The script is interpreted when the user displays the card. Each action the user performs may trigger a response in the script. This response might be to display another card, to perform some complex calculation, or to fetch information from another card.

Although both types of hypertext system may be used for prototyping user interfaces, the next section will concentrate on page-based systems, as in the experience of the authors these are more useful.

Use of hypertext for rapid prototyping

The use of hypertext for rapid prototyping relies on actions being simulated by the display of another page. To take a simple example, suppose it is necessary to simulate a selection from a menu. The menu is to have three options, which result in either a menu, or one of two different forms being displayed. To do this in Hypercard, a page is created that looks like the menu, and another page for each of the menu options. Links are created from the menu to all the other pages, and these are designed to be triggered when the particular item on the menu is selected. This is shown in Figure 6.6.

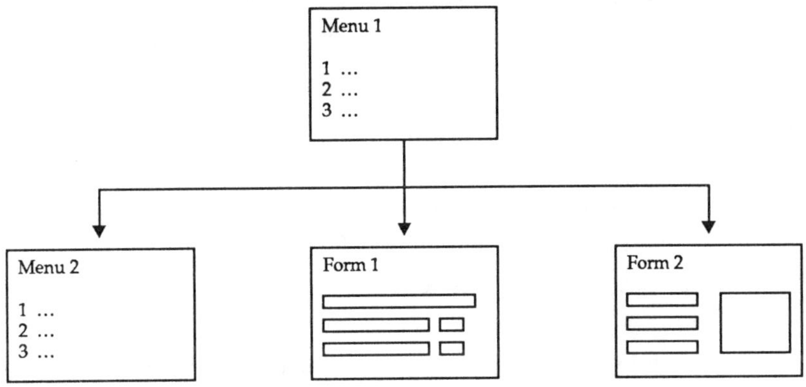

Figure 6.6 A prototype system built in hypertext which uses menus

The network of screens can be extended to create the complete prototype. If a script language is available in the system, then some of the application program can be simulated as well. For example, some pages could be loaded with information that can be fetched on certain user commands. These pages act as a database, and are never actually displayed to the user.

By changing from one page to another, very subtle changes can be made to the screen. These changes can give the appearance of things that could require complex graphical programs. A prototype once built by the authors contained a 'zoom' facility on a map. This allowed the user to select a point on a map and, in a series of stages, zoom into the highest level of detail at a particular point. This was done by creating many images of the map at different levels of detail, and holding each on a different page.

The prototype was totally impractical as a real system, due to the vast amount of duplicated data However, it did demonstrate the idea with very little programming effort. The prototype system design has now become more practical due to the falling costs of disk memory. Indeed, since the prototype was built, the British Broadcasting Corporation has produced just such a system on their optical disk-based Doomsday project.

An interesting case study is reported by Bødker (1989), using a technique known as cooperative prototyping. A patient case record system for municipal dental records was prototyped in Hypercard. The potential users of such a system were interviewed in front of the prototype. As suggestions were made as to possible ways in which the system could be modified, the interviewer either noted them down, to be dealt with later, or modified the system on the fly in front of the interviewee. The main point about this is that if a prototype can be modified very quickly, then very rapid progress can be made by this method.

Hypercard has achieved a high reputation for user interface and application prototyping. The impression usually given in the literature is that Hypercard is easy, even for non-experienced users. However some authors, for example Jones (1990), have recently started to question this.

The key points about the suitability of Hypercard for prototyping are as follows:

- It is not easy for non-programmers to use, other than for trivial systems; it is a sophisticated software development environment.
- It is most suitable for investigating user requirements, and for building prototypes with limited functionality.
- It is not suitable for fully-functional prototypes, for prototypes with extensive number crunching, or with critical real-time requirements.

6.5.5 Use in prototyping

Graphical systems are important for the rapid prototyping of user interfaces. Some systems, like forms generators or Hypercard, enable a mock-up of an interface to be constructed quickly, and relatively easily. Other systems, like the X Window System, are suitable for product-quality interfaces, and are much more complicated.

When prototyping a user interface, a clear distinction must be drawn between a prototype as a *model* of the real system interface, and a prototype to *investigate* system interface behaviour. The former requires a user interface that looks and behaves like the real interface, so that the user's interactions will be close to their interactions with the real system. The latter requires a user interface that is *similar* to the real interface, but which can be much simpler, and need not provide the same functionality. Once the aims of the user interface prototype have been decided, the selection of the appropriate graphical technique becomes much easier.

6.6 Configuration management systems

When using evolutionary development, the elapsed time between software releases is relatively short. This means that the number of releases that can exist is potentially quite large. The configuration of such systems must be managed with great care.

There will be many old systems that will need to be referenced to find out where a particular bug has been introduced. There will be old versions of the system that are still being used, and which need to be rebuilt in order to test or modify them. As change requests come in from users, some users may even ask for previous versions of the system back, as they contain features which are now needed.

As the use of software tools increases software development productivity, one of the dangers that must be avoided is that more code can lead to greater chaos. All these different problems suggest the need for a configuration management.

6.6.1 Configuration management

Configuration management can be defined as:

> 'The discipline of identifying the items which form the configuration of a system at discrete points in time for the purpose of controlling changes to the configuration and maintaining the integrity and traceability of the items which form the configuration, throughout the system lifecycle.' (Cooper, 1989)

It is characterised by the following tasks:

- configuration identification
- configuration control
- status accounting
- configuration auditing

Configuration identification

Configuration identification is concerned with answering the following question:

> 'What items of software went into this particular release?'

Figure 6.7 illustrates a small system configuration with several modules. The shaded boxes represent the modules in the system; the unshaded boxes are not in the current configuration.

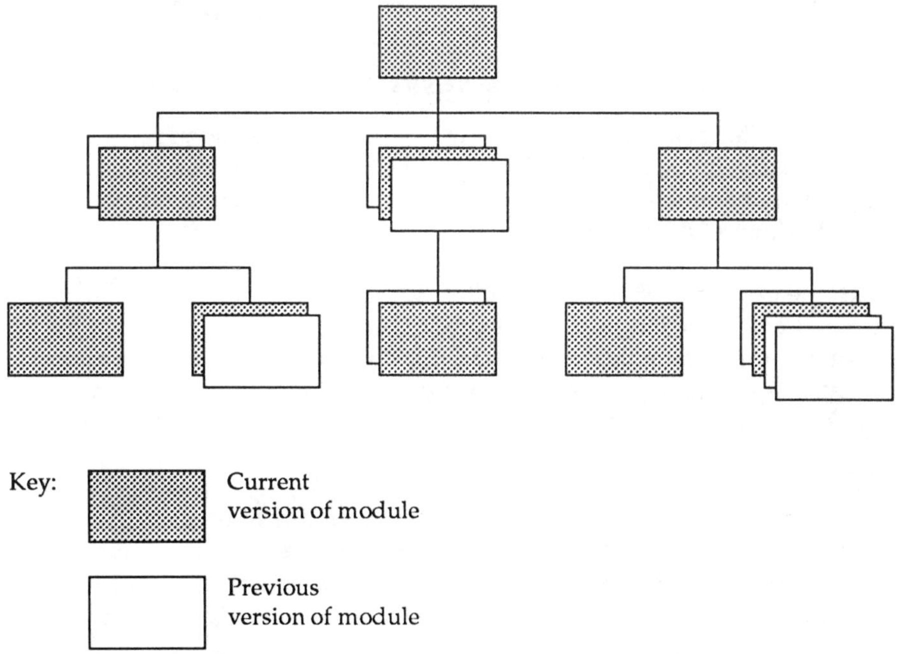

Figure 6.7 An example configuration

Configuration identification is essential for the rebuilding of a specified system release, with any set of subsequent upgrades or patches. When the release is rebuilt, there must also be a rebuild of all the appropriate documentation that goes with that release. In order to do this:

- Each module must be uniquely identified.
- It must be possible to recreate each version of each module.
- The modules that go to make each release must be recorded.

The larger a system is, the more vital it becomes to get this right. For example, the VAX VMS operating system before version 5 had 8,300 source files. If each file is not uniquely named, and its history recorded, then it becomes impossible to rebuild such a large system.

If formal methods are used, the configuration management system must also keep track of the equivalence of the various executable specifications.

Configuration control

The task that configuration control attacks is that of controlling the changes made to modules, and also the configuration of modules that go together to make up any one release. Software engineers must not be able to update the modules in an ad hoc fashion; the updating must take place in an orderly manner.

This is achieved either by a strict access control mechanism, or by well-disciplined developers[8]. Each new release of any module must only take place after the appropriate procedures have occurred. For example, a module should not be integrated with the rest of the system until it has undergone unit testing, and is found to be fault free.

There may be different threads of the development going on at the same time, each updating their own version of the system, and each requiring their own set of access controls. These versions may be brought together in a large integration exercise. This requires *strict* configuration control, otherwise it is very easy for complete confusion to occur.

Status accounting

The various modules will always exist in a certain *state*. For example, a set of states for a module could be:

- defined – specified but not under development
- development – undergoing development
- testing – being tested by another developer
- released – having completed the tests successfully

[8] Reliance on software engineers always runs the risk of the late-night debugging session which 'fixes' several modules, whose names are then forgotten by the next morning.

A module must exist in one of these states. Figure 6.8 shows a state diagram of the paths through the states; a state table could also be used to represent this information. A status accounting system keeps track of the state of each item in the system, and ensures that it always follows a valid path through the states.

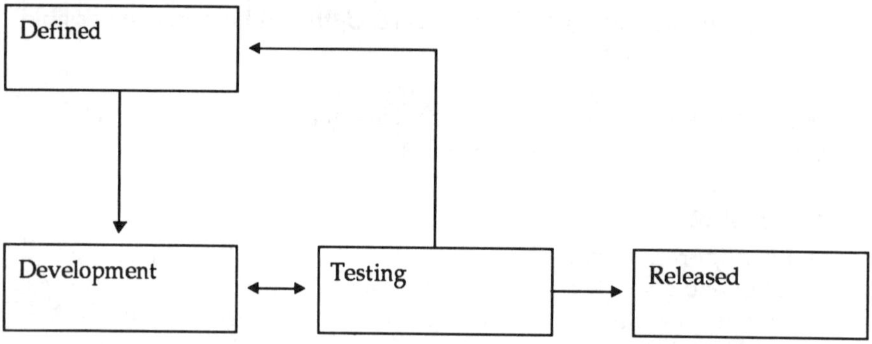

Figure 6.8 Module status state diagram

If this is not done, a module could be released for testing before it has completed development, and thus testing would start on a version that was incomplete. Alternatively, a module could get released before it had been tested.

Similar state tables can be drawn for the documents in the system. For example, a change request document may have states of: defined, assigned, closed (rejected), and closed (completed).

Configuration auditing

In order to maintain a consistent quality of product, it must be possible to audit the development of a system. An audit is a simple check to make sure that the correct procedures are being carried out. In the case of configuration management, it ensures that the modules are being given the correct identification, that configuration control is being used properly, and that the modules are in the correct state. This may be a semi-automated process if a full configuration management system is in place.

Configuration tools

One of the basic tools in the configuration management system is a DBMS which stores:

- Each version of each module.
- The status of each version of each module.
- Each configuration, ie a list of the modules making up each configuration.

There are three basic methods of storing all the various versions of the modules:

- Hold full copies of every version.
- Hold baseline copies of the main releases, and *deltas,* ie changes from the baseline.
- Hold the latest copy, and *reverse deltas,* ie changes to reproduce old versions.

The DBMS must also:

- Control the use of module identifiers.
- Ensure the proper movement of a module from one state to another.
- Apply adequate access control to the modules.

An automated configuration management system should contain a database that performs the above operations automatically. However, in some systems it may be necessary to perform these tasks manually.

6.6.2 Use in prototyping

The changes undergone by software systems developed under a normal lifecycle model are sufficient to warrant a configuration management system. When working under an incremental or evolutionary prototyping strategy, the number of versions and changes becomes frighteningly high. It becomes vital that a configuration management system is used.

If there are many user sites, each site will have to be updated as the evolutionary process continues. It is inevitable that at some stage the various sites will get out of step. Some will ask to miss out on a new release, because it is not relevant to them. Some will find a bug that only occurs because of the way that they use their system, and will want to go back to a previous version, or obtain a temporary patch. So the site that is releasing the systems must keep track of the various versions. When a problem arises at a site, it must be possible to recreate the version of software running at that site, in order to reproduce the system and the problem.

This description of a multi-site, multi-version system is one that is common enough with large systems, such as operating systems. With evolutionary development, that situation can become just as chaotic, even with much smaller systems with fewer users. Anyone who tries to do a serious evolutionary prototyping project without a configuration management system is likely to get into serious trouble.

Selected reading

CASE tools

Fisher, G E
Application software prototyping and fourth generation languages, US National Bureau of Standards special publication 500-148, May 1987

Gane, C
Computer aided software engineering: the methodologies, the products, and the future, Prentice-Hall International, 1990

Rock-Evans, R
CASE Analyst Workbenches: a Detailed Product Evaluation - Volume 1, Ovum Ltd., London, 1989

Formal methods

Berg, H K, Boebert, W E, Franta, W R, and Moher, T G
Formal methods of program verification and specification, Prentice-Hall, 1982

Programming languages

Horowitz, E
Fundamentals of programming languages, Springer-Verlag, 1984

Willis, C P and Paddon, D J
Modula-2: A software engineering approach, Pitman Press, 1991 (in press)

Graphical systems

Goodman, D
The complete Hypercard handbook, Bantam, 1987

Myers, B A
Tools for creating user interfaces: an introduction and survey, *IEEE Software,* Vol 6, No 1, January 1989, 15–23

Software configuration management

Babich, W A
Software configuration management: coordination for team productivity, Addison-Wesley, 1986

Buckle, J K
Software configuration management, Macmillan, 1982

7 Case studies

Introduction

Four case studies are presented in this chapter. Each is based on a real situation, in which one or both of the authors have been involved in a managerial or team leader role. None of the projects were done as an experiment in prototyping; all were done for commercial reasons. It is because of this fact that some of the details have had to be changed.

Respect for commercial confidence prohibits us from publishing any of the technical details of the projects that we worked on, or the names of the companies we were employed by, or contracted to. Only the technical details have been changed, whereas the aspects of the project that make it interesting as a prototyping project have been left intact, for example:

- the nature of the prototype
- the success or failure of the project
- the order of events
- the plans, and what actually happened
- the use that was made of the prototype
- the reaction of the users
- the incidental stories

and so on. Any changes to the technical aspects have been kept to a minimum, and when a change in the story has been made, the technical details are only subtly different from the original. Thus an attempt has been made to keep the moral the same, in order to supplement this book with valid examples of prototyping[1]. The projects cover a wide variety of problems with very different features.

7.1 Sales demonstrator

This is an example of the use of a prototype to sell a product. It was not created rapidly, but used a very small development team, and was therefore very cheap. It was used by the customer to get a foothold into a new market.

7.1.1 Introduction

Customer profile

The customer's main business was hardware manufacture. It employed approximately 80,000 people, and its main products were personal computers, a small Unix workstation, communications boards, and cables. As a by-product of this work, several software products had been produced. These products had been developed by various parts of the customer's company, between whom there was little coordination. There was no sales department whose main purpose was to sell these software systems.

Project origin

One of the sales and marketing departments, responsible for small companies, took the initiative to sell systems which included a substantial amount of software, in order to enhance the sales of its hardware. It felt that three to five years would be needed to change the image of the company sufficiently to make large-scale software sales viable.

With the backing of the sales and marketing division, it set about changing the image of the company. It was decided that the best way to show off the software products would be to create a prototype application targeted at a particular market sector. The prototype was to show the use of a database product and a file server, and was to be aimed at medical general practitioners.

Description

The prototype system to be built had to show off the customer's database and file server products, running on their hardware; it had to be capable of being extended at a later date to include other products that the company wished to sell. Finally, it had to be something that a doctor could understand and relate to. There were no defined functional goals.

---

[1] Of course, no guarantee can be given regarding the technical merit of the ideas presented, as none of them have been tested by the authors.

The prototype system was one that might be used in a typical doctors' practice. It had terminals to be used by the doctors themselves, one for the receptionist, and one for a nurse. Each of these terminals presented a different rôle, and displayed different things. The database contained details of appointments and patient records, but was not designed to be able to handle large amounts of data. People seeing the system were to be able to relate to it, and imagine it in their own surgery.

Project goals

The goals of the project were to provide a system demonstrating the use of various hardware and software products. The system was to be based on an application that might be used in a general practice. (Later, several other market sectors were added.)

Functional requirements

The functional requirements were very simple:

- an application based on a medical general practice

Constraints

In contrast, there were quite detailed constraints for this project:

- use of customer's file server
- use of customer's database
- use of customer's personal computers
- use of customer's Unix workstation
- use of customer's network cards
- use of customer's cabling system
- to be completed at low cost

Quality goals

The quality goals were not very strict:

- demonstration quality only
- 'flashy' user interface

7.1.2 Discussion

The problem that the prototype had to solve was to enhance the customer's image, so that people would believe that the company was a serious contender for both hardware and software systems. In order to do this, the prototype had to show all the products working together, and it had to look impressive. The main problem was one of education: the products existed, but the potential customers needed educating with the knowledge that the company was in the market place.

The prototype needed to be self-explanatory. It had to model a system that used the products being sold. It had to evolve to include other products at a later date, and so also had to be evolutionary. It had to be believable.

The prototype was to be based around a modern style of user interface that used windows and a mouse. The user interface had to look good, and invoke the software products that were used. While driving the user interface, the person demonstrating would talk about the various products. The user interface was not for sale, but it nevertheless had to look good in order to catch the attention of its audience.

At an early stage in the project, it was decided to develop a scenario. The scenario was to take the audience through a short story based on the typical events in a general practice. The scenario had to be very carefully designed so that it would be an accurate representation of a real situation, and would use all of the products. It had to be sufficiently long to include all the products, and not too long so that people lost interest. It had to use realistic data, so that doctors could relate to it. The scenario turned out to be the crucial focus for the project.

7.1.3 Planning the prototype

Strategy

An evolutionary development strategy was adopted for this project. The system evolved as more products were added, and as the number of scenarios were increased. The main emphasis was on getting the scenarios right, therefore the first part of each evolutionary cycle was to design the scenario to be demonstrated. This provided the focus for the technical development work.

What to prototype

The combined use of the software products on the hardware infrastructure was being demonstrated. Thus the model was of an application with real products, and a mocked-up user interface. The major modules in the system are shown below. Existing products are marked by an *; all the other modules were prototyped.

- Medical data service
    - Database
        - File server *
        - DBMS *
        - Database schema and access

User services
- User interface
- Service invocation
- Print server *

Management *

Mail service *
- LAN mail *
- WAN mail *
- Unix mail gateway *

Tools and techniques

The user interface was built using a fourth generation language. Existing software products were utilised, which provided a high degree of software reuse.

Using the prototype

The prototype was only to be used for demonstrations. The audience were not to operate the system, only to view it. The demonstration was to be scenario based, ie it was to follow a simple story making use of the system.

Project organisation

The customer was represented by the manager of the sales and marketing department responsible for sales to small businesses. Within the development team, the project manager essentially took a back seat role, managing the budgets. The team leader played a major part in developing the scenarios, liaising with the customer representative, and managing the work on a day to day basis. The team consisted of one full time developer, and a number of others brought in from time to time.

Decisions were made at formal review meetings, held bi-monthly, between the team leader, project manager, and customer representative. More informal discussions took place outside these meetings between the team leader and the customer representative.

Project plan

The project plan was divided into phases of six months each; the end of each phase was considered a major milestone. The project was extended on a yearly basis.

Quality reviews

The scenarios were informally reviewed by the client representative, and a specialist in the particular market sector at which it was aimed.

Milestones

Milestones were every six months, at the end of each phase.

Budget control

The budget was set on a yearly basis by the client, based on discussions with the project manager. Within the year, it was controlled on a day to day basis by the team leader.

7.1.4 What happened

After the initial approach from the customer, the problem was discussed, and it was decided that the best approach was to build a prototype using a fourth generation language that could access the software products. A one year budget was agreed, with milestones set after six and twelve months.

Phase one

The first thing that was done was the selection of the tools, in particular a fourth generation language. The main criteria for selection were:

- ability to access other software products
- an impressive looking user interface

The development team set about building the system; the lesson of designing the scenario before designing the system had not yet been learnt. The system design included many interesting and novel features, such as diaries linked with the appointments database, and so on.

The first system was built on a personal computer. It did not use any of the required software products, nor the network. It was a prototype of the prototype, designed to check if the customer understood what the developers were doing. While it was being built, the scenario was being designed. The scenario eventually chosen showed only the basic features that demonstrated the use of the system, and not the clever ideas.

The scenario started with the doctor examining the appointments for the day. The first patient arrived, and the doctor called up the patient's notes on the screen. It was decided that the patient required a vaccination, and so the doctor used the appointments system to book the patient in to see the nurse. The scenario then switched to the nurse, who checked through the following week's appointments in order to place an order for vaccines.

The scenario was designed to show people working in the same building accessing data via a shared database. The system was reviewed informally. A specialist in the general practitioner's sector saw it, and said it would not work for a number of reasons:

- It is rare for the doctor to make an appointment; it is usually the receptionist.
- Common vaccines are kept in the pharmacy, the nurses only order special ones.
- The jargon used was wrong in several places.
- The displays on the screen did not look like the paper forms that the doctors were used to using.

The judgement on the scenario did not reflect on the use of the file server and database. Nevertheless, the scenario and system design were altered to take these factors into consideration. A receptionist was added to the scenario to make the appointment; the vaccine required was changed to a more unusual one that was unlikely to be kept in the pharmacy; the jargon was altered, and the screen layout changed to use standard medical forms.

Unfortunately, before the software could be rewritten, the main programmer on the team left to start a new job, and there was no one else with the necessary training. External contractors were asked to take on the work, and they presented themselves as a top-class team. No other companies were available at short notice to do the job. The contractors did not use the chosen fourth generation language, because they claimed they did not have time to learn it. They said that they had their own system under which software could be developed very quickly.

After four weeks work, the contractors appeared to have little to show for their efforts, and it became apparent that they were struggling. The parts that they had developed were demonstrated on a VT100 terminal, and looked very old fashioned. The team leader realised that a mistake had been made, so one of the more experienced staff was quickly trained to take on the work. She learnt the fourth generation language, wrote the software, and beat the external contractors after giving them four weeks start. Their contract was terminated as quickly as possible!

The system was demonstrated to the customer representative, who approved moving on to the next phase.

Phase two

Having got the software to run on a stand-alone computer, the next step was to integrate the file server and database. A demonstration system was built with three personal computers, a local area network, and a Unix workstation acting as a file server and database server. The user interface software was rewritten to use the database server, rather than its own internal database.

The scenario remained the same, having been approved by the customer. The only difference was that the three people involved (doctor, receptionist, and nurse) had their own screens appearing on different computers. Each computer terminal was labelled 'Doctor', 'Receptionist', and 'Nurse', and they were arranged in such a way that the demonstration moved across the room, from one to the next. The system was set up in a demonstration area at the developers' premises.

During this phase, the customer's company underwent some peculiar reorganisation that the developers could not understand. At each meeting, a different customer representative would appear, and each had a different view of the project. It would have been impossible to continue the project had not the project manager insisted that the developers carried on with the original plan. Eventually it all settled down with the original customer representative, who seemed totally unaware that any changes had happened at all. This is one of the problems that can occur in any project. In this case, fortunately, it turned out all right.

The system was demonstrated to the customer representative, and several of his senior management. The general reaction was good, although one person seemed to have missed the point completely when he asked, 'Can you change the colour on the screen?'. A complete copy of the system was built and installed in the companies own demonstration site in London[2].

A three day long exhibition was held at this site to which most of the customer' top managers were invited, as well as their own customers. The aim of the demonstration was to spread the idea within the company that it was moving towards a new market. There were several stands at the exhibition showing off other new systems that the company had to offer. The prototype system had the most interest shown in it, chiefly because it was dynamic, and was not just a black box, or a board full of components. All the visitors had, at one time or another, visited their general practitioner, and so could appreciate the scenario.

---

[2] This was a very strange place, in the heart of London's docklands – not a very salubrious place at the time. After going down a shabby road, a dirty looking building appeared that one might think was derelict. The entrance hall was lit by a single naked light bulb. A flight of stairs led to a dimly lit landing with bare boards, but entering the demonstration area was like walking into a different world. Hidden lights shone on the receptionist's designer desk. Wading through a thick pile carpet into a second room, the gently lit tables were waiting for the demonstration computers. In one corner free drinks were available to anyone who had the nerve to pour one out and risk damaging the highly polished surfaces. Hidden behind the screens that provided the backdrop to the demonstration area was a mass of wires and plugs, using the same adapter to take the power for almost everything in the room out of a single cracked socket.

As a result of the exhibition, several other parts of the business which had their own software products wanted them built into the prototype. These were included in the plans for the next two phases.

Phase three

The software products that were added in the third phase were:

- a mail system
- a print server
- a simple user interface shell for Unix system managers

In order to include these items in the demonstration the scenario had to be changed. This time, the scenario was altered first, and then the system re-built. This change in procedure proved very useful, as all the code previously written was re-used.

The new scenario was a modification of the old one. The doctor now used a standard form to mail the nurse to say that the patient required a vaccination, and the receptionist also got a copy. The receptionist put the appointment in the appointments database. The nurse printed the appointments for the day on the printer, read the mail, and realised a special vaccine had to be ordered.

The demonstrations at the end of this phase included a stand on the periphery of a conference for general practitioners. Several other companies had stands there as well, and were trying to sell systems of a similar nature. The most telling comment that was made to the demonstrators at the stand was from someone who was clearly visiting each stand in turn. He said that this was the first demonstration he could actually understand; the last one had given a demonstration of a database used to store a library catalogue, with the opening line: 'Now, imagine this book is a patient'.

Phase four

The software components added in the fourth phase were:

- a network planning tool
- an extension to the mail system, that ran over a wide area network
- a mail gateway to Unix mail

Again, the scenario was updated first. The new scenario included the arrival of a new doctor at the practice; the network was then replanned, and the system manager's user interface tool used to add the new doctor into the system. When the patient arrived, he not only had to take the vaccine, but also had to make an appointment with the nearest hospital.

The appointment was made by sending mail through the Unix gateway. It was considered unlikely that the hospital would use the Unix mail system, but the customer thought the audience would be unlikely to know that, and so it didn't matter! A second patient then arrived who was on holiday, and required emergency treatment. A request for the patient's medical records was mailed by the doctor to the patient's home practice, using the wide area network.

Having rewritten the scenario, the system was again re-designed and implemented. The Unix mail was sent to the Unix workstation, but the wide area network proved more difficult. It was not obvious as to how to show the wide area network being used.

Eventually, it was decided to install an X.25 switch to represent the network. The main advantage of this was that it had several lights on the front that flashed when data was going through it. The data was sent to another system in another room.

The audience never asked for proof that the message had got through, and were always quite happy to accept the word of the demonstrator that it was working when the lights flashed. After a series of demonstrations one day it was noticed that the remote system had never been switched on. As this had not affected the demonstration in the slightest, future demonstrations often left the remote system turned off, although this was never mentioned to the audience.

Various demonstrations were made, and a duplicate system was set up at a demonstration centre in London. Staff manning the demonstration centre were trained in running the system.

Phase five

The complete set of products that the customer wanted to demonstrate had now been incorporated into the prototype. They were satisfied with the inroads they had made into the general practice sector, and now wanted to expand the market. New scenarios were written aimed at several other market sectors, namely:

- solicitors' offices
- accountants' offices
- private schools
- management consultants

Each was sufficiently close in concept to the original idea to make the job of rewriting the software easy. The scenarios were written first, as they were the most important thing to get right; the rest was relatively easy.

And afterwards ...
The software was modified to go into trial sites, as the customer had realised that not only could they sell the software products, but also software applications tailored for a particular market sector. Their long term attempt at breaking into the software marketplace had begun. It had needed that two and a half years, not only to change the public image, but also to change the internal view of the software part of the business.

7.1.5 Retrospect

A number of lessons were learnt during this project:

Scenarios
When demonstrating software to an audience who may not understand the computer jargon and the concepts that are being shown, a scenario is of tremendous importance. The scenario is something they can relate to, and which they will remember. Of course, this applies to any piece of software that is being demonstrated. If the system is a prototype, then it is vital to design the scenario before designing the software. This is akin to writing a specification before the design.

The story line in the scenario must be simple, but memorable. It should make use of everything that is to be demonstrated. The demonstrator should explain both the technical background and the story line. This enables non-technical members of the audience to follow the demonstration.

The scenario needs to be accurate, in that it must represent a reasonable set of actions for the players, and must use terminology that the audience will understand. It need not have a formal requirements analysis. Local expertise of the problem domain is often useful.

Demonstrations
Demonstrations are enhanced by the use of handouts that not only explain the technical work, but also take the reader through the story line. This will help them to refresh their memories as to what happened. Wall boards illustrating the story line are also useful.

During the demonstration, no data should be entered; it should all be preset. Entering data tends to distract the audience, and leads to breaks in the presentation. If the speaker is operating the keyboard, it can also lead to breaks in eye contact.

The audience should not be allowed to use the system themselves. If the prototype has been set up without a requirements analysis, and without making it robust, then most people will find some fault or other. If the prototype has been built to show the sort of things that *could* be done, then no-one can expect the system to be perfect. This simple fact is very hard to explain to a potential customer who complains that something is just not right.

The prototype system

The purpose of the project was to explain the software products to potential customers, and to show the products being used to solve realistic problems. This it did, and so it can be concluded that the project was a success.

The system in this case was not built rapidly, and might not be considered a rapid prototype. But the time taken is not as important as the degree of success in achieving the goals of the prototyping. Furthermore, the prototype was built at comparatively low cost, and at the rate the customer was prepared to pay.

7.2 The secure file transfer network

In this study the customer approached the developers with a very clear set of requirements. A world-wide file transfer network was required, one that was secure even from unauthorised people within the company. It was required in a twelve to eighteen month timeframe, and was seen as important to the working of the company. A prototype needed to be built in order to verify the design, and it had to be completed within very tight deadlines.

7.2.1 Introduction

Customer profile

The customer was a large, multinational chemical company. Most of the customer's sites were in the United Kingdom, but there were several in other countries, particularly the United States of America. The company had seen the need to standardise on a particular operating system for their computers. They had chosen Unix as a system to migrate to eventually, as this was seen as having the most open system architecture.

Project origin

The customer had set up a small team to write a requirements specification. The team had been at work for about four months, and had produced a document which was a cross between a requirements specification, a functional specification, and a design, as it contained elements of all three. The development team were first approached for a few days consultancy to review the document, as the customer considered that it was important to get an external view, particularly on the design aspects.

During these few days, the development team showed the customer representative some of the work that they had done. The customer representative then said that the project plan included the building of a prototype before the development started, and asked if the development team would like to bid for the work. The project plan did not contain any reason as to why the prototype was to be built.

It is not atypical that the customer makes certain technical decisions, which are not well thought through. In this case, they wrote a requirements specification that contained many aspects of the design and functional specification; they also made a decision to build a prototype with no clear reason as to why, other than that they had heard it was the 'right thing to do'. This is where the developers have to tread carefully, not to ruffle too many feathers by debasing the ideas, but to try and get a compromise solution.

Description

The organisation had around 1000 Unix based machines throughout the world; with a potential expansion to 10,000 within the following five years. Some sites had many machines; some had only one. The sites were mostly in the United Kingdom, but several were in other countries.

Data was transferred between machines on a regular basis. This was done in a variety of ways; some sites used electronic mail, some sent data on disks via a courier, some sites had file transfer programs, and some had to re-enter the data. The main requirement was to develop a single file transfer network between *all* the sites.

The data transferred was confidential, sometimes even within the company itself, and so it was necessary to encrypt all the data before it was sent. Because the data had to be secure a public key cryptogram was chosen. The requirements study had selected a particular encryption package, and had also chosen FTAM[3] as the file transfer protocol.

The users of the system were well educated people, but not necessarily with any previous experience in using computers.

Project goals

The overall goals of the project were to provide secure file transfer between all the world-wide Unix machines in the company, using public key encryption and FTAM file transfer.

---

[3] FTAM is an international standard protocol for file transfer.

Functional requirements

The main functional requirements were:

- encrypted file transfer
- public key encryption
- centralised key management
- simple addressing

Constraints

The main constraints were:

- use of FTAM file transfer
- Unix operating system
- use of named encryption package
- Ethernet and token ring local area networks
- X.25 wide area networks
- installed, running, and supported within twelve months, with a second release giving full functionality within eighteen months

Quality goals

The main quality goals were:

- up to 10,000 machines supported
- 99 per cent availability
- two megabyte data transfers completed within ten minutes
- usable by intelligent, but computer-naive operators

Goals of the prototype

The goals for the prototype were as follows:

- To build a system using the same components as specified in the design, with the following exceptions:
  - no centralised key management
  - no distribution lists
  - no addressing
  - the user interface code could be different
  - the hardware could be different

- The components that had to be the same as the final product were:
  - the FTAM package
  - the encryption package
  - the networks

- The prototype system was to demonstrate:
  - end-to-end encrypted file transfer over a local area network
  - end-to-end encrypted file transfer over a wide area network

- The prototype system did not need to demonstrate:
  - simultaneous, multi-user access
  - aborted attempts, ie no significant error recovery required
  - robustness
  - usability

The whole system was to be demonstrated to the senior management in the customer's company in ten weeks time. The date of the demonstration had already been fixed.

7.2.2 Discussion

The problems at the start of the project were:

- The document was not a complete requirements specification, and it included aspects of design and functional specification. The classic lifecycle model had already been broken.
- A prototype was specified by the project plan, but the reasons for developing one were left unstated.

Most of the components in the design were understood, and many of them already existed, and so it was thought that the most difficult part of the problem was likely to be at the integration stage. The requirements were quite firm, and so there seemed little point in using a prototype to verify them. However, it was quite reasonable to use a prototype to verify the design of the system, and so the team leader agreed with the customer representative that the purpose of the prototype was to verify the design.

Another problem that was addressed by the prototype, but which was not perceived as a problem at the beginning, was the need to estimate the cost of the whole development project.

The problem was one of verifying a hypothetical design. It was therefore experimental in nature. Furthermore, any parts of the design that were shown not to work were to be redesigned. The prototype was to include all aspects of the design, in that all the major components were to be represented, either with the actual code, or with a mock-up that had the same characteristics. In this way, it could be seen whether the components worked together or not.

The knowledge gained from this would also enable the development team to estimate the cost of the whole development effort. The hard parts of the system could be determined, and the major risks identified.

7.2.3 Planning the prototype

Strategy

The goal of the project was to build a throw-away prototype, with an emphasis on getting a working system, and not worrying about writing maintainable code. The top risk items for the project were reassessed on a weekly basis.

What to prototype

The main things to prototype were the file transfer and encryption package, initiated from a simple user interface. The major modules in the system are shown below. Existing products are marked with an *; modules not in the prototype are marked with a †. All the other modules were prototyped.

- Secure file transfer network
  - File transfer
    - FTAM *
    - FTAM access
  - Security
    - Encryption package *
    - Encryption package access
    - Key management †
  - User interface
  - Network
    - LAN *
    - WAN
  - Management
  - Addressing †
    - Address storage †
    - Address translation †

When to prototype

This was already set by the timescale; it was a late prototype built in the early parts of the design stage.

Tools and techniques

The prototype was to reuse existing components. A fourth generation language was to be used to build the user interface. FTAM and encryption packages already existed, and were to be included. A network filing system was also to be used. Finally, some daemon software from another project was to be reworked.

Using the prototype

The prototype was only to be used in experiments performed by the development team in order to test the design. It had then to be demonstrated to the customer's senior management as part of a presentation of the results.

Project organisation

One customer representative was the sole contact with the customer company for the whole period. The team leader ran the project from day to day, as well as being the design authority.

The team consisted of many people; only one worked full time for the whole of the ten weeks, and all the others were brought in for short periods of time to do specific jobs.

Weekly meetings were held between the team leader and the customer representative, at which all major decisions were made. Meetings between the team leader and team were held on an ad hoc basis when the need arose.

Project plan

A rough plan was drawn up for the ten weeks. Specification and design of the prototype were to be done over the first four weeks. Development of the user interface code was to overlap this, and go on for five weeks. The other software was to be developed towards the end of the design stage. Integration was to take place over the last three weeks, with the last week being dedicated to preparing for the demonstration.

Quality reviews

The specification and high-level design were informally reviewed by the customer representative at the weekly meetings. The code was not reviewed, apart from the team leader checking that it worked.

Milestones

The only milestone was the demonstration at the end of the project.

Budget control

The contract was fixed price. Within the development team, the cost was controlled by the team leader. Within the developer's organisation, the management decided not to worry about going over the contract price. This was because there was a strong chance of them getting the contract to do the whole development project afterwards, provided the prototyping job was done well. The cost of the prototyping project was, therefore, only limited by the availability of the development staff.

7.2.4 What happened

After the initial approach from the customer, the management in the development organisation decided to treat the prototype as a loss leader. It would accept a higher cost than the contract price, and it accepted the disruption of other projects in order to pull the right staff in for the various jobs.

A contract was drawn up with the customer, stating the extent of the prototype, and the purpose – which was to verify the system design. The agreement included:

- the price – which was fixed
- the goals – to verify the design
- the project control – by weekly meetings
- the deliverables – a presentation of the results which would include a demonstration of the prototype

The development team were very keen to get the contract for the full system.

Week one

The initial specification was written, stating what functions were to be implemented, and what functions needed to be demonstrated.

The development environment was chosen. All the software components were readily available except the encryption package, which was ordered by the team's administrative officer. The main team members were selected, and they started winding up their current work.

The signed contract with the customer was sent to the finance department, so that they could set up the necessary budgets, and bill the customer.

The highest risk item for the project was noted as being the lack of available, suitably experienced people. The team leader notified his managers in order to make sure that other team leaders were told of the priority that this small project had.

Week two

The specification was refined and agreed. The substance of this amounted to little more than one sheet of paper. A high-level design was written, similarly on one sheet of paper; this proved easy as the high-level design had to conform to the design that was to be tested.

During discussions with the customer representative, it was realised that the user interface to the system would be more important than originally expected. It became apparent that the people to which it had to be presented were not particularly technically minded. This meant that it would be important to impress them with more than just a verification of the design.

Outside of the meeting with the customer representative, the development team decided to put more effort into getting the user interface to look nice, despite the fact that this would cost more, and was not in the contract. The user interface specialist installed the latest version of the fourth generation language on her PC, and started experimenting with screen designs.

A lack of suitably experienced people was still the top risk item.

Week three

The design was refined, and each module interface was specified on a single sheet of paper.

The user interface experiments continued. The best screen layouts were used as the basis for the implementation. The customer representative again stressed the importance of the user interface.

A clerk from the finance department telephoned the team leader to ask what project they were working on. He did not have a copy of the signed agreement that had been sent two weeks previously. The team leader sent another copy.

With the increased importance of the user interface now recognised, the top risk item became the possible lack of time to complete this module. People had been promised for this, so staff availability was no longer a high risk item.

Week four

The design documents were completed, and the first working version of the user interface software was nearing completion. This invoked about half of the required functions.

Some daemons needed writing to control the flow of data through the system. A specialist was brought in from another project to work part time on this. A senior manager explained to his team leader that this was a high priority project, and that it was important that it was completed. The team leader interpreted this as meaning that his specialist should work on the prototype half time, for a maximum of three weeks.

At this point another team involved in writing system management software heard about the project. They too were interested in getting a part of the contract to develop the whole system. Some of their work, which was scheduled to be completed in about three months, could be useful to the project, and so they offered to reschedule it to include it in the demonstration. This idea was accepted, and the design was modified to include an interface to a management module. None of the other interfaces were changed, as it was considered too late in the day to do this.

The team leader suddenly realised that the encryption package, ordered three weeks previously, had not arrived and asked the team's administration officer to chase it.

A different clerk from the accounts office telephoned to ask what project the team was working on. He knew nothing about the conversation with the other clerk the week before, whose name the team leader had forgotten. A second copy of the contract was sent to the accounts department.

Progress on the user interface was going well, and so this was dropped as a high risk item. The lack of time for daemon development was promoted to this position. This was prompted by the other team leader's attitude towards lending staff.

Week five

The user interface software was completed, and demonstrated to the customer representative. The response time proved to be very slow. After some discussion it was decided that, although a fast response time was not part of the original requirements, it would be necessary to speed it up bearing in mind the increased importance of the user interface.

The user interface specialist did some experiments to find the source of the slow response. This proved to be the new version of the fourth generation language, which was designed for a 386-based PC, rather than the 286-based PC which it was currently on. The decision was taken to port the user interface back to the old version of the 4GL. It was anticipated that this would take several days, as the differences between the two versions of the languages were more than just minor ones. The user interface specialist started working fourteen-hour days.

The daemons appeared to be progressing as expected, and were predicted to be complete within their allotted three weeks. The system management team joined the project, and immediately started work.

The encryption software had still not arrived. The administrative officer chased it again; the firm supplying it promised that it would arrive within two days. Work on the encryption software was already behind schedule.

The team leader got a telephone call from one of the supervisors from the accounts department, who asked what was going on. This time the team leader took a copy of the contract round to the supervisor personally. The supervisor found the relevant forms to start a new project. There were two, one for contracts over £25,000, and the other for contracts under £10,000. There seemed to be no procedure for projects between these prices. The team leader left the supervisor to sort it out, and saw her heading towards her bosses office as he left.

The top risks were the porting of the user interface software, which was extending the schedule, and the lack of any encryption software, which did not arrive after the promised two days.

Week six

The user interface specialist worked the weekend to port the code. It was demonstrated to the customer representative at the weekly meeting, and it was agreed that the response time was now acceptable.

The daemon specialist had not quite finished by the end of the week. He said it would not take too much work to complete it now, and to avoid any conflict between team leaders and management, said that he would finish it off without telling his team leader. His work load was not very high, and he could easily hide the work away.

The system management team had rescheduled their work, and had two people working full time developing the software. A possible lack of time to integrate the management software was noted, and it was agreed with the system management team that they could run separate demonstrations if this proved the case.

The encryption software had still not arrived. The team leader chased it this time; he telephoned the supply company, demanded that it was ready to be collected within two hours, and drove to the company to collect it.

The late arrival of the encryption software was considered the top risk, with the possible lack of time to complete the daemons a close second.

Week seven

The user interface software was stable, and only required minor adjustment.

The daemon development continued in secret at the same rate as before. This apparently went unnoticed by the other team leader.

The user interface specialist transferred her attention to the encryption software. Very quickly she discovered a flaw in the design: the encryption package could not have one encrypted disk and one unencrypted disk at the same time. The system was quickly redesigned, the changes were circulated, and the user interface modified to cope with this change.

The system management software proved harder than expected, and was not going to schedule. The team leader left them to complete if they could. This problem was considered low priority as it was not part of the original contract.

The accounts supervisor's bosses boss called the team leader. She explained the procedure for contracts between £10,000 and £25,000. A special budget had been set up to cope with this situation. Several projects used this budget, which was therefore over £25,000 per year, and so could be processed. Apparently it was easier to do this than to set up a new procedure. This solved the budget problem.

Possible errors in the redesign due to the encryption problems, and the late delivery of the daemon software, were considered the top risks.

Week eight

The user interface software was integrated with the encryption package. After a few problems, this work was completed.

The daemons were complete except for one bug: a file disappeared at apparently random times. The bug could not be duplicated with certainty, but happened too frequently to be considered a minor risk. The daemon specialist left on two weeks leave. Just before he went, he went through the code with the team leader, who took on the job of finding the bug.

The system management team were still behind schedule, but were catching up. The integration system was assembled in the laboratory, and the software mounted on it.

The daemon bug was now the top risk item.

Week nine

The system was integrated. By the end of the week, it all seemed to work. The daemon bug had been found and fixed. On the Friday, the daemon bug reappeared. The team leader prepared to work through the weekend. One of the accounts clerks telephoned the team leader, and said that she had heard that he had found a way to have a project between £10,000 and £25,000. She wanted to know how it was done.

Week ten

The team leader and one of the team members worked all weekend. They discovered a major design flaw in the daemon code. The daemons were largely rewritten, and then worked. The count-down for the last week began.

Monday – integration tests were run with the new daemons in place. It was decided to move the integration system to the demonstration area before attempting to integrate the management software.

Tuesday – the team tried to relax as the technicians moved the hardware to the demonstration area, and started to assemble it there.

Wednesday – the integration tests were run again. They failed. There was a minor panic, until someone realised that as the machines had changed their location on the network, the network addresses would all be different. After reconfiguring the machines the integration tests worked.

Thursday – the integration of the system management software failed. It was decided to run it as a separate demonstration.

Friday – a demonstration was given to the customer's senior managers. It started with a brief presentation of the goals of the system, which were to test the design. While the demonstration was in progress, one of the managers arrived late. After the demonstration was finished, there was a general discussion.

The manager who had arrived late immediately criticised the user interface, and appeared very angry that the money on the prototype had been 'wasted'. After things calmed down a bit, it became apparent that he had expected a prototype of just the user-interface, with little functionality behind it. He was surprised that the system actually worked, but did not like the user interface at all.

And afterwards ...

The development team were asked to bid for the contract for the development of the complete system. The team leader put together a very detailed project proposal and costing. This bid was presented, along with a second demonstration of the prototype, to even higher management. The customer realised that, having built the prototype, the team leader was in the best position to estimate the cost of the project.

Eventually, the project was cancelled, as the perceived benefits did not match the cost.

7.2.5 Retrospect

Success or failure?

The goal of the prototype as stated in the contract was to validate the design, and this goal was achieved. The main features of the design were tested, and those that were found not to work were modified so that they did work.

One of the problems encountered was that some of the customer's managers had a different view as to the goals. The development team had completed their contract, but it was not clear that this contract was correct. The contract stated the requirements for the project. More care should have been taken to ensure that these requirements were correct, or at least that everyone had the same view of the requirements.

One of the results of the prototype, that was not a stated goal, was an estimate of the cost of the whole system. That estimate was treated with a high degree of confidence by both the development team and the customers. The result of this was that the business case for the project could be re-evaluated, and, whereas previously it had been accepted, it was now rejected. The prototype prevented a system from being developed whose costs exceeded the expected benefits. A project kill-point was reached, and the project was correctly stopped.

As far as the developers were concerned, it may be considered a failure. As a loss leader, it failed to gain a further contract.

Other lessons learnt

Prototyping a design is a good way of understanding the full cost and performance of a system. Items which seem quite small during the design can take a disproportionate time to sort out. These come to light during prototyping. At the end of the prototyping, the degree of confidence in the cost estimates is much higher than at the beginning.

In developing the prototype so rapidly, it was very important to have one person who understood the design very well – a design authority. There was little time to go through a formal review process for any of the code. This meant that the design authority needed to understand the design completely.

Specifications and designs that fit onto one sheet of paper are acceptable in a throw-away prototyping project, provided that they are accompanied by discussion. They are not intended to be used after the project, and the author is always available for discussion in cases of ambiguity.

The technique of using specialists to do small jobs works well as a way of developing software rapidly. It does tend to disrupt other projects, and cannot be used for all projects without a massive scheduling problem.

7.3 Document storage and control system

This project shows how, by using evolutionary development, a system with uncertain requirements can be developed into a good product. It also shows how ideas generated during the middle of a development can still be successfully included.

7.3.1 Introduction

Project origin

The ideas for this project started with the developers. Document storage and control systems were used in all the development projects, but none of them had seemed particularly useful to the developers. They had systems forced upon them by the project quality control system, which were not much used. These systems added to the administrative burden of the developers rather than easing it.

The developers put forward a proposal to design a new document storage and control system, their main aim being to build one which would be helpful to them. If such a system could be built, it might be sold as a product at a later date to recoup the investment cost. The idea was accepted, and an eighteen month budget was allocated for two people.

Description

A document storage and control system is one which allows documents (typically specifications, designs, code, and test reports) to be stored and indexed. It controls the access to these documents, so that while a document is out for updating, no-one else can change it.

Existing systems were only used for archiving completed material, and for maintenance documents. However, it seemed that a new system could be useful as a source of information, and perhaps provide some real help for the users.

At the start of the project, the ideas were fairly vague; no clear requirements were laid down. The purpose of the project was to build a 'better system', whatever that meant.

The ideas outlined at the beginning of the project included:

- integration with electronic mail and a word processor package
- inclusion of multimedia documents
- better search facilities
- document reading facilities, so that documents didn't have to be printed out

Project goals

The main goal of the project was to build a prototype document storage and control system which was more useful than those available commercially. The idea was that people would *want* to use it, and as they used it they would find new ways of using the facilities.

Functional requirements

There were few functional requirements:

- storage of documents
- retrieval of documents
- version control of documents
- control of access to documents

Constraints

The only constraints were time and money:

- A working system had to be produced within eighteen months.
- The project budget limited the man-power to an average of two.

Quality goals

The quality goals were:

- simple to use
- much easier to use than existing products
- robust enough for an in-house trial

7.3.2 Discussion

The main problem in this project was the lack of tangible goals. The requirements could be met by taking an existing document storage and control system and improving the user interface, but this did not really satisfy the spirit of the project goals. There was no obvious route to tackling the problem, and no obvious starting point. The problem relied on a creative attitude, on developing ideas, and testing them. This process was largely exploratory.

This problem lends itself quite naturally to an evolutionary development strategy. In the classic lifecycle model the creative part dies out shortly after the functional specification stage, whereas in the evolutionary model, ideas can still be generated and included in the system right up until the beginning of the last cycle.

7.3.3 Planning the prototype

Strategy

An evolutionary development strategy was used. This concentrated on generating new ideas and testing them.

What to prototype

At first a simple document storage and control system was built. Later it was extended to include new features. The system was developed with full functionality, and was robust enough to be used within the department. Some features were not developed as well as they might have been, in particular those concerned with the management of the system. This was considered to be of lesser importance. It was not an unimportant aspect of the system, but one which was unimportant as far as the purpose of the prototype was concerned. The major modules in the system are shown below. Existing products are marked with an *; modules not in the prototype are marked with a †. All the other modules were prototyped.

Document storage and control system

- Document storage
  - File server
  - Database
- User interface
  - X Window System *
  - Icon control
  - Document display
  - Window control
- Document control
  - Access control †
  - Version control
- Management †

Tools and techniques

Development initially took place using Hypercard. Although this proved a good starting point, some technical flaws proved too difficult to solve. Hypercard was useful in generating ideas, despite the fact that the code developed was completely thrown away.

The next platform was based on Unix workstations sharing files on a file server. The software was written in C++, and the user interface was built using the X Window System, and Interviews, a public domain software library supported by X.

Using the prototype

As the system was being developed, it was used by the developers for storing their own documentation and code. It was also demonstrated to other people within the company on several occasions.

Project organisation

The day to day running of the project was done by the team leader, who had an average of one and a half staff throughout the project. Various other people were brought in to brainstorm ideas. The overall control was in the hands of the project board. This consisted of three senior managers who met at the end of each phase of the project. The team leader reported to the project board at every meeting.

Project plan

The development was to be in six three-monthly stages. The first stage was to investigate other projects, research, and products that might be relevant. The other stages were to be evolutionary steps in the development cycle.

Quality reviews

At the end of each stage, the code and documentation went through a formal quality review. No specifications or designs were reviewed formally, as these were apt to change. The project board approved the general direction that the project was moving in at each of its meetings.

Milestones

Milestones occurred at the end of each stage, and were marked by a project board meeting.

Budget control

The total budget for the project was fixed at the beginning of the project. The expenditure was estimated by the team leader at the beginning of each stage, and approved by the project board at its meeting. The team leader had to keep within ten per cent (either way) of this budget.

7.3.4 What happened

Stage one

The investigation stage started with a literature and product search. The literature search was done using a library database, but the majority of the results were not relevant. The product search examined various packages currently available on the market.

The results of the search were that most products were found to allow retrieval based on the project name and type of document. Some allowed keywords, and some used full text retrieval. A few used a complex query language. Current research in this area seemed to concentrate on better forms of retrieval, using simpler techniques.

A previous project within the department, to buy a document control and storage system, had produced a full requirements specification. This stated that the requirements for retrieval were to be based on document number, project, and document type.

The main problem that was perceived by many of the users seemed to be surrounding the problem of retrieval. The products currently available were based on the fact that people were able to retrieve something if they *knew* it was available, and had sufficient information about it. It was generally not possible to find information which they didn't know about, nor to find old information that they had read, but had now forgotten the details of.

Many of these products were text-based, and gave little support for diagrams, whereas the research projects tended to have graphical user interfaces. There was a general feeling that if the tools gave better support for diagrams, then diagrams would be used more in the documents.

A report was completed on this investigation. The board meeting at the end of stage was run with the two board members. The team leader and administrative officer were also present. The meeting ran very smoothly with no problems.

Stage two

It was decided to build a system as quickly as possible, in order to get something working. The fastest tool available to the developers was Hypercard, so this was chosen as the basis for the first system. To provide a common database for several users, a file server was used.

The initial aim was to build a system that performed the essential functions, but had a better user interface than other available systems. A simple folder-based system was built, with the data stored on the shared disk.

Two problems occurred. Firstly, some technical problems arose with the file server. It proved impossible for several users to have access to a file at the same time. At the time no other file servers were available on the hardware that was being used. Secondly, it was the intention to use the department itself as the first trial site for the final system. The department had recently changed its development environment to be based around Unix workstations. The document system would also have to change operating system.

The software that had been built was scrapped, and the decision was made to build afresh on Unix workstations. The time spent on building a Hypercard system was not considered wasted, as the developers felt much happier about what they were doing, a lot of experience had been gained, and several new ideas had been tried out with the user interface.

It was at this point that another, much larger project started. The senior managers saw the new project as being very important, and when human resources became scarce, the document storage and control project was put on 'hold' for six months.

The project board met at the end of the stage. They stopped the project, and said that there should be no problems about restarting it in six months. It was assumed that since the software was being rewritten, it would not matter too much if the project was stopped at this point.

Stage three

The project was restarted six months later. Apart from the team leader, the project team had changed completely. Instead of picking up where it left off, the project was effectively started again. The new team had to be re-educated, not only in the purpose of the project, but also in the ideas that had already been generated. Although these ideas had been documented, the *flow* of ideas had stopped.

Development on the Unix workstations proved slower. The system was again based on folders, with a commercial full text retrieval system. Retrieval was seen as the main problem, and so several brainstorming sessions were held to try to resolve it. A lot of ideas were generated, mostly based around new types of search keys, but they did not meet the project's goals, ie to develop a system that people would want to use.

The company's administration now decided to rationalise all ongoing research projects, including this project. A team was set up to do this, and they started by interviewing the team leaders on all research projects. The interview was based on a questionnaire, with a set a set of keywords which were seen as the key goals. The aim of this was to associate several keywords with each project, and to use this to look for a significant overlap between projects.

Stage four

The first fully working system was completed. The user interface was developed on the X Window System, and Interviews. These took some time to get used to, but when learnt, they proved a very fast way of developing user interface software.

The system used an iconic representation for folders, and a graphical dialogue to build up complex searches. The database stored the type of word processor used to create each document, and this was invoked whenever the document was opened. This solved the problem of different document formats.

The rationalisation project published its report. What was written about the document storage and retrieval project showed that the interviewers had got totally the wrong idea. Instead of seeing it as a research project, they had seen it as an in-house development of a software engineering tool. They suggested that all work on including diagrams in the system be stopped, as there was another research project that was investigating multimedia documents. They finally suggested that, since the project was based on a network, it could be integrated with the work of a network project.

These ideas were dangerous. The project could be seriously set back if it was forced to spend time integrating with a network project which had been designed for something else. There was a serious danger of the system not being used because no diagrams could be included. Finally, it was certainly serious if this rationalisation project had mistaken a research project for an in-house development project. A lot of effort was spent trying to correct things. The 'no-diagrams' idea could not be quashed; it was left as a politically expedient compromise.

Someone from the rationalisation project was appointed to the project board. The board meetings now took on a different character. Instead of concentrating on the ideas generated during the last stage, the focus turned onto what had been planned for the current stage, and what had actually been delivered. This emphasis is one that typifies development projects, but seemed inappropriate for research work.

Stage five

During a brainstorming meeting at the beginning of this stage, a new idea was suggested that received wide acclaim. Instead of the traditional retrieval mechanism, or a variation on it, a 'messy desk metaphor' would be used.

This idea was based on the concept that many people store documents on a messy desk, with piles of papers everywhere, but still know exactly where everything is. They can retrieve documents with a high degree of efficiency, because they remember the location relative to all the other things on the desk. They also use other visual clues, such as the colour of the cover, or the size of paper used.

The new metaphor was to work like this: each document was to be represented by an icon, and each icon had a position on an infinite plane. Each document would also have a colour, which showed itself on the icon, and also on the colour of the title bar of the window when the document was opened. The user had a view of the infinite plane, on which it was possible to zoom in or out to gain a closer view of a particular region. Finally, the users could place other objects on the plane, which could not be opened, but were visual clues. These objects could be selected from a standard set, in the shape of everyday objects.

The idea was that the users would place the documents where they wanted, on the plane. They would generally group like items together, for example items on a given project. If someone wanted to tell someone else where a document was, they might say 'In the project X pile, just behind the coffee cup'.

The new system was built. It seemed far more acceptable to the users than the existing full text retrieval systems.

Stage six

The last stage of the project tidied up the software. The system was then used in the department. It generally received a good reaction. The messy desk top metaphor was well liked, although it had not been tested on a very large-scale project.

This stage concentrated on demonstrating the system to other people in the business. Two reactions are worthy of note:

1 One person on the (now reorganised) rationalisation project said that the system was excellent, and asked if we had considered developing the system to hold diagrams. It was explained that there were other projects working on this, and that this project had been told to steer clear of that particular area of work.

   Someone else made the comment that the fact that a document had diagrams in it had nothing to do with the substance of the project. This, of course, was what the team leader had argued six months previously.

2 Another person could not see what had been done beyond providing a different style of interface to a database system. This was very difficult to explain. The only real explanation that could be given was that this document system was being used by real users, and that they were keen to use it. They were now finding new ways of doing things, and it was really being used to the full. The reply was that the old system did everything that the requirements specification said it should, and that all this project had done was to provide a new user interface.

   The implication was that a lot of money had been spent on developing a small item of code for the user interface, and that this was poor value for money. What he did not see was that the effect of the small item of code was that users would now use the system to the full, whereas before they would use it only when they were forced to. The value of the code was therefore very high.

And afterwards ...

The system was demonstrated to several of the companies customers who showed considerable interest. Whether it is taken any further, only time will tell.

7.3.5 Retrospect

The generation of new ideas is not something that can be turned on and off at will. It takes several months of concentrated effort in a particular area before ideas start to flow regularly. Putting the effort into evolutionary development complements the process of generating new ideas.

As the software develops, so it sparks off new thoughts. The evolutionary nature of the software enables the developers to include their ideas in later versions of the software. Far from being pressured into sticking rigidly to a specification, the developers are encouraged to think of new ideas, although these must be added to the system in a controlled way. This project was very small, and so did not need much control.

It is important in such a project to retain the same team as far as possible. The flow of ideas does not peak until several months after the start of the work. Changing staff in the middle of the project stops the flow of ideas dead. The process has to be restarted.

The team must be prepared to throw away code that does not appear to enhance the development. The management must allow them to do this.

One of the most difficult problems encountered in this project was that of explaining what was going on. The people who saw the system tended to be oriented towards products, and classic software development. The concept of not knowing what is to be delivered at the start of the project was, on the whole, alien to them. The idea of spending a lot on generating a small thing was also alien to them, despite the fact that the small thing was very valuable. They tended to have the concept that all code is of equal value.

One of the hardest challenges that management has in controlling research projects is that of knowing where to stop. Blue skies research can be characterised by the development team being given a budget, but no specific goals. Pure development is characterised by the goals being fixed and unalterable. Commercial research is an inevitable compromise, but the point at which to set the goals and the flexibility the developers have are the most difficult problem. The developers will always find the goals too inflexible, whereas the management will always find them too flexible. Therein lies the dichotomy of research.

This project achieved its goal of developing a system that would be used because people liked using it. However, it was a qualified success in that the management had difficulty in seeing the point of it.

7.4 Manufacturing automation

Among a catalogue of prototyping projects that achieved their goals, at least to some extent, it is important to present the other side of the coin. This is the story of a failed project, which, one can surmise, would not have failed quite as tragically had a different approach been taken. The project would have benefited either from evolutionary development, or from planing a throw-away prototype at the beginning, so that developers and customers both knew what they were building.

7.4.1 Introduction

Customer profile

The customer was a large manufacturer of car components, selling to the big car companies, and into the spares market. They had around fifty factories, and were in the middle of a somewhat uncontrolled process of introducing manufacturing automation. Each of the divisions of the business had, in the past, introduced automation on their own initiative. The company had then given a large budget to a controlling group to coordinate this work, and to introduce automation as a new direction for the company. This department, over a period of about two years, developed a lot of expertise in the area of manufacturing automation, particularly from the hardware point of view.

Project origin

The automation group realised that they might make use of their expertise beyond the confines of their own company. They decided that they would embark upon a new venture – they would commission a platform of software and hardware for factory automation. This could then be sold to other manufacturing companies throughout the world.

They approached the developers, a software house, with a view to building the system. For the software house, it was the largest project they had ever undertaken, and, very pleased with such a large contract, they took it on. The customer ran a six-month start-up project during which they wrote a requirements specification and business case.

Description

The customer had identified two market sectors to justify the development of a manufacturing automation system. One sector was internal, ie they intended to supply the system to their own company, and therefore save on the costs of buying externally. The second was the external market sector. These sectors were similar in many respects, but did have slightly different requirements.

The system to be sold externally was a configurable manufacturing automation system, ie one that could be configured for the particular factory into which it was to be installed. It would provide centralised control of the automation process.

Three major project phases were planned. The first was to be delivered in eighteen months, the second in thirty six months, and the third in forty eight months. The idea was that the first system should be the most basic, establishing a foothold in the market. The second was to contain more advanced features, some of which required long term development, and so had to be started at the beginning of the project. The third stage was to be based on an advanced architecture. This required a long period of study in order to get the right design built into the system from the start.

All three projects were to be started at the same time, to a greater or lesser degree. It is the first of these three phases that is examined here.

Project goals

The main goal of the project was to produce a product quality, configurable manufacturing automation system within eighteen months.

Functional requirements

The requirements specification contained many functional requirements, and went into great detail on some points, and little detail on others. In essence it specified:

- robot and machinery control on the shop floor
- centralised control and programming
- a network linking the various items

Constraints

The main constraints were:

- specific computer hardware, including make and model
- specified robot hardware

It is important to point out that the reasons behind the model of shop floor computer being specified were to do with cost. The business case was based partly on the cost of this specific model being used, as the next model up in the range was too expensive.

Quality goals

Few quality goals were defined in the requirements specification, even though the development was aimed at producing a product quality system.

7.4.2 Discussion

The main problem for the developers was that the requirements specification was essentially a wish list. It contained list of all the things that the customer had thought was a good idea. There was no priority put on the items, and the time available was too short to build everything. The customer seemed to indicate a willingness to negotiate on these items, so the project was started on this basis.

A second problem was that the work was breaking new ground for both the customer and the developers. The customer was not used to selling software products, and the developers were not used to projects of this size. The customer had not yet established a presence in the market place, but was planning to start to ship products within six months of the launch of the product – a very short time.

A fundamental problem was that of communication between customer and developer. The requirements specification was a wish list because the customer had no past experience in writing specifications. They had some idea of what they wanted, but little idea of the cost. A second problem, probably equally as important, was that of communication between the customer and the market place. In order to develop openings into the market place, the customer had to show credibility.

Yet another aspect to the problem was that the developers had little experience of managing a project of this size (several hundred man-years in total), and so had little knowledge of the expected problems and costs.

All aspects of this project seem to cry out for a prototype to be built. Firstly, the lack of credibility of the customer in the market place would have been enhanced by a prototype system that could be demonstrated. This was, in fact, realised halfway through the project, unfortunately with somewhat disastrous consequences.

The customer's lack of understanding of the nature of the project was also one which could have been helped with a prototype. A prototype system would have been the right tool to focus on the major requirements of the system, and one which would have provided the customer and developers with a basis for their discussions.

Finally, the developers would have been able to see the true scale of the problem, and would have been able to estimate the size of the project far more accurately after building a prototype.

7.4.3 Planning the project

Strategy

The classic lifecycle model was used. Starting with the requirements specification provided by the customer, there was to be a functional specification stage, a design stage, a coding stage, and an integration stage.

System structure

The major modules in the system are shown below. No part of the system was prototyped, and very little use was made of existing modules.

- Factory automation system
  - Communications
    - Low-level communications
    - High-level communications
    - Networks
  - Shop floor systems
    - Robot control
    - Device monitor
  - Control centre
    - Database
      - DBMS
      - SQL-like interface
      - Database schema and access
    - Production line set up
    - User interface
      - Screen display
      - Print service
    - Emergency shutdown

Tools and techniques

Conventional third generation languages were used. The aim was to avoid third-party software being used, and to develop as much of the code as possible in-house, to retain intellectual property rights.

Project organisation

The customer had several representatives on the project board. A project manager reported directly to the project board. About ten team leaders reported to the project manager; each team had between one and five staff working on the project. This project meets the criteria for a large-scale project as defined in Chapter 5.

The project board met once every two months, at which progress on the deliverable items was reported. The project manager had weekly meetings with the team leaders, at which progress was reported, and any problems covering more than one team were discussed.

Project plan

The plan had:

- six months requirements specification
- two months functional specification
- two months design
- six months coding
- two months integration

Quality reviews

All documents and code modules were formally reviewed. The review procedure insisted that documents were sent out five working days before the review meeting. At the meeting, the reviewers reported only on document errors. All errors had to be corrected within five days, unless the document was so bad that it needed re-doing, and therefore re-reviewing.

Milestones

Milestones were set at the end of each stage and at certain crucial points in between.

Scope changes

Changes in the scope of the project, ie changes to the requirements specification, had to be formally agreed by the project board.

Budget control

The contract was on a time and materials basis. The total budget was set by the customer six months in advance. Team members had to supply weekly time sheets to say what they were working on, and for how long. The project board had to have an emergency meeting if the cost went over ten per cent of that planned.

7.4.4 What happened

This is only a partial history of this project. The project was too big to relate all that happened. The stories that are told here have been selected to illustrate the need for prototyping, and for amusement and amazement.

Months one to six – the requirements specification

After setting up initial agreements with the developers, the customer started working on the requirements specification and business case. None of the developers thought to suggest that the customer might need some help in writing the requirements specification.

At this stage the activity of the developers was low, their main task being to supply a report on current practices in manufacturing automation, and the future trends suggested by research activities. The group that did this work then formed the architectural group for the longer term projects that were to deliver in three or four years time.

The developers spent some time organising their teams, so that they would be ready to start work on time. An administration office was established, one of its tasks being to develop a project document database. One person wrote the requirements specification for this system, which was reviewed by the other people working in the administration office. A system was purchased on the basis of this specification, installed, and commissioned. At the same time, the administration office set up a review procedure for all the documents produced by the project.

The requirements specification was finished and reviewed by the customer. It was then released to the developers. The document was around a hundred pages long, and appeared to be a wish list of everything one could possibly want from manufacturing automation. There were no quality goals worth speaking of, only functional goals.

When the requirements specification was given to the rank and file of the developers, they could not believe what they saw. The message that they were very unhappy about working with such a document was passed back to the customer, via the project manager, and the project board. Unfortunately, by the time it got back to the customer, the message had been severely watered down.

Month seven – the functional specification

A team was established to write the functional specification. There were large gaps in the requirements specification, and much effort was spent in correcting this. At first the functional specification was written directly from the requirements specification. It soon became apparent that there was too much to do in the allotted time and budget.

The customer's business case was accepted by their higher management. This was a great relief to the developers, as they now expected to be assured of work for several years to come.

Month eight

The customer held several meetings with the project manager regarding the requirements. Several of the points in the requirements specification were simplified in some way or other. The customer did not actually change the requirements specification, but accepted that the changes would be made. These changes were formally recorded in the minutes of these meetings.

Since the requirements were still changing, the functional specification could not be completed in the allotted time. The time was extended by a month. The customer said that the time should be made up later on.

One of the team members, who was writing the section specifying the computers for the shop floor, left the project. He finished his work, based only on the original requirements. He did not realise that changes were taking place, nor that he could request changes to the requirements.

Month nine

As the functional specification neared completion, the leader of the database team began to realise that it would be impossible to complete his work in time. The main problem appeared to be with the interface. The requirements specification stated that the interface had to be SQL conformant[4]. It was this in particular that was going to be the problem.

He went to talk about it with the project manager. They agreed that the customer would probably not mind another interface, provided that it was close to SQL, as many other changes had been approved. Of course, this would have to be checked with the customer, so they agreed to change the text of the specification and ask for approval at the next meeting. In any case, as a formal check on the new wording, the customer would have to sign approval of the functional specification.

At the next board meeting, the discussion on the changes to the database was the last item on the agenda, and it was passed over without comment. No formal agreement was made to the change, but neither was any agreement made *not* to change. Two days before the deadline to produce the functional specification, the database team leader asked the project manger what was going on.

The project manager told him to make the change anyway, and let the customer approve it, or not, during the formal review. As there was not much time to add substantially more text, the words 'SQL conformant' were taken out and replaced with 'SQL convergent', which seemed to convey the correct meaning,

---

[4] SQL , structured query language, is a standard query language for database systems.

ie it would be close to SQL in concept, and could migrate to SQL in a future release.

The review of the 150 page functional specification took place at a two hour meeting. The errors recorded in the meeting concentrated on the details of the wording, rather than on any variance from the requirements specification. By the time the database section was reached, towards the end of the document, everyone was hurrying in order to finish on time. No-one commented upon the change of wording.

The functional specification was now complete, reviewed, and approved. Unfortunately, the word processor on which it had been written was incompatible with the project document database. The administration office were surprised that there were diagrams in the document, as the database could not cope with anything other than vertical and horizontal lines. They suggested that a restriction be put on the type of diagrams that could be included in future documents. Eventually they agreed to storing copies of diagrams in a filing cabinet, and the text was transferred into the database.

Month ten – the design stage

The design stage started a month late. The functional specification appeared to be incomplete in a number of places. This was largely because the specification team had run out of time again, and had not wanted to extend the timescales further.

Ten or so team leaders were assembled to form the design team. They had worked on various projects, and had used different design strategies. The design team leader chose a design strategy known to himself, and which he considered the best, but which was new to about half the team. No budget or time had been allocated to re-educating people.

The functional specification was distributed by hard copy, rather than by reference to the copy in the project database. This was for two reasons; firstly many people resented being forced to use a database that they considered unsuitable, and secondly, the lack of diagrams in the database made the document unusable. Even when copies of the diagrams had been stapled to the back, it proved much harder to read than a hard copy of the original.

Late changes to the specification were also circulated in the same way. Inevitably some people got missed out in this process.

Month eleven

The goals of the design stage did not state the detail to which the design would have to go. In order to complete the design within the allotted time, only the high-level design was done. The component-level design was left to the teams to do during the coding stage.

The database interface was designed, but because of the decision not to include interface designs, it was omitted from the high-level design document. The customer was, therefore, not given the opportunity to see it.

It was at this stage that the architectural team, which had been working independently of the developers, completed a huge thirteen volume document, which was the first draft of their work, and which covered all possible aspects of system architecture in manufacturing automation. As this was a related project, many of the team leaders were required to spend time reviewing the massive tome. This took far longer than expected, and consequently the coding work started late.

Month twelve – the code stage

The coding stage began with the detailed design. As the team leaders completed their detailed designs, there were many different attitudes to the project database. Some people ignored it, but some people used it all the time for day to day working.

The result of this was that there was no definitive source for any document. Those documents that were in a different word processor format tended to be put into the project database in bit-map form – the only way that they could be stored. This was useless for retrieval purposes.

The team leaders were asked to produce their project plans. The team leader for the low-level communications system used a computer-based project planning tool, but took far longer than all the others, and came back with a plan that detailed all his teams activities to within a day for the next six months.

The customer booked a stand at a manufacturing automation show due to be held in three months time. Their representative said that he wanted to demonstrate what had been built by that time at the show. From his point of view, the coding stage would be halfway through, therefore half of the code would be available for demonstration. The developers were in no position to show anything. For one thing, most teams planned to spend the first two months on low-level design, and secondly, incomplete code is impossible to demonstrate.

The customer suddenly decided that a prototype system was to be built in three months.

Month thirteen

A small team of some of the best developers were taken off the mainstream development work in order to work on the customer's prototype. They prepared to work long, hard hours for the next three months.

The customer's higher management re-evaluated the business case for the project. Due to changes in the market place, the internal market looked unviable without the support of the external one. The external market now became vital, and the launch of the product at the exhibition became a critical part of the product strategy.

Month fourteen

The team developing the software for the shop floor computer found that it would not fit into the model of machine they had. They continued development on a larger model. Their team leader was not the same person who had written the functional specification, and did not realise the importance the customer had put on the model of the machine.

The team working on the low-level communications found that the day to day plan did not hold. It had to be replanned every time there was a slip of any sort. This was done about once a week.

Month fifteen

The administration office complained that nobody was using their project database. At this stage everyone was very busy, and took no notice. Eventually a meeting was held. The administration office now realised that the requirements for the documentation system had not included consultation with any of the developers. There was no money available to redo the requirements analysis, nor to buy a new database. The result, of course, was that more time was wasted in looking for missing documents.

The customer representative was shown a demonstration of the database, and suddenly realised that it did not conform to SQL. A meeting was hastily arranged between the team leader, the project manager, and the customer representative – who was very angry. The team leader showed the customer that he had approved the changes in the functional specification.

The low-level communications team continued to replan their part of the project on a weekly basis. Each slip required a reorganisation of the daily schedule.

The prototype system was finished after a frantic weekend. The equipment was flown out to the exhibition site. The exhibition proved a qualified success.

Month sixteen

Some of the modules were integrated. There were a lot of problems that were traced to individual misunderstanding of the design documents.

The low-level communications team had yet another slip in a delivery. The planning package could no longer cope with fitting everything in to the allotted time. Suddenly their plans extended by four months. The customer was shocked.

Month seventeen

The customer was told that the shop floor computer had to be a larger model to meet the functional specification. The business case was reassessed, and it was found that the unit price was now too high for the product to be viable.

Month eighteen

The customer was now without a valid business case. The project was cancelled.

And afterwards ...

Most of the teams had worked excessive amounts of overtime. Because of the accounting system that the company used, the customer was charged on the number of days worked, however long each day was. The employees, however, were allowed to take time-off in place of the overtime that they had worked. Little work was done for the following few months as staff worked off their overtime, and took their holiday entitlement. This had to be paid for by the company.

A lot of valuable code, mostly ninety per cent complete, was thrown out as a result of the project being cancelled, and no-one had the money to finish it off.

7.4.5 Retrospect

Some of the problems encountered in the project were due to inexperienced management, but many more were due to a lack of communication.

Poor communication between customer and developers allowed the development of the database to continue for so long, when the root cause of the problem was not tackled. The real problem was that not enough time had been allowed for the developer to complete an SQL conformant interface. The customer was totally unaware of this. The customer, on the other hand, had been so sloppy in writing the requirements specification that it was not at all clear that an SQL conformant database was needed.

The customer did not understand the requirements for the system. They did not define the requirements properly, and that led to an overrun on the timescales.

This lack of understanding was the cause of several problems. If a prototype had been built, or if the system had been developed under an evolutionary development strategy, then the understanding of what was being built could have grown with the product.

The prototype was built at the wrong time. It took the best staff out of the development, and set them to developing a system that only had the goal of selling the product. This, in itself, was not a bad thing, but the timing was wrong. Had the prototype been built earlier on, it would have served other purposes as well. Not only would it have given everybody a better understanding of what they were building, but also it would have focused the work on the more vital areas, it would have produced a better idea of the cost of the system, it would have produced a better design, and it would not have taken the best developers out of the mainstream development work.

The problems associated with reliance on computer-based project planning were highlighted by this case study. The one team that relied on the planning tool were blinded by the ease at which projects could be planned in so much detail. They did not step back and use common sense and past experience to see if their plans would work.

7.5 Conclusions

The cost of developing software is, on the whole, high. The probability of failure can also be high. The risks involved include not estimating the costs, underestimating the development timescales, attempting to stretch the limits of computer science, and very often building the wrong system. The cost of failure is the cost of reworking the software, the cost of the development being written-off, or at worse the failure of the company to move in its chosen direction. It is a kind of poker, the stake being the development cost, and the pot being the achievement of the project goals.

The use of rapid prototyping is like being able to cheat, but legally, at the game! It allows you to buy an extra ace, or a look at the pack before upping the ante. However, it is not really cheating because the other players are allowed to do the same – although they usually don't.

In the secure file transfer project, the goal was to build a system for passing data; the stake was the development cost, which was not known. The prototype was used, unknowingly at the time, to buy information about the development cost, after which the cost was considered too high. The hand was folded at the loss of the ante, avoiding the loss of a much larger stake.

In the sales demonstrator project, the goal was to encourage new customers; the stake that would eventually have to be put up was the development of a complete system. The prototype was used to buy an order up-front, instead of merely hoping that the system would sell.

In the document storage and control project, the goal was to develop new ideas, in order to have a better product than the competition. The stake was again the development cost. The prototype was used to buy the ideas, and to test their acceptability.

In the factory automation project, the goal was to break into a new market, and the full development cost was put up as the stake. The risks were not reduced by prototyping; nothing was done to ease the path. The project could have been a success; the company could now be the market leader in factory automation products. The possibility was there, it was a risk which was taken – and lost. The players bid on a straight, and lost to a full house. The sad thing is that a prototype would have helped. A proper risk analysis would at least have let the company understand what they were playing against.

The risks are always high in any software development project, the stakes are correspondingly high, and the potential rewards are great. No-one should enter the game without a sound analysis of the risks, and without managing these risks in a proper fashion. Those who do not will surely leave the table with empty pockets, while others enjoy their misfortune.

Prototyping is one way in which the risks can be managed. It is not the only way by any means, but it is the one that this book has attempted to present as a technique for the software engineer, who is also, we hope, a risk manager.

Selected reading

Boddie, J
Crunch mode
Prentice-Hall, 1987

Brooks, F P Jr
The mythical man-month
Addison-Wesley, 1982

References

Alavi, M
An assessment of the prototyping approach to information systems development, *Communications of the ACM*, Vol 27, No 6, June 1984, 556–563

Alexander, H and Potter, B
The use of formal specification and rapid prototyping to establish product feasibility, *Information and Software Technology (GB)*, Vol 29, No 7, September 1987, 388–394

Appleton, D S
Data-driven prototyping, *Datamation*, Vol 29, No 11, November 1983, 259–268

AT&T
UNIX System V Release 3 Programmer's Reference Manual, Issue 1, 1987

Baker, F T
Chief programmer team management of production programming, *IBM Systems Journal*, Vol 11, No 1, 1972, 56–73

Blum, B I
The life cycle – a debate over alternate models, *ACM SIGSOFT Software Engineering Notes*, Vol 7, No 4, October 1982, 18–20

Bødker, S and Grønbœk, K
Co-operative prototyping experiments. In: *Proceedings of the 1st International Conference on Computer Supported Co-operative Work*, September 1989

Boehm, B W
A spiral model of software development and enhancement, *Computer*, Vol 21, No 5, May 1988, 61–72

Boehm, B W
Software engineering economics, Prentice-Hall, 1981

Boehm, B W
Software engineering, *IEEE Transactions on Computers*, Vol C-25, No 12, December 1976, 1226–1241

Boehm, B W, Gray, T E, and Seewaldt, T
Prototyping versus specifying: a multiproject experiment, *IEEE Transactions on Software Engineering*, Vol 10, No 3, 1984, 290–303

Brooks, F P Jr
No silver bullet: essence and accidents of software engineering, *Computer*, Vol 20, No 4, April 1987, 10–19

Brooks, F P Jr
The mythical man-month, Addison-Wesley, 1982

Budde, R, Kuhlenkamp, K, Mathiassen, L, and Züllighoven, H (eds)
Approaches to prototyping, Springer-Verlag, 1984

Business Week
It's late, costly, incompetent – but try firing a computer system, *Business Week*, McGraw-Hill, 7th November 1988, 164–165

Cieslak, R, Fawaz, A, Sachs, S, Varaiya, P, Walrand, J, and Li, A
The programmable network prototyping system, *Computer*, Vol 22, No 5, May 1989, 67–76

Collins dictionary of the English language
Collins, 1979

Computer
Special issue on formal methods, *Computer*, Vol 23, No 9, September 1990

Connell, J L and Brice, L
The impact of implementing a rapid prototype on system maintenance, *AFIPS Conference Proceedings: 1985 National Computer Conference*, 15th–18th July, Chicago, AFIPS Press, 1985, 515–524

Cooper, R
The fundamentals of configuration management in a software development environment, *Software Tools '89*, Blenheim Online Publications, 1989

Coulouris, G F and Dollimore, J
Distributed systems concepts and design, Addison-Wesley, 1988

De Marco, T
Controlling software projects: management, measurement and estimation, Yourdon Press, 1982

De Marco, T
Structured analysis and system specification, Yourdon Press, 1978

Dijkstra, E
Selected writings on computing: a personal perspective, Springer-Verlag, 1982

Drucker, P F
Management, Heinemann, 1975

Dupuy, A, Schwartz, J, Yemini, Y, and Bacon, D
Nest: a network simulation and prototyping testbed, *Communications of the ACM,* Vol 33, No 10, October 1990, 63–74

Floyd, C
A systematic look at prototyping. In: *Budde et al,* 1984, 1–18

Foster, J R, Jolly, A E P, and Norris, M T
An overview of software maintenance, *British Telecom Technology Journal,* Vol 7, No 4, October 1989, 37–46

Giddings, R V
Accommodating uncertainty in software design, *Communications of the ACM,* Vol 27, No 5, May 1984, 428–434

Gilb, T
Principles of software engineering management, Addison-Wesley, 1988

Goodman, D
The complete Hypercard handbook, Bantam, 1987

Gordon, J E
Structures or why things don't fall down, Penguin, 1978

Harel, D
On folk theorems, *Communications of the ACM,* Vol 23, No 7, 1980

Hekmatpour, S
Experience with evolutionary prototyping in a large software project, *ACM SIGSOFT Software Engineering Notes,* Vol 12, No 1, January 1987, 38–41

Henderson, P
Functional programming, formal specification, and rapid prototyping, *IEEE Transactions on Software Engineering*, Vol 12, No 2, February 1986

IEEE Software
Special issue on formal methods, *IEEE Software*, Vol 7, No 5, September 1990

IEEE Transactions on Software Engineering
Special issue on formal methods, *IEEE Transactions on Software Engineering*, Vol 16, No 9, September 1990

Johnson, S C
Yacc: Yet Another Compiler-Compiler, *BSD Unix Programmer's Manual*, supplementary documents, University of California, Berkeley, California

Jones, M L R
Hypercard – the legend, British Telecom internal report, 1990

Jordan, P W, Keller, K S, Tucker, R W, and Vodel, D
Software storming: combining rapid prototyping and knowledge engineering, *Computer*, Vol 22, No 5, May 1989, 39–48

Jörgensen, A H
On the psychology of prototyping. In: *Budde et al*, 1984, 278–289

Lee, E
User-interface development tools, *IEEE Software*, Vol 7, No 3, May 1990, 31–36

Lesk, M E and Schmidt, E
Lex - a lexical analyser generator, *BSD Unix Programmer's Manual*, supplementary documents, University of California, Berkeley, California

Lewis, T G, Handlooser III, F, Bose, S, and Yang, S
Prototypes from standard user interface management systems, *Computer*, Vol 22, No 5, May 1989, 51–60

Lientz, B P and Swanson, E B
Software maintenance management, Addison-Wesley, 1980

Luqi
Software evolution through rapid prototyping, *Computer*, Vol 22, No 5, May 1989, 13–25

Martin, J and McClure, C
Software maintenance: the problem and its solution, Prentice-Hall, 1983

Maude, T I and Willis, G J
Rapid prototyping: the management of software risk, Pitman, 1991

Mayhew, P J and Dearnley, P A
An alternative prototyping classification, *The Computer Journal*, Vol 30, No 6, 1987, 481–484

McCracken, D D and Jackson, M A
Life cycle concept considered harmful, *ACM SIGSOFT Software Engineering Notes*, Vol 7, No 2, April 1982, 29–32

Mills, H D
Software productivity, Dorset House, New York, 1988

Mills, H D and Dyson, P B
Using metrics to quantify development, *IEEE Software*, Vol 7, No 2, March 1990, 14–16

Mullery, G P
CORE: method for controlled requirements expression, *Proceedings of the 4th International Conference on Software Engineering*, New York, IEEE, 1979

Nichols, K
Performance tools, *IEEE Software*, Vol 7, No 3, May 1990, 21–30

Nielsen, J
The art of navigating through Hypertext, *Communications of the ACM*, Vol 33, No 3, March 1990, 296–310

Nosek, J T
Organisational design choices to facilitate evolutionary development of prototype information systems. In: *Budde et al*, 1984, 341–355

Oman, P
CASE analysis and design tools, *IEEE Software*, Vol 7, No 3, May 1990, 37–43

Pressman, R S
Software engineering: a practitioner's approach, McGraw-Hill, 2nd edition, 1987

Ratcliffe, B
Early and not-so-early prototyping – rationale and tool support. In: *Proceedings of the 12th International Computer Software & Applications Conference*, IEEE Computer Society Press, 1988, 127–134

Rentsch, T
Object oriented programming, *SIGPLAN Notices*, Vol 17, No 9, September 1982, 51–57

Rockart, J F
Chief executives define their own data needs, *Harvard Business Review*, Vol 57, No 2, March–April 1979, 81–93

Royce, W W
Managing the development of large software systems: concepts and techniques, *Proceedings WESCON*, August 1970. Reprinted in: *Proceedings of the 9th International Software Engineering Conference*, Monterey, California, IEEE Computer Society Press, 1987

Salvendy, G (ed)
Handbook of human factors/ergonomics, John Wiley & sons, 1986

Sanders, P, Johnson, M and Tinker, R
From Z specifications to functional implementations, *British Telecom Technology Journal*, Vol 7, No 4, October 1989

Smith, D B and Oman, P
Software tools in context, *IEEE Software*, Vol 7, No 3, May 1990, 14–19

Swartout, W and Balzer, R
On the inevitable intertwinning of specification and implementation, *Communications of the ACM*, Vol 25, No 5, July 1982, 438–440

Tanenbaum, A S
Computer networks, Prentice-Hall, 1981

Tracz, W (ed)
Software reuse: emerging technology, *IEEE Computer Society Press*, 1988

US Government Accounting Office report FGMSD-80-4, 1979
Reported in: *ACM SIGSOFT Software Engineering Notes*, Vol 10, No 5, October 1985

Weinberg, G M
Overstructured management of software engineering, *Proceedings of the 6th International Conference on Software Engineering*, Washington DC, IEEE Computer Society Press, 1982, 2–8

Whyte, R R (ed)
Engineering progress through trouble, The Institution of Mechanical Engineers, London, 1975

Zahniser, R A
Levels of abstraction in the system life cycle, *ACM SIGSOFT Software Engineering Notes*, Vol 8, No 1, January 1983, 6–12

Zave, P and Yeh, R T
Executable requirements for embedded systems. In: *Software specification techniques*, Gehani, N and McGettrick, A D (eds), Addison-Wesley, 1986

Zelkowitz, M V
Resource utilization during software development, *The Journal of Systems and Software*, Vol 8, 1988, 331–336

Zipf, G K
Human behaviour and the principle of least effort, an introduction to human ecology, Addison-Wesley, 1949. Reprinted by: Hafner, New York, 1972, 35-37

Index